THE
GROWTH
ENGINE

THE GROWTH ENGINE

A Guide to Building a World-Class Business Development Function in Professional Services

**WALT SHILL, ANDI BALDWIN
ERIKA FLOWERS, JACOB PARKS**

WILEY

Copyright © 2025 by Profitable Ideas Exchange. All rights reserved.

Published by John Wiley & Sons, Inc., Hoboken, New Jersey.
Published simultaneously in Canada.

No part of this publication may be reproduced, stored in a retrieval system, or transmitted in any form or by any means, electronic, mechanical, photocopying, recording, scanning, or otherwise, except as permitted under Section 107 or 108 of the 1976 United States Copyright Act, without either the prior written permission of the Publisher, or authorization through payment of the appropriate per-copy fee to the Copyright Clearance Center, Inc., 222 Rosewood Drive, Danvers, MA 01923, (978) 750-8400, fax (978) 750-4470, or on the web at www.copyright.com. Requests to the Publisher for permission should be addressed to the Permissions Department, John Wiley & Sons, Inc., 111 River Street, Hoboken, NJ 07030, (201) 748-6011, fax (201) 748-6008, or online at http://www.wiley.com/go/permission.

The manufacturer's authorized representative according to the EU General Product Safety Regulation is Wiley-VCH GmbH, Boschstr. 12, 69469 Weinheim, Germany, e-mail: Product_Safety@wiley.com.

Trademarks: Wiley and the Wiley logo are trademarks or registered trademarks of John Wiley & Sons, Inc. and/or its affiliates in the United States and other countries and may not be used without written permission. All other trademarks are the property of their respective owners. John Wiley & Sons, Inc. is not associated with any product or vendor mentioned in this book.

Limit of Liability/Disclaimer of Warranty: While the publisher and authors have used their best efforts in preparing this book, they make no representations or warranties with respect to the accuracy or completeness of the contents of this book and specifically disclaim any implied warranties of merchantability or fitness for a particular purpose. No warranty may be created or extended by sales representatives or written sales materials. The advice and strategies contained herein may not be suitable for your situation. You should consult with a professional where appropriate. Further, readers should be aware that websites listed in this work may have changed or disappeared between when this work was written and when it is read. Neither the publisher nor authors shall be liable for any loss of profit or any other commercial damages, including but not limited to special, incidental, consequential, or other damages.

For general information on our other products and services or for technical support, please contact our Customer Care Department within the United States at (800) 762-2974, outside the United States at (317) 572-3993 or fax (317) 572-4002.

Wiley also publishes its books in a variety of electronic formats. Some content that appears in print may not be available in electronic formats. For more information about Wiley products, visit our website at www.wiley.com.

Library of Congress Cataloging-in-Publication Data is Available:

ISBN: 9781394277872 (Cloth)
ISBN: 9781394277889 (ePub)
ISBN: 9781394277896 (ePDF)

Cover Design: Wiley
Author Photos: © Profitable Ideas Exchange

SKY10121711_071525

For Matt.

Contents

Preface   *ix*

PART I   THE PROBLEM AND THE PROMISE   **1**

1   **The Problem – Why Professional Services Firms Fail
     to Scale Business Development**   **3**

2   **The Promise – You Can Build an Engine**   **15**

PART II   SERVICES   **23**

3   **Knowing What You Do – Service Definition
     and Discipline**   **25**

4   **Service Development and Expansion**   **43**

PART III   CLIENTS   **61**

5   **Knowing Whom You Serve**   **63**

6   **Double Down on Current Accounts**   **81**

7   **Winning New Clients**   **105**

PART IV   TALENT AND PERFORMANCE MANAGEMENT   123

8   **Hiring and Harnessing Talent**   **125**

9   **Talent Development – Building Your BD Capability**   **141**

10   **Motivating the Team – Incentives and Rewards**   **159**

PART V   OPERATING MODEL   **175**

11   Structure for Scale – Supporting Growth Leaders   **177**

12   Aligning Marketing and Business Development   **199**

PART VI   DATA AND MEASUREMENT   **221**

13   Measuring What Matters   **223**

PART VII   PUTTING IT ALL TOGETHER   **253**

14   Managing Change   **255**

15   Going for Growth – Where to Go from Here   **265**

Appendix: Business Development Maturity – Reader Assessment   *271*

Bibliography   *281*

Acknowledgments   *283*

About the Authors   *287*

Index   *289*

Preface

Ian Bremmer, CEO and founder of The Eurasia Group, published a report in 2011 on global risks. In that report, he warned about the rise of a "G-Zero World." He was making a play on the Group of Seven (or the G7), an elite club formed in 1975 comprising the largest free-market countries. While the G7 controlled global markets and institutions in the post – World War II world, Bremmer was making the case that, in 2011, they were losing their grip on power as economic influence became more decentralized – away from the United States, Canada, and Europe.

A similar dynamic is at work in the world of professional services. Whereas once professional services were ruled by an elite club, today the number of advisory firms across law, consulting, finance, marketing, and engineering has proliferated. Whereas McKinsey, BCG, and Bain once experienced limited competition, today there are more than 800,000 consulting firms across the globe, ranging from single-shingle shops to 400,000-employee behemoths. Whereas once graduates of the best law schools (the "T14") only wanted to work with firms like Skadden or Jones Day, today super-star lawyers serve clients while working across the Am Law 200, as well as hundreds of prestigious boutique firms.

To paraphrase Thomas Friedman, the world is getting flatter. Technology has allowed experts to serve clients all over the world. Freed from the constraints of geography, those experts have narrower and narrower niches as they seek to differentiate what they do from others. The accountant next door no longer does the audit for the local car dealership. Today, she is a partner in a firm that specializes in ERC tax credits or helps drive out med-tech costs for community and regional hospitals in 50 states.

This is good for the marketplace as it gives rise to innovation and more experts are moving around with their ideas. More than a few of those single-shingle firms are founded by leaders spinning out of the behemoths, eager to take their unique, niched skills to market in their own way. And even more frequently, experts bounce from one big firm to another, in the face of firm reorgs or better offers. Many people we interviewed for this book have a resume that feels like a tour of top firms (Deloitte, to AlixPartners, to EY, to Capgemini). Few firms are led exclusively by "lifers," presenting both challenges around culture and change management, as well as opportunities to bring in talent to drive growth.

We're seeing similar changes on the customer side. Buyers have also become decentralized; rarely is a project sold to an individual buyer – and even if it is, there are certainly other influencers. Successful sales of services often mean winning over a dozen or more stakeholders. And these client stakeholders are moving around more frequently than they used to as well. This, again, represents both challenges in staying embedded in your client accounts, as well as opportunities to win new work with your fans when they move on.

Adding to the change in this landscape is the recent influx of private equity (PE) into professional services. PE firms have seen the benefits of strong cash-flow and ample growth opportunity in the professional services industry, often in pursuit of mergers and acquisitions (M&A) that allow firms to double their geographic footprint or bring winning services to new industries. This book is not about M&A – we could write a whole book about driving growth via acquisition. This book is about how to build the business development engine inside firms that can propel them toward sustained growth,

x

Preface

whether pursuing acquisitions or not. But this is timely for those who have – or are seeking – outside capital, because growth capital comes with growth expectations. Winning new work in a professional services business is different than winning new work in a SaaS or CPG business, but absent a clear road map from you, investors are known to put forward (or force) "sales plans" that are bound to fail. You cannot just hire 10 more salespeople to ensure 10× growth in your practice that does data privacy consulting for large ecommerce businesses. That sale is far more complex than giving someone a script and a list of names.

As fast as expertise has spread from a few firms to many, expertise about how to *run* a growing firm has not kept pace. And this is a problem. To build asset value in an advisory firm, one must do two things exceptionally well: One must design their organization (people, process, and technology) to serve clients at scale, and one must also *grow* a small – and then large – company well. Weakness in either area will gate growth.

Our particular obsession is around this second piece: how professional services firms grow. Our team has written two books on the subject – one on how to find and serve new clients, *How Clients Buy*, and a second on how firms expand relationships within the clients they already have, *Never Say Sell*.

This book is about a third critical subject: how do professional services firms *manage and scale their growth efforts* from the go-go days of entrepreneurship, when "sales" looked like founders calling their friends, to a state-of-the-art business development machine that's consistently up and to the right.

Being curious, we decided to dig in and unearth best practices around business development in professional services firms, asking ourselves how firms replicate those practices to drive decade-after-decade growth. This book is a road map for anyone looking to grow their professional services organization with lessons, tools, and best practices that can apply to the Chief Growth Officer at a Big Four consulting firm as well as to the 10-person law practice that just opened up shop around the corner. Whether you lead a practice or just joined a growing firm, what follows is a helpful guidebook to give structure and direction to how you deploy time, energy, resources, and capital to grow.

We are excited to share with you what we found.

A Note on Words

Words matter. Our previous book title, *Never Say Sell,* was not selected at random. Our industry exhibits an historic aversion to the word "sales," not wanting the exchange of their expertise for profit to be confused with a desperate used car salesman trying to offload a lemon. Our belief is that part of this aversion to the word "sales" has created an aversion to doing what is needed to build a growth engine in professional services firms. As an industry, we've come to develop a language with which we're more comfortable: we talk about "business development" or "BD," and "growth," and "go-to-market strategies," to avoid saying "sell." We talk about "account expansion" or "client development" to avoid talking about "cross-selling." And we as an industry do this for good reason. Indeed, we are not just trying to "sell" our expertise to anyone walking down the block – we're looking for those who are truly in need of the expertise we have to offer. We seek the mutual benefit of truly *serving* those who are in need of help, which in turn builds our own business.

You will see all of the different words outlined above used in this book, often reflected in the quotes from those we interviewed, whose language we wanted to maintain.

In addition to "growth" vernacular, you'll see us talk about those driving growth in multiple ways: partners, growth leaders, managing directors, account executives, sales leaders. Firms are structured differently and use different titles, but we are confident you'll understand what we are trying to say when we write about the people who bear the responsibilities of firm growth.

Among the authors and those quoted, you will also see a few different words used to talk about the work firms do for their clients – services, service lines, offerings, practices, solutions.

Our hope is that readers of this book will work in firms varying in size from 5 to 500,000. Large firms will inevitably be a combination of many business units or practices. While some of the concepts in this book are written about as "firm" best practices, many others are equally relevant at the practice level, and we hope they provide a roadmap to think about growth for your "business" – whatever that scope is.

Finally, and not surprisingly, you'll see the word "client" used abundantly throughout this book. When we write about a client, we mean a person. We mean the Northwest Regional VP of Operations at Walmart who went to the University of Washington, has two kids, and enjoys the occasional trip to Vegas. We mean the Supply Chain Director at John Deere who just moved over from Caterpillar and is getting their bearings in the new company while working on a young adult novel on the weekends to feed their creative desire. We will use "account" or "client account" when we are talking about Walmart or John Deere. We are in the relationship business, and we have relationships with people – not companies.

Now, let's dig into the good stuff: how we organize ourselves to build relationships with *clients* to expand *accounts* by providing new *services* and *developing business* that will *grow* our firms.

xiii

Preface

Part I

The Problem and the Promise

Chapter 1

The Problem – Why Professional Services Firms Fail to Scale Business Development

Investors have a way of popping the balloons of our high hopes.

Andi and Jacob walked out of the meeting room at the Marriott Marquis Chicago after eight packed hours. They'd shaken about 50 hands and had five (or more) cups of coffee each while sharing the story of Profitable Ideas Exchange (PIE), our small but growing consulting firm based in Bozeman, Montana. Over the course of the day, they spoke with more than a dozen potential investors, practicing their pitch for capital that could help PIE unlock its growth goals over the next 10 years. Andi is the CEO and Jacob is the president of PIE, a firm of about 75 that helps large professional services firms build bridges to their target market.

The conference was organized around companies like PIE having "speed dates" with different investment firms. Andi and Jacob were excited to meet potential investors and had been eager to share the stories of PIE's success over the last 25 years.

They walked in that morning with freshly pressed shirts and caffeine-fueled excitement, but as the day progressed, the duo quickly found wrinkles emerging on their shirts – and their confidence. Each investor group kept asking how PIE planned to scale the firm's business development function to meet their revenue goals for growth. At first, Jacob responded by highlighting PIE's track record of success: "We've grown steadily for the last 10 years. We *know* how to win new business. We've grown 15% a year with the energy of our current team. We won't sleep at night unless we're growing." Jacob's confidence was met with skepticism.

Catching the L at the end of the day, furrowed brows replaced the morning's smiles. Jacob read the frustration on the face of his long-time business partner and felt it too. "They kept talking about the 'return on invested capital dynamic' associated with adding new salespeople and they seemed to get freaked out when we said that business development would fall to us as senior rainmakers." Jacob paused, reflecting on his 20-year tenure at PIE. "I mean, expertise and gray hair are what sell professional services. We might not be totally gray yet, but clearly, *we are* the growth strategy. It feels like they're saying they don't believe us – or believe *in us*."

"And that is exactly the problem," Andi confirmed, finally beginning to smile. "Sure, we could grow the firm to $20 million, but we know that what we're doing now won't be enough to get us to $200 million, or even $50 million. No two people could do that on their own in a business like ours."

When Andi and Jacob got back to Bozeman, they convened with Erika and Walt. The four of us, the authors of this book, realized we had a problem to solve.

"I know we've been working to operationalize our approach to client management so we can teach our newer, more junior consultants," Jacob reflected to the room of his partners. "We want to get more operating leverage on the business. I get that. It makes sense. I think those investors were saying something similar. They want to see us operationalize our go-to-market efforts. They want to invest in companies that have a real business development machine."

"You're right," Andi added. "We need to build a team that operates like an *engine* – that isn't so dependent on a few of us. We need growth of the firm to go beyond our own relationships and rolodexes, and we need to show how profits can be reinvested into strategic growth initiatives with knowable returns. We know we sell work based on relationships, but we still need a plan to scale those relationships."

Erika – PIE's chief client officer – chimed in, "Predictable growth. Of course. You weren't talking to venture investors. You were talking to growth investors, and they need a *replicable* growth model before they put cash in harm's way."

"And that's what we want, too," said Andi. "We shouldn't be investing our profits back into the company unless we see a path for that investment to help us scale."

Walt jumped in, nodding vigorously. "This is exactly the challenge nearly every firm runs into – trying to scale business development in professional services is like herding wet cats. Few firms have figured out how to do that well." Walt knew what he was talking about: a former McKinsey partner, global managing director at Accenture, and global head of sales for ERM, PIE's three leaders felt lucky to have him as a board member, trusted advisor, and friend.

The group breathed a collective sigh of relief – not that anything had been solved. Rather, it felt good to be on the same page and finally put words to what suddenly seemed obvious: PIE, and professional services firms more generally, need to operationalize and manage business development just as they manage other key parts of their businesses. Professional services firms need growth engines.

* * *

Indeed, if a firm is to grow, building a replicable process around business development (BD) is *imperative* and a prerequisite for sustained growth. Without a growth engine, professional services firms atrophy as the rainmakers lose enthusiasm on their way to retirement.

5

The Problem

Even in a people business where growth is a function of reputation, referral, and relationships, **we have conviction that there is a way to create a growth engine** – an operation not solely reliant on a couple key rainmakers, acquiring other firms, or luck.

Why Building the Engine Is Hard

The four of us – Andi, Jacob, Erika, and Walt – collectively have more than 80 years running professional services firms. Our firm, PIE, adds another 25 years of growth history, data, and lessons learned to that resume. We've spent many of those years grappling with these exact challenges and listening to our clients share similar frustrations.

We knew we couldn't solve the problem of scaling a BD function on our own, so we talked to more than 100 of *you* in a year-long series of interviews. We asked Partners, CEOs, CMOs, and CGOs across consulting, legal, financial, and technology services firms: What does good look like? How do you build a growth engine? What's worked and what's failed? What made you want to tear your hair out, and what made you celebrate a banner year? What does best-in-class look like and, importantly, how do you get there?

If these interviews taught us anything, it's that everyone has this same question rattling around in their head: how do you build a sustainable, resilient, and scalable growth engine in professional services?

Good news: Hundreds of firms have found myriad ways to drive excellence in how they develop clients and lead go-to-market efforts; we can learn from their examples.

Our goal is to help those who are leading professional services firms or practices better understand how to successfully scale their growth function. We want to unpack how great firms go to market, how they define and expand their market, who they hire, and what they ask those rainmakers to do. We want to explore what training looks like and how success is enabled. We're here to understand the best tools to measure performance and how effective sales teams can be supported by structure. We're going to tease out when and how incentives are most effective and examine best-in-class business development processes.

Before we do that, however, let's look at some of the systemic challenges that make this so hard.

Challenge #1: Selling Professional Services Is Different

While this book is not about *how to sell* professional services (we have written about that previously in *How Clients Buy*), the unique way in which services are sold is an important piece of what makes building a scalable growth function so challenging. In *How Clients Buy,* PIE's former CEO, Tom McMakin, wrote about the Seven Elements (Figure 1.1) of a client's buying journey as they consider engaging with a professional services firm.

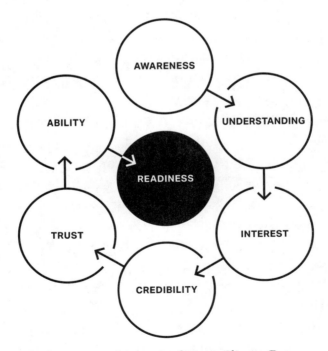

Figure 1.1 The Seven Elements of How Clients Buy.

The Seven Elements show the pre-conditions that must be in place for a client to engage with a professional services firm: The buyer must be **aware** of you; they must **understand** what you do; they must have an **interest** in what you do (it meets a need they have); they must find you **credible** and believe you can deliver on the work competently; they must **trust** that you will have their best interests at heart even when they don't fully understand what you are doing; they must have the **ability** (or budget authority) to buy from you; and, most importantly, they must be **ready** – the timing needs to be right.

Professional services firms share some of these same sales preconditions with those who market and sell goods. The difference is that buyers evaluate widgets and hardgoods based primarily on features and attributes (for example you buy a pair of jeans based on things like the fit, color, feel of the denim, hem length, and pocket style), whereas in professional services, the "product" is expertise. You don't need a personal relationship with the denim designer to know you like their jeans. When choosing an accountant or attorney, people engage based on who they **trust** and find **credible**.

Services are what economists call "credence goods," meaning that clients depend on service providers to both diagnose a problem *and* solve it. Credence goods are inherently hard for customers to evaluate, even after they make the purchase, and the traditional sales playbooks don't apply. Someone might be an excellent mechanic, but at the same time they charge you double for a service you don't need (diminishing **trust**). Equally, a mechanic might be as honest as the day is long (you'd trust them to babysit your kids) but might not be very good at servicing your new electric vehicle (diminishing **credibility**). Hiring a consultant is more like hiring a mechanic than buying a new pair of jeans: the client must trust that their consultant is working in their best interest, even when they don't entirely

8

The Growth Engine

understand the problem, and they must feel confident that the consultant is very, very good at what they do.

The amount of patience required to engage with new clients also makes BD in professional services different. Sales cycles are often long. Erika recently closed a deal after three years of quarterly check-in calls, two lunches in New York, and persistent email and LinkedIn follow-up. You would never see your local Verizon sales rep courting you for three years of lunches to get you to switch from T-Mobile. This is because the size of the prize is entirely different; a few lunches are easily worth it for a $500k contract for PIE, but probably not worth it for a $140/month cell phone plan.

This is why seasoned rainmakers tell new professionals to stay connected with their web of relationships. The people in your network might know you, understand exactly what you do, have a need with which you can help, feel like you are great at what you do, trust you implicitly to do the right thing, and have the money to buy … and still not be *ready* to engage. How many times have you been *this* close to sealing an engagement only to learn that your client is pushing "pause" on a project until they get through a reorganization, complete the acquisition, or seat a new CFO? As Ross Hunter, CEO and founder of CopyLab says, "The biggest challenge with business development is patience."

The influx of PE investment in professional services only exacerbates this problem. PE firms typically overlay the same growth models they've successfully applied to scale SaaS businesses, where big investments reliably translate into quick growth. In professional services, this model breaks down, driving perverse incentives that seek quick wins in lieu of the long-term investment in relationships. Building and scaling a growth organization is not as simple as writing a script for a salesperson, throwing money at advertising, or even making sure you have a big booth at all the conferences. Selling services at any size or scale is complex.

Challenge #2: Your Salespeople Are Different – They're Also Doing the Work

Verizon's salespeople are responsible for selling Verizon cell phones. Their sales reps have one job and one mission. They are *not* also responsible for designing, building, and packaging the cell phones. This is not so in professional services.

Ally Brophy, senior marketing manager at the New England accounting and advisory firm Baker Newman Noyes, puts it well, "Our business developers are our Partners, who are also doing client work, who are leaders of the firm, while also handling internal communications and developing and mentoring the next generation. It's just a lot." Indeed, it is ... a lot.

Top rainmakers do the work because "delivery sells." A successful law firm partner is great at business development, not because they are good at advertising themselves; they are great because day in and day out, they demonstrate their expertise as they manage complex legal challenges and deliver strong client outcomes. Having a history of generating those outcomes fuels increased revenues by way of reputation, referral, and relationships.

"Simply hiring a big shot, high-dollar salesperson won't work because they don't have the time in or knowledge of our market," said a friend of ours who runs a middle market accounting firm to his new private equity sponsor's partners. Instead, you must build business development capacity among those most able to win new work – often your best deliverers and client whisperers. In firms where billable hours reign supreme, this is no small feat. A billable hour is a jealous partner to an hour of unpaid business development.

Another ancillary challenge with this model is that successful partners sometimes squat on accounts. Why would a partner put one of their most precious relationships at risk by letting a colleague, whom they may barely know, pitch other work? This behavior is often reinforced by poor incentive structures that fail to reward collaboration, encouraging rainmakers to hold tight to the keys to their kingdoms. Mike Martin, client development lead and principal at ZS Associates, deeply understands this challenge, and is one of many who have tried new avenues to address it. He explains, "We put a premium on collaboration and reflect that in our sales credits. We also encourage senior partners to find new territories and it is expected that they will make room for up and comers."

Challenge #3: Managing the Unmanageable

Because "sales" is considered a dirty word in professional services, we don't talk about it. This has led to it being *wildly undermanaged*. Says Michael Pittendrigh, national managing partner of Consulting and Private Business Advisory at Grant Thornton Australia, "Partners often operate independently. How do you unite them into a cohesive partnership rather than a group of individuals under the same infrastructure? How do you demonstrate the need for a unified movement over siloed strategies?" Dozens of others we spoke with, who also lead successful firms and practices, are pondering same questions.

The egos of a powerful team of rainmakers compound these challenges, making anything beyond organized chaos feel like a win. If your top rainmakers believe they have succeeded due to their genius and personality, they have no interest in being "managed." Partners are entrepreneurial and have built their careers (and perhaps their fortunes) on their client relationships. Why would they let someone else tell them what to do when they've proven they know best? From a management perspective, this can feel like the difference between being a coxswain on a smoothly operating rowing shell and being the captain of a very unruly pirate ship.

Layer the complexity of professional services organizations and the markets they serve on top of this team of rogue players and you're left with a complicated, albeit powerful, mess. Shobha Meera is the former head of global sales and marketing for Capgemini Financial Services and is the current executive sponsor for Group Sustainability Services – America after serving as the firm's chief corporate responsibility officer. She says, "When you are with a large professional services organization offering a range of services and expertise, you are by definition serving multiple client stakeholders with their respective priorities and imperatives. You'd have to be incredibly fortunate to experience beautifully laid out organizations where all stakeholders are perfectly aligned and agendas are nicely connected and flow seamlessly. In reality, organizations are usually complex, with their particular challenges and interdependencies, and with the human factor of wanting to retain a degree of control. Successful business developers are masters of navigating this complexity while creating value for clients and their organizations."

Challenge #4: We Never Learned to Use a Measuring Stick

We all know the importance of having rigorous data gathering systems and metrics when it comes to the work we do with our own clients. However, the professional services industry has largely avoided the same rigor around disciplined processes and measurement when it comes to managing their own growth.

Sure, we measure what matters: did we grow this year? Are we profitable? But we don't keep track of the questions that might help us predict our growth. Do we track leads and contacts? Do we measure opportunities and win rates, pipeline growth, and time-to-close? Do we compare professionals with each other? Do we commission success in a way that works? Critically, do we have accurate and comprehensive data that *allows* us to measure what we want to? Most firms either don't measure at all or fail to measure the things they can actually manage.

Challenge #5: The Pain of Making Change Is Higher Than the Pain of Not Growing

The challenges around change management are as prolific as the changes required to build a world-class growth engine. Even when firms are aligned around where they want to go and have agreed on how to get there, an unwillingness to change plagues teams looking to move forward. This happens for a few reasons:

1. **Inertia:** Newton's first law of motion holds as true here as it does in physics. An object in motion will stay in motion and an object at rest will stay at rest unless acted upon by a net external force. Creating change requires external forces to adjust the day-to-day habits, activities, behaviors, and outcomes of a professional services organization. As firms grow and mature, the force needed to change direction also grows. People are inherently resistant to change, reverting most easily to well-trodden pathways.

2. **Impatience:** "You can't make a massive change in something as critical as your sales structure or your incentive structure and expect to see results in a few months," says Jim Batterton, former senior vice president and general manager at Kyndryl and IBM. "It takes time, and lots of people are unwilling to be patient." We agree.

3. **Sales Culture:** Trying to get a bunch of proud, independent rainmakers to shift directions collectively is like herding cats. The entrepreneurial culture of professional services firms combined with intelligent, motivated, and independent sales executives present both strengths and challenges when it comes to change management. As firms grow, the natural tendency to add bureaucracy and process can stifle and frustrate those who have largely operated as independent entities.

4. **Poor Communication:** *How* change is communicated and reinforced is often as important as *what* is communicated. Too often, firms start with the "what," and fail to do the work up front to clearly understand and communicate the "why" for change.

5. **Inconsistency:** Without a clear change management framework, firms struggle with ad hoc approaches to change that create confusion and frustration, and ultimately demotivate teams. If partners can't trust that today's incentive structure or growth priorities will be the same tomorrow – or will be delivered consistently – why should they get on board?

Building the Engine

A few weeks after that original Chicago debrief, the four of us – Jacob, Andi, Erika, and Walt – reconvened in Bozeman, sitting outside the PIE office as the first signs of summer began to show. The mood matched the sunshine and light breeze shuffling the pile of papers and sticky notes strewn across the table. The recent flurry of PE activity had sparked countless conversations within PIE and with PIE's clients, and our minds were spinning. Although the infusion of capital was putting growth pressure on the industry, it also presented an opportunity. "We need a road map," Walt said. "We know what good looks like, we just need to spell out the steps to transform a few successful rainmakers into a world-class growth engine."

This book promises to deliver just that and demonstrate how any professional services firm can mature and scale their business development function to build a sustainable and successful model for growth.

Chapter 2

The Promise – You Can Build an Engine

Adrian Newey is the uncontested best when it comes to designing Formula One cars. He is coveted by team principals and top drivers alike – they know that he will make their cars faster, and he will put them on the top step of the podium. His cars have won 12 World Constructor's Championships and hundreds of Grands Prix during his time with teams like Williams, McLaren, and Red Bull Racing.

What is his secret? Why is it that when Newey is around, the cars find that extra tenth of a second that puts them at the front of the grid? Unsurprisingly, it's not one single thing. As Newey describes it, "The aim is to have a car where all the different elements—aerodynamics, suspension, tires, engine—work together, so you get a balance that is greater than the sum of its parts" (Newey, 2017). He wins because he seamlessly combines every element, making sure each piece and player is top quality and in harmony with each other.

Jeffery Immelt, the former CEO of GE, has been known to characterize the ultimate growth goal as knowing that when you put your foot on the gas, the car will go forward. But as Les McKeown, author of *Predictable Success*, writes, "The reality is that the leaders of most organizations can't say any such thing. For them, when they step on the gas pedal, the car may or may not go forward. And if it does go forward, it may or may not go in the direction they expected or desired."

How, then, do managing partners, chief growth officers, CEOs, practice leaders, and founders connect the gas pedal and steering wheel with their intention to grow their firms? What are they doing with their tires, their aerodynamics, and their suspension, to help them find that extra tenth of a second?

We found that firms who are the best at driving predictable, sustainable growth are powerfully disciplined in how they approach business development. Nothing is left to chance. They know what they need to do, and they hold themselves accountable to doing what they say.

The Disciplines

Firms and practices with high-octane growth engines have rigor around five disciplines, which will serve as the structural backbone of this book. This is a road map for firms to navigate the business development maturity curve (see Figure 2.1) and move from Entrepreneurial to World-class across each of the five disciplines outlined below:

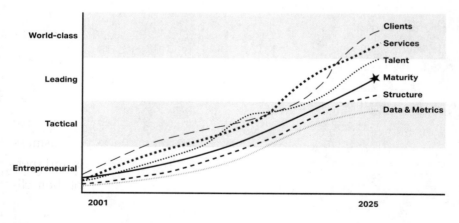

Figure 2.1 The business development maturity curve.

- **Discipline 1: Services.** World-class firms know exactly what they do best and where they have a right to succeed. They have narrowed their focus to be number one in the places they know they can win and have adopted a checkerboard strategy to cultivate a collection of adjacencies over time (see Chapter 4). World-class firms build their strategies for investing in new services based on direct feedback from their customers, and often pilot new services with top clients.

- **Discipline 2: Clients.** World-class firms know who they serve and understand their target buyers inside and out. They are disciplined in who they chase. World-class firms have rigorous account-planning. They are so engrained in their top client firms that they may even co-create account plans with their clients. Consistent growth can be expected from current clients and surprise client losses are exceptionally rare.

- **Discipline 3: Talent and Performance Management.** World-class firms are able to harness high-achieving, competitive, independent rainmakers to predict and control the BD weather. World-class firms have both formal and informal training and development processes to ensure they have a pipeline of future rainmakers and that their best stories are scaled across the enterprise. They have developed a collaborative, growth-focused culture supported by reward systems aligned to firm goals, ensuring they can attract and retain top performers.

- **Discipline 4: Organizational Model.** World-class firms develop BD structures that support their strategy. They have trusting relationships and true alignment between business development and marketing, buoyed by shared goals and metrics around company growth and deep knowledge of their clients and prospects. As World-class firms develop their structure and build support around their rainmakers, they are thoughtful about each role that is created and how the role will ultimately make sellers successful, while maintaining team cohesion and excellent client experience.

- **Discipline 5: Data and Measurement.** World-class firms do the hard thing: they look at themselves consistently and ask, "How are we doing?" They set up key performance indicators (KPIs), measure themselves, and they do not let themselves off the hook. If something – or someone – is not performing, they take action. They use data to make decisions and inform changes, and they build systems to ensure they know what the future looks like, so that growth can remain predictable. World-class firms also make thoughtful investments in technology to support their growth and – importantly – hold people accountable for using the technology consistently and correctly to ensure it is harvesting value for the organization.

The Stages of Maturity

The five disciplines are the pistons, valves, and camshafts that go into building your growth engine. But greatness is not born overnight, and not one of the firms we interviewed claimed to have it all figured out on day one. A firm's maturity (Figure 2.1) is a combination of where they fall along each individual discipline. For example, a $200M legal consulting firm might have a robust talent development model that is Leading compared to peers, but lacks discipline in who they serve, taking a more Entrepreneurial approach to client definition.

Building a growth engine is the story of maturation over time, and synergy between disciplines distinguishes firms with World-class business development functions.

The four stages of maturity can be characterized as follows:

- **Stage 1: Entrepreneurial.** In the **Entrepreneurial** stage, firms have, well, an Entrepreneurial culture. Individual partners more or less act on their own priorities and impulses, and there is no formal structure or strategy for growth. This works well in the nascent days of a firm, where the founder partners are also the IT directors and marketing happens at their kitchen tables on Sunday night.

- **Stage 2: Tactical.** In the **Tactical** stage, some structure emerges, perhaps with teams developing under different partners as the firm starts to go to market by industry, geography, or service line. This stage is characterized by early players deputizing new hires to get modest leverage on their business development efforts.

- **Stage 3: Leading.** In the **Leading** stage, the team is thoughtful and organized about their go-to-market strategy, the business development function is centrally managed, and accountability is in place. The firm is clear about where it wants its growth to come from – distinguishing between new logos and current client expansion. The firm has a clear point of view about how new opportunities are created and an active pipeline that is used to forecast revenues and drive hiring. It measures win-loss ratios and understands the relationship between those ratios, pricing, and profitability.

- **Stage 4: World-class.** When firms are **World-class**, business development reaches a "flow state," humming along like a race-winning Formula 1 engine. Marketing and BD are fully aligned, growth is predictable and scalable, and every element of the function operates at such a high level that, should there be a hiccup in one area (say, training processes slip, or a new incentive structure falls flat), all the other elements are strong enough to course-correct swiftly and minimize engine sputters. Critically,

The Promise – You Can Build an Engine

STAGES OF MATURITY

FIRM CHARACTERISTICS

ENTREPRENEURIAL

- Excitement and creativity; organized like a pirate ship with disdain for process
- Services are like "snowflakes" — every project is very customized
- Client list is founder's rolodex and whoever they can get in touch with
- Attracts entrepreneurial people (often in the image of the founder) and has no formal BD training
- No support structures for those doing BD
- No data strategy or visibility on performance; all that's measured is "are we growing and making some money?"

TACTICAL

- Feels like a roller coaster; lots of activity with unpredictable success
- Service definition emerges, with a focus on one core service offering
- Ideal Client Profile (ICP) is defined; a target list of clients is developed
- Emergence of sidewalk coaching (juniors tag along on client visits) and some collaboration; incentives in place but confusing and frustrating
- Organized on paper; limited BD support roles and structure emerge
- Opportunities tracked on various spreadsheets and limited or misleading metrics

LEADING

- Confidence and some complacency — practice and market leaders operate in silos, thinking "why make changes if we're growing?"
- Well known within marketplace; positive reputation
- Process for developing new services based on client/market feedback
- Deep client relationships and account planning in place to expand accounts
- BD training is formalized, and the firm leverages skill sets to drive growth
- Support structures and roles are built around those driving growth
- Rigorous data collection and strong visibility into firm performance; CRM informs forecasting and hiring

WORLD-CLASS

- Proactive, orchestrated, forward-looking, and focused on continuous improvement; go to market as "one-firm firm"
- Known as top player in the field and sought after by prospective clients
- Solutions development for clients, providing the right mix of services; new services developed in collaboration with top clients
- Sophisticated account planning and expansion based on trust throughout firm; hyper-sensitive to client needs and responsive to client feedback
- Employer brand draws top growth talent; formal, impactful BD training underpins a "growth" mindset across firm; incentives drive collaboration
- Growth operates like a true engine — the right roles are filled with the right people driving toward shared objectives
- Highly transparent performance and team recognition; CRM is embraced and used consistently so shared, up-to-date data can propel the business

Figure 2.2 Firm characteristics at each stage of maturity.

The Growth Engine

if a founder or top-selling partner leaves the firm, it does not derail the firm's growth. World-class business development engines are forward-looking, insight-driven, and market-creating. Because the firm is going to market as "one firm" – the entire organization functions as a cohesive unit – management can seamlessly shift money from a legacy practice (high profit; low growth) and allocate that capital to firm-wide bets (high growth; investment stage) without the fear of frustrating teams.

Importantly, maturity does not always equate to time or size. Figure 2.2 shows the general characteristics at each stage. While **you cannot skip a stage** in the progression from Entrepreneurial to World-class, you are also not *guaranteed* to move up the curve with time or growth in size. Firms may also fall back a stage in certain disciplines if focus is pointed in the wrong direction.

Business Development Maturity – Reader Assessment

The model of five disciplines and four stages serves as a heuristic. Where are you on your journey up the business development maturity curve? The answer is a combination of your development across each discipline. Are you at a Tactical stage with your talent but World-class on structure? What aspects of talent are holding you back from making the jump from Tactical to Leading or World-class? As you read the rest of the book, we encourage you to scribble notes (yes! mark up our book!) and use the "Business Development Maturity – Reader Assessment" found in the Appendix. Doing so will allow you to track and prioritize your thoughts and do what is most important when you are done reading this book: sit down with your colleagues and start the discussion. What does your current maturity curve look like? Where do you go from here to build a BD engine that even Adrian Newey would envy?

Part II

Services

Chapter 3

Knowing What You Do – Service Definition and Discipline

Erika felt like a total fraud. She was in her second year of professional ski racing with the start of the season just weeks away, and things were not going well at a pre-season training camp with the U.S. Ski Team.

In cross-country skiing, there are two primary types of skiing: classic and skate. Within those, there are a series of sub-techniques that skiers rotate through based on terrain. Double-poling is a sub-technique of classic skiing where skiers use only their arms to propel themselves down a groomed track. For the best in the world, double-poling is a secret weapon to pull out on flats and often used at the end of races to fly past competitors. For Erika, double-poling was her nemesis. She never had a ton of upper body strength, and she found herself losing ground to competitors any time the terrain called for double-poling. Being with the U.S. Ski Team only magnified this weakness, putting a spotlight on the strengths she *didn't* have in front of the coaches she most wanted to impress.

Erika spent the entire camp exclusively practicing double-poling, willing her upper body to somehow get stronger. By the end of the week, she was still meters behind, with sore lats and triceps. She was on the verge of tears when she skied by Matt Whitcomb, the U.S. women's head coach. Matt has a smile that starts with his eyes (especially when talking about fly-fishing), and he treats his athletes like his equals. As Erika skied by, he gave her a hearty "Nice work –you're doing great!" but Erika didn't feel great.

A few weeks later, Erika sent Matt a note asking for feedback to help her improve her double-pole. When she opened her email the next day, Erika was surprised by Matt's response:

> "Ah, the double-poling thing. Don't worry – you're already a great skier. People too often dismiss what they are good at because they think being hard on themselves and focusing on *new* skills will make them faster. You know what happens when this type of person gets faster? I don't either, because they usually don't get faster. That constant, subtle stress of *not* acknowledging the great things you already have going? That wears a person out. All these different styles are just a different way of breathing. I learned years ago to stop focusing on weaknesses – on missing skills – in athletes I coach. Too many athletes choose to focus on: what *else* do I need to do better? Meanwhile, your talents – your real strengths – are being ignored. Instead, identify your strengths. Learn them a little better. Love them. And hone them. You're an excellent skate skier, and you're unbelievable on hilly terrain. Lean into this. Be the world's fastest skate skier on hilly terrain. Make these strengths super strengths."

The super strength of a professional services firm? Your service niche. Building a truly World-class growth engine, like building a World-class athlete, starts with what you do really well. How does your firm stand out in the market? What is the thing you are known for that earns you a spot at the proverbial U.S. Ski Team camp to begin with? Whether you are a small firm with a single service or a practice lead in a global consulting firm with 20+ service lines, identifying your super strengths is key. These give you a right to win.

When we think about the clients we work with in professional services, this ability to identify, sharpen, and lean into their strengths is the single biggest key to unlocking the growth potential of a practice and a firm. Start by strengthening your strengths and concentrate on developing your differentiated superpower, widening the distance you already have ahead of your competition. This is important for three reasons:

1. **You become known for your niche.** If someone asks you what the best restaurant in the United States is, your mind tends to shut down in the face of so many delicious choices. But if someone asks you who serves the best smashburger in Austin, Texas, your mind might just go to Biggie's Yardbird at the Armadillo Den. When you are strongly niched, you are top of mind when a client has the need you serve. There are a thousand providers of mid-market legal advice, but perhaps by leaning into the help you have given American companies setting up production facilities in Mexico as they navigate local regulations (the law firm of Von Wobeser in Mexico City does exactly this), you become known as the go-to firm for this sort of work.

2. **When you niche yourself, you get better at what you do.** As Malcolm Gladwell writes in *Outliers*, "Practice isn't the thing you do once you're good. It's the thing you do that makes you good." Investors say that Warren Buffett is successful with his wholly owned companies because, assuming long hold periods and strong reinvestment opportunities, capital compounds (which is to say, money multiplies quickly).

27

Knowing What You Do – Service Definition and Discipline

Intellectual capital works the same way. Automate tax provision in Canadian retirement funds for a decade, and you get good at it – maybe even learn a trick or two that wouldn't be obvious to a newbie. This builds efficiency, builds your reputation, and drives growth.

3. **The more you deliver the same work you are already good at doing, the more margin you can realize.** You have the equipment, you know which subcontractors will finish on time and within budget, you spend less time planning how to execute the project, and your brain slips more easily into high productivity when faced with a familiar task.

But, but, but …

… we love to innovate.

Sitting in front of a whiteboard and imagining all the possible things you could do for a client is fun! Founders have the gift of seeing unmet needs and designing solutions, but they often lack the patience to scale the first need they uncovered (and solved) before moving on to another unmet need. Further, founders are often fearful of putting all their eggs in one basket, feeling the pull to diversify so they are not so vulnerable.

Let's take Althea as an example.

Althea was going a million miles an hour building her new firm. She had worked at a leading technology consultancy on their major annual conferences – well-attended, ecosystem events. Part AI wonderland, part vendor hall, part commiseration-over-cocktails, and part C-suite strategic huddles, these were complicated parties to throw. She had been the impresario at the center of it all.

When the firm downsized their events team, Althea spun out and set up her own conference company.

28

The Growth Engine

Soon, she had two clients that had attended her previous events and wanted her to design a similar conference program for their companies.

Althea hired a team and rented offices in suburban Dallas. The open-floor-plan space was a hive of activity with recent graduates, a few interns, and two tenured, trusted marketing hands making things happen for clients. The team's meticulous planning and preparation led to a successful first event and a happy client.

The next Friday afternoon at a favorite restaurant in McKinney, Texas, Althea brought together her team. Instead of debriefing how they could use this first success to get new introductions or win more event work with this client, Althea asked the team, "What else should we be doing for our clients? What other services should we offer?" She loved to brainstorm, and looking for new ideas seemed more fun than focusing on what they already knew.

The ideas came boiling over the transom. "Let's build their registration sites." "What about food and beverage? There is money in that." "What they really need help with is driving executives to the events. We should offer to recruit."

Althea loved this kind of energy. She could feel it. She was building a business.

That night, Althea visualized the org chart in her mind. She'd be the CEO and have a CFO and a CIO (finance and technology were not her strong suit). She'd hire a salesperson. Then under her would be four operating divisions – Conference Content, Food and Beverage (F&B), Venue and Logistics, and Attendance. Suddenly, building her firm to $100M in bookings didn't seem too far-fetched. She wondered if she should take on a financial partner. First, though, she'd have to build a proper website to let clients know of her expanded service offerings.

Althea's firm could now offer a lot more to her clients, but that also meant she was competing against other, much larger firms that

Knowing What You Do – Service Definition and Discipline

could bring economies of scale to their bids. She had nothing to bring to the table but a case study from her last company where she had been responsible for content and attendee experience but had not generated attendance, managed F&B needs, or built registration sites. Experience in these areas seemed important to the clients on whose work she bid. Because cashflow was tight, she was unable to hire the best, most experienced talent. Most importantly, though, she was no longer a superstar. Her brand, which used to be the "Conference Content Queen," had been diluted to "a bit player in the $994 billion global events industry."

Althea's pipeline of new work dried up. She had exhausted her network, couldn't win bid work, and no one was beating a path to her door. She had a sincere desire to grow quickly with many service lines, but it ended up harming the business.

Firms often find they build their reputation on one service, then over time learn they have earned the right to expand that offering into an adjacency. When we asked firm leaders how they expanded their service lines, the most common answer was, "Our clients invited us." This has certainly been true for us at PIE. Historically, we have executed business development tasks on behalf of professional services firms, but now we also conduct training for business development teams, because our clients started to ask us, "Would you ever train our team in BD best practices?"

So, all of us have a dilemma: It's equally true that strongly niched firms succeed by being known, by compounding expertise in a particular domain, *and* that good work begets opportunity to expand service lines. From the interviews we conducted, there was a strong consensus that you go narrow first and then expand your services from there. Service expansion happens over time, and you can't get to the place where you are offering multiple strong, growing services unless you start from the place of being sharply defined. Layer on new offerings too early and you risk not being known for anything. Wait too long and you risk exhausting the vein you are currently mining or missing an emerging market you have a right to serve. Let's dig into finding the sweet spot (Figure 3.1).

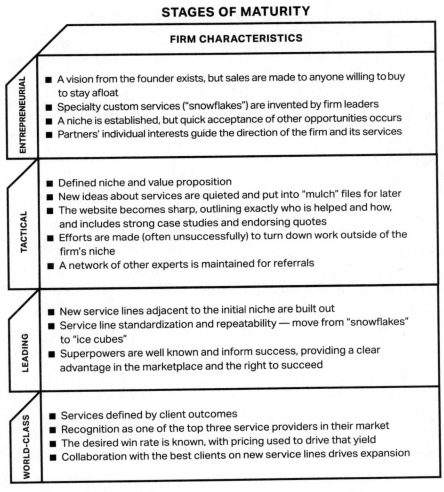

Figure 3.1 Firm characteristics at each stage of maturity – service definition and discipline.

Jump 1: Entrepreneurial to Tactical

Preach the Niche

The first step in moving up the maturity curve is an exercise in focus – a client might need someone to provide support across a wide range of challenges, but your firm may not have the expertise to adequately serve *all* their needs. A practice's niche is the overlap on a Venn diagram between what you are great at, the problems your target audience needs solved, and what the market is willing to pay for. Blair Merlino, co-founder at 9point8 Collective, notes that many firms go about this backward and spend too much time "selling a solution that is looking for a problem." Instead, firms should figure out what problems people will pay to have solved and then create a solution, based on your strengths, to serve that need. To shift from an Entrepreneurial to a Tactical firm in the Services Discipline, the key task is to identify this service niche and then strengthen that position.

1. Define your unique value proposition.

A common mistake firms make in building and selling services to clients is failing to define and communicate a clear value proposition. When firms or practices can articulate their value proposition, they experience increased sole source work, higher competitive win rates, faster client decisions, and they win larger projects.

A strong value proposition is a clear and concise promise of the specific benefits or outcomes a client will achieve by hiring your firm. The most powerful value proposition addresses specific client needs – explicit or implicit.

Create an effective value proposition by narrowing in on what you are known for in your market – in the pond (or lake, or ocean) where you compete. Don't forget substitutes for what you do. Being brutally honest here is both important and difficult – few firms or partners objectively assess competitive position. Investing in a systematic process to listen to clients helps generate better real-time market feedback to inform this analysis. To define your value proposition, ask yourself "What are we known for? What do we do better than anyone else? Where have we made a real difference?"

A strong value proposition has three elements: features, advantages, and benefits. **Features** describe the service – what you actually do for your clients. **Advantages** explain how you are uniquely suited to help – why clients should choose to work with you. **Benefits** explicitly describe how the service will directly meet or address client needs – how it will *make their lives better*.

Once you have a clear statement in hand, put it to the test. Does it:

- **Differentiate:** Does it describe how the service is unique in some way from competitors?

- **Substantiate:** Does it explain how the service solves a specific problem or captures a specific opportunity, and does it provide evidence that your firm can deliver the value promised?

- **Resonate:** Does it quantify the value in some way and address not only the rational benefits, but also the emotional benefits, which are often the strongest decision drivers?

A good example of a strong value proposition might be:

"We write CSRD-compliant reports on mandated climate-related disclosures for large, multinational companies that operate in the European Union. Our writers all worked for the EU, helping draft the disclosure requirements. Our work is 100% guaranteed. Your CSRD disclosures will not be returned for costly rewrites. Clients tell us we hit our marks, deliver reports that are not audited, save their companies unneeded follow-up costs, and free them to build shareholder value. To date, we have written disclosure documents for 68% of Fortune 500 companies."

33

Knowing What You Do – Service Definition and Discipline

The statement above clearly defines features of the service (climate-related disclosure reports that are CSRD-compliant), advantages (guaranteed work, experienced writers, credible and reliable), and benefits (saves money and time to focus on shareholder value).

2. Identify your superpowers.

The second dimension of identifying your niche is to name your practice's superpower. Like Erika, you may be a cross-country skier, and your superpower is skate skiing up steep terrain. Or perhaps you're a technology service provider and your superpower is advising on sustainability-informed technology strategies. A "superpower" is not what you do and the benefit of the work, it is *how* you do the work. Identifying your superpower is important because, along with your unique value proposition, it describes where you have the *right to win*.

Take Biologics Consulting, for example. A DC-based firm with 80 professionals, Biologics helps pharmaceutical and medical device companies navigate the product development process that culminates in U.S. Food and Drug Administration (FDA) approval. Their solutions include support around regulatory strategy, nonclinical development, clinical development, chemistry, manufacturing and controls development, medical device development, medical writing, regulatory approvals, and regulatory operations. Their unique value proposition? They clear the way for smart people who invent better medicine to scale their products. Their *superpowers* include understanding the FDA inside and out (a bunch of folks on the team used to work there), empathy for the craziness and inexperience of start-ups (it wasn't that long ago they were a start-up), a knack for reverse engineering process, and the fact that everyone on the team is detail-oriented, scientifically literate, astute at designing process, and never misses a deadline. Understanding these superpowers will sharpen your focus around how you are best suited to help clients.

Jump 2: Tactical to Leading

If the signal characteristic of being in the Entrepreneurial stage of Service Discipline is an *ad hoc* scatteredness, and the Tactical stage is marked by niche discipline, Leading firms distinguish themselves by a *focused doubling down* on service lines and *informed expansion* aligned to the business.

1. Standardize service delivery.

Now that you are clear on your niche, invest in the resources needed to scale your services and equip your business development leaders with the knowledge and materials to talk to clients about those services. This becomes even more critical as you look to add additional service lines (see Chapter 4). Kevin Clem, chief growth officer – Corporations and Community at Harbor Global, says, "The biggest inhibitor for our company is people saying, 'I don't know what we do,' or 'I don't know who to go to.'" For every primary service offering you bring to market, build out standardized materials to support the sale and delivery of your services (we will expand on this in Chapter 11).

These resources should include:

- Boiler-plate collateral (decks, videos, one-pagers)
- Client case studies
- References
- Conversation starters
- Intro email drafts
- Articles/white papers
- Workplans and frameworks for delivery
- Standardized benchmarks to evaluate service delivery

Not every rainmaker in your firm needs to know every detail of every client engagement, but they need to be able to clearly articulate what you do and have the tools to support that conversation with prospective clients. Standardization of service delivery allows for structural analysis, and repeatable, scalable tools and processes that can be applied regardless of service type. As Walt puts it, "You want to start moving away from snowflakes to develop ice cubes." While every client will be different, the less time the team must spend reinventing something totally one-of-a kind, the more time they can spend selling and delivering on the ice cubes that promise strong margins.

2. Orient your service model in the market.

In *Managing the Professional Services Firm,* David Maister writes that clients seek out professional services firms for three distinct types of services: expertise, experience, or efficiency. Each model can make money and be successful, but each balances margin and the need for consistent work in a different way. Orienting the type of work you do allows you to make better decisions around who you hire, the clients you are best equipped to serve, how you deliver, and, critically, how you bring those services to market.

Expertise firms serve clients seeking help on large, complex, one-of-a-kind issues that require creativity, intellect, innovation, and a partner with a track record of solving "rocket science" problems. Elite strategy and law firms fall into this category. For example, an Expertise problem might be developing an interpretation of new data privacy regulations to build a global policy that differentiates you from competitors. This work is high-margin and episodic at best. It is the "big brain" approach to consulting.

Other firms rely on their extensive **Experience** to bring value to their clients. Experience firms serve clients seeking help on issues that may be complex but have been previously faced by other companies in their industry or functional area. The solutions need to be tailored to the specific client needs, but they are grounded in a history of solving similar problems. Experience firms win work because they've "done it successfully before." This is the "gray hair" approach to consulting.

Finally, some firms rely on **Efficiency** to deliver value. Efficiency firms deliver people, process, and technology that perform a needed function for a client at a low cost. Often, the client knows what needs to be done and how to do it but lacks the internal capacity to execute. An Efficiency problem could be a routine audit of a single business unit or the management of an outsourced IT function. This work typically has lower margins than Experience or Expertise work but can produce steady, reliable revenues when executed at scale. While trust and credibility are still required for these sales (they can be very high-dollar contracts), price and speed-to-delivery are also differentiators, as there are more options available in the marketplace.

Maister's framework requires us all to ask, "How do we face the market?" "What is our niche and how does it make money?" The secret is to focus on one corner of the triangle (see Figure 3.2). Competing

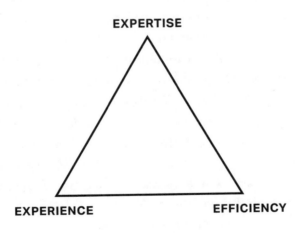

Figure 3.2 Types of professional services firms, adapted from the Discipline of Market Leaders Framework by Michael Treacy and Fred Wiersema.

in the middle means you are unclear about your value proposition, and you risk losing distinction and getting beat by someone in a corner. Orienting yourself at the pointy end of the triangle also informs how clients buy from you and hence, how you win work.

Beware the temptation to try to be something you're not. Where you sit in the triangle depends on what your clients say and how they actually think about engaging with you – not what you hope to be. You may want to say you're rocket scientists, but if your clients see you as an efficiency play and make their buying decisions that way, that is where you live.

3. Practice saying "no" to protect the things to which you should say "yes!"

Grabbing at new work that comes your way is tempting, especially when you're hungry to grow quickly. But Arjun Davda, director of Market Growth & Business Development for one of the Big Four in Canada, shares a lesson from his experience earlier on in his career: "A client said to me, 'I really want to give you guys a chance at some work. I trust you. I love the story you're telling. Based on the rapport we're building, I'd like to give you a shot at a very specific scope of work for our data team....' I thought to myself, 'Argh!' That specific area is not our sweet spot. I was so tempted to say yes. But I told him, 'to ensure our relationship kicks off on the right foot, I want to guarantee our team knocks it out of the park for you – leaving zero doubt in your mind that we have earned the right to be a partner of choice for you . . . but if we take this on, this is not the impression I'm going to leave you with because this project isn't squarely in our wheelhouse.'"

Arjun's decision paid off in spades.

"As a business development director measured by revenues, acquisition of new logos, and strategic prospecting, saying 'no' was incredibly difficult—but that 'no' had a multiplier effect. Over the next eighteen months, that individual brought me opportunities worth 10x that one project because I knew our best capabilities, and he understood them as well. Looking back, it took courage to say no to something that was not in line with my performance metrics, but it was the right answer for long-term value creation for clients."

Call it the irony of professional services growth. When you give a genuine "no," you are usually building credibility with your clients and better positioning yourself for growth.

Finally, know that all of us are helpers. We live and breathe client service, so saying "yes" feels better than saying "no" – even if "no" guards our niche and fuels our long-term growth.

So how do you know when to say no? Ask yourself – or your team – these questions before committing to a new project:

- Do we have the resources to execute this project well or does it create reputation risk?
- Will this project hurt our margins?
- Will this project take focus away from bigger priorities?
- What percentage of our work is now moving outside our niche? How would I (and my partners) describe what we do right now?
- Who are we doing this work for? Will taking on this work cause clients to start thinking about our capabilities in different (perhaps more desirable, perhaps less desirable) ways?
- Would the time spent delivering this non-niche work be better spent growing our core service offerings?
- Is the overall market for our core services changing? Is this indicative of a need for us to change our service portfolio or are we just reacting to a temporary dip in current sales?

39

Knowing What You Do – Service Definition and Discipline

Think critically with your team about the answers to these questions. If something is clearly a risk, discuss whether it's worth taking. Saying "yes" might be an opportunity to impress people who can open the floodgates to new business for you, or it could lead to gobbling up your capacity on low-margin work – including those who could otherwise be selling.

As Mukund Rao, president, Global Markets at Xoriant and former chief business officer of BFSI for LTIMindtree, puts it, "Focus is important to any growth strategy. You need clarity about what you are going to do and what you are not going to do. Understanding the organization's strengths and doubling down on those is key." Strengthen your strengths.

* * *

Jump 3: Leading to World-class

World-class firms or practices know exactly which pointy end of the triangle defines their services, and their services are fully formed around client needs and outcomes.

1. Define services by client outcomes.

World-class firms establish eminence in the market by telling a consistent story about who the firm is and the value its services provide for clients. Clients, marketing teams, partners, and even junior associates need to be able to clearly articulate not just what you do, but *how* what you do *solves client problems*. Too often, professional services providers explain what they do by the activities that comprise billable hours. Instead, challenge your employees to articulate the value story. For example,

What we do: At PIE, we coordinate executive roundtables, interview executives, draft agendas, and facilitate conversations between our clients and their target market.

The value we provide: We help our clients strengthen critical relationships, win work, and grow their practices by building substantive bridges to those they most want to serve.

How do you know this is right? Ask your clients what value you provide for them. If you survey 15 clients, can they tell you what your firm does? Can they speak to the unique value you provide? An extra benefit is that they may even identify another superpower for you – perhaps the value you are driving is broader or deeper than you know. Let them tell you directly.

2. Utilize pricing to drive margin.

As Paul Boulanger, former group operating officer, Strategy and Consulting at Accenture, knows, "Pricing is incredibly important because it drives more profit than volume does." When you've done the work to prove to the market you are the best at what you do, you earn the right to charge a premium for that service. The power of niching is that it allows you to build reputation, references, and a history of success that positions you as the best in breed with a pricing model to match.

In addition to value-based pricing, World-class firms drive more predictability in their revenue stream by extending contract length or shifting to a retainer model. When scoping work for a client, start with the business case. This allows World-class firms to shift from providing individual point solutions for discrete problems to comprehensive and integrated business solutions.

Walt recalls a conversation with a client during his time at McKinsey. The client came back to them and said, "You're twice as much as our three other bids." Walt's response? "Yes, we are. And we're twice as good." By leaning into your superpowers, you win more work while also earning the right to charge more than your competitors and delighting clients.

* * *

41

Knowing What You Do – Service Definition and Discipline

Erika eventually did get better at double-poling. She never won races that way, but over time and with diligent practice, she became competent on the flatter terrain, where her competitors had historically outsprinted her. But even as she improved, Erika spent more of her time skate skiing, practicing transitions on hills, and strengthening the muscles and technique that made her fast in the first place. The races she did win (those that ultimately qualified her for World Cups) were hilly 10k skate races where her turnover and ability to maximize glide on each ski propelled her to the front of the pack. With time, she also began winning skate sprints and eventually 50k races across a wide range of courses and terrain.

As firms mature, so too does their ability to do more than one thing well within their niche. World-class firms are dynamic organisms that continue to learn and improve, broadening in how they help clients. In Chapter 4, we cover how firms can expand their service offerings over time in the same way Erika built on her 10km skate skiing talent to win other types of races.

Chapter 4

Service Development and Expansion

Aaron rushed down the stairs to grab a drink with Jacob after a half-day account planning workshop with PIE. "Let's get after it," he said with gusto. Jacob is from Spokane and Aaron is from Eastern Oregon. They have the same dirt under their fingernails.

Aaron looks more like a guy who runs the local power company than he does a master of the universe. But, as one of a small group of managing directors at elite consulting firm L.E.K., he is, in fact, a *consigliere* to software CEOs and finance titans, operating from his 33rd-floor office in San Francisco's Financial District.

"We have been hyper-successful doing due diligence for private equity firms. It's great work. They call at eleven o'clock on a Friday night and say, 'Can you stand up a team starting tomorrow to dig in?' These acquisitions are big and require a skilled team able to be deployed, in many cases, yesterday. It's no joke, but we get the call because we can get it done."

He sipped his bourbon, put the glass down, and said with that not-to-the-manner-born smile, "When you can do hard stuff, there are margins to be had."

Over the last decade, Aaron has built a preeminent diligence practice serving software companies. He has mined that vein as relentlessly as a gold-rush '49er, and it has been a productive vein – enriching him and his partners. When a wet-behind-the-ears Stanford Graduate School of Business grad suggested the firm should expand from its commanding heights as leader of the diligence niche to offer more services, Aaron laughed and said, "Nah. We've got a good thing going here."

Still, one thing was bugging him: every time his team exhaustedly fell across the finish line of a diligence assignment, they said the same thing. "We're building these annual recurring revenue (ARR) models showing how the subscriptions stack like annuities over time, but the PE guys never ask us to dig into their pricing models. We can see from our work, they are leaving a ton of money on the table."

Circling the ice in his empty glass, Aaron looked at Jacob and said, "I didn't think I would ever say it, but I'm contemplating standing up a new service line around software pricing. We're there. We're in the room. It would be criminal for us not to offer to help."

In our interviews with leading rainmakers in professional services, they all say the same thing, "mind your niche." And yet as firms move from Tactical to Leading, they begin to expand that niche by *thoughtfully* broadening their services.

But what is thoughtful?

Thoughtful is listening to your clients, and playing checkers instead of chess.

Most firms are triple-matrixed by geography, industry, and services. As you look to explore white space, consider only one adjacency at a time. This means that when you're beginning to look at new services, you should start with offering them to your current customers – by geography and industry – before adding "newness" to one of those dimensions as well.

This is Aaron's strategy (see Figure 4.1). Stand up a new service (pricing) selling to the same clients (PE firms) who are investing in the same domain (software companies with recurring revenue) in the same geography (United States). Change only one thing – the service, namely helping PE firms think about pricing as they make

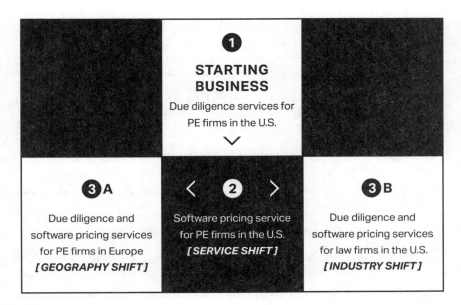

Figure 4.1 Aaron's sample checkerboard expansion strategy.

an investment. It's a new service, but it's also closely aligned to the service currently being provided; it's part of the same value chain. That seems doable and is *high reward and low risk*.

After a few years, once Aaron has proven his sensitivity modeling and software pricing prowess to current clients and developed great case studies in the United States, he then earns the right to begin calling on firms in Europe. He takes this one step at a time, slowly expanding along the way.

As firms develop maturity around service expansion on the journey to building a growth engine, they go through four key areas of evolution. They sharpen their focus on client feedback and market input to inform new services; they create process around go/no-go decisions on new service lines; they underpin these efforts with clear success metrics to ensure ROI; and they develop teams who can manage complex sales for large accounts (Figure 4.2).

STAGES OF MATURITY

FIRM CHARACTERISTICS

ENTREPRENEURIAL

- A quick acceptance of work that has never been done before occurs, with no clear process for determining new service investments
- Dabbling in offering new services happens without central decision-making around firm investments
- Attempts are made to "play chess" by jumping into ideas where the right to win has not been earned

TACTICAL

- Ad hoc processes are set for collecting client feedback on unmet needs
- Pressure is felt to expand service offerings, and a service development team is established
- Expanding services result in fits and starts, with more misses than wins
- Innovation occurs in an ad hoc manner

LEADING

- Focus is placed on service expansion
- A systematic process for client feedback is in place, often conducted by a third party
- Client Advisory Boards (CAB) are leveraged to more deeply understand client experience and needs, and to maintain key relationships
- A process is in place to decide on which adjacencies to pursue
- A process exists for evaluating "build vs. buy" decisions for new services
- A process is established for measuring the success and continuation of new service lines

WORLD-CLASS

- Ongoing innovation is driven by clients via formal advisory boards, co-creating new service lines with clients
- A formal portfolio of innovation is fully funded with clear on-ramp, off-ramp, and decision-to-scale inflection points
- Alignment in the long-term vision for the evolution of the firm's services
- Account teams are skilled in solutions selling, offering multiple services to client accounts
- The addition of Alliance partners strengthens the service portfolio

Figure 4.2   Firm characteristics at each stage of maturity – service expansion.

Jump 1: Entrepreneurial to Tactical

To begin maturing your organization around service expansion, complete the following:

1. Establish a service support team.

Establish a small team responsible for enhancing your existing and emerging services by creating marketing assets and delivery assets that are updated after each project and organized for quick use by your business development drivers. Deploy someone to meet with your service leaders(s), understand what they do and the delivery materials needed, and create a package for them to leverage in conversations with current and prospective clients. Make it as easy as possible for account leads and rainmakers alike to confidently engage with their clients about new and different ways they may help.

2. Demonstrate your capabilities in adjacent service areas.

One of the most significant jumps firms make is the shift from providing one service for one client to multiple services for one client. This requires scaling trust and breaking free from the narrow niche you've become known for...or at least widening that road a bit. As you consider other ways you could be helping clients, start with small moves laterally across the checkerboard. There are three strategies Tactical firms employ to build buy-in for new service offerings:

- Test supplementary services that complement your existing niche. Rather than making a diagonal dash all the way across the checkerboard of opportunity to build a new stand-alone service line, experiment with services that make your existing offerings even better.

- Offer to pilot a new service for a discounted rate (or for free) with a trusted client in exchange for feedback to help co-create the offering. This allows you to demonstrate your growing capabilities while simultaneously gathering valuable client input to evolve the service line in response to your best customers.

- Fail fully. Many Entrepreneurial firms like to experiment with lots of different offerings but sometimes discount an idea too quickly before giving it an opportunity to fully mature. Screen for a false negative by guaranteeing sufficient time and resources to test a new service offering before throwing in the towel. Is your new idea failing because you put your B-team on the project to minimize risk? Or did you fail to see returns in the first six weeks when really the offering requires a six-month sales cycle? Write down the list of considerations you would need to see to give a new offering a realistic chance at succeeding to ensure you don't cut it off at the knees before it can really fly.

Jump 2: Tactical to Leading

While Tactical firms begin to broaden their focus by incorporating general client and market input, Leading companies build strong processes for prioritizing new service development to ensure success. In Leading firms, everyone knows how decisions are made about launching new services, clients are deeply involved, a clear market need is determined, and plans are set out to measure ROI and evaluate continued investment. Leading firms also develop strength around evaluating "build v. buy" decisions to understand when to develop a new service in-house, and when to acquire outside expertise.

Leading firms do the following:

1. Seek out and respond to client feedback

Walt says, "In my experience at McKinsey, Accenture, and ERM – and decades of talking to others in the industry – it's unbelievable how systematically we *under-listen* to our clients. Want to know what clients need? Ask them!" While Tactical firms brainstorm new service lines based on their thoughts and predictions, Leading firms engage programmatically with their clients to co-create the future.

There are three main ways to secure useful feedback:

1. **Double-up on accounts.** Leading firms typically have at least two professionals serving a client: a senior partner who defines the engagement and a junior partner who leads the team doing the work. This approach not only leverages lower-paid talent to ensure margin, but also "matches levels." A senior partner may sell an engagement to a CFO needing an integration plan for a recent acquisition. Once sold, the junior partner runs a team that interacts daily with the CFO's team. The senior partner periodically checks in with the CFO to ensure the project is on track because the CFO's team is more likely to complain about misalignment to their boss than to the junior partner.

   Once an engagement is completed, the senior partner has two more tasks: getting feedback on the project and identifying opportunities for more work with the client. Leading firms take this conversation seriously, using a structured approach to capture feedback, including standard questions asked across clients.

   This is not a check-the-box interview to ensure deadlines were met. It is a deeper conversation with the CFO about their organizational goals and whether the project achieved the desired outcomes. Such conversations lead senior partners to report back to the firm with insights like, "I hear from multiple clients that CFOs want to start thinking about integration earlier during diligence. We should consider offering due diligence services to CFOs to better support our integration service line."

2. **Send your client a project-based survey or an annual survey.** While surveys can be a useful tool to understand general client feedback, they also present an opportunity to ask your clients what else they would like you to help them with.

   The most popular surveys follow Fred Reichheld's Net Promoter Score (NPS) methodology. In his 2003 *Harvard Business Review* article, "The One Number You Need to Grow," Reichheld, a Bain consultant, posited that the best predictor of customer loyalty behaviors (including repeat and expanding purchases) is the answer to a simple question: "On a scale of 0-10, how likely would you be to recommend us?" This produces a score, the NPS. This methodology can be used to survey clients, employees, and other stakeholders. It is quantitative in nature, allowing leaders to compare scores across divisions, markets, and service offerings.

   While this is beneficial, it should be complemented with substantive, qualitative feedback around current and prospective service offerings. Mark Hawn, managing partner at EY, agrees, "There is no firm that robustly listens to clients. NPS is a crutch." Although surveys provide consistent and quantitative feedback for the practice or firm, they are just one piece of the puzzle and cannot replace conversation.

3. **Leverage a client advisory board (CAB).** As Bruce Press, principal at ZS, says, "We've got a mantra internally that is focused on doing the right thing for clients. The only way we

know that we're doing the right thing is by asking them – and really listening." Current services should continuously evolve (and adjacent services should be developed) based on direct, consistent feedback from your best customers.

Leading firms gather client feedback, input, and ideas and strengthen client relationships through robust client advisory boards (CABs). The first rule of a CAB is to do no harm. The second rule? Add value. The purpose of the CAB is not to sell services but when done well, sales will be a natural outcome. The primary purpose of a CAB is to listen – to deeply understand client needs, issues, and challenges. Second is to understand strengths, weaknesses, and opportunities of existing services and understand how your services stack up against competition. Third is to explore what extensions or adjacencies might be helpful.

Walt recalls an experience during his time at Accenture, sitting in on a CAB meeting with Cisco Systems. After Cisco led a fairly lengthy presentation to their clients about a new service they were planning to launch, one of the advisory board members jumped in, "Microsoft has already developed this and is way ahead of you. Don't waste your time on this." All of the other clients in the room agreed. Cisco System's CEO, John Chambers, shut down the project the next day, saving his company untold time and resources they would otherwise have put into a losing product.

To understand where you have a chance to succeed most readily and ensure you're not wasting your time, consider asking your best clients some of these questions:

- What do you most value about working with us?
- What makes us stand out?

51

Service Development and Expansion

- What are the strengths and weaknesses of our current offerings?

- What do you really need help with, or wish you could out-source, that you can't seem to find a partner for?

- What expense would you incur if you can't find someone who offers that service?

- If we were able to offer this new service, would that add value to you? What would you be willing to pay for this new service?

- Where is the industry headed and what future needs do you anticipate?

- What is the competition doing? What else should we be considering?

- Would you be open to piloting a project with us around this new service?

2. Establish a process for deciding on new service investments and measuring their success.

Caroline Chick is Partner and Managing Director at CCS Fundraising, the world's largest fundraising consulting firm. "We've been around for 76 years, and for a long time we did one main thing – built and managed fundraising campaigns for non-profits." However, over the last decade or so, CCS started to identify a few different places where clients were asking for their help. What were previously considered one-off "custom" projects for clients have become additional key service lines – services like data analytics and training and leadership development for fundraising teams. Caroline co-chairs CCS's Innovation Committee, where they have defined processes for testing new service line ideas with clients and collecting client feedback to inform priorities.

But how?

Prioritizing involves understanding the intersection of your clients' needs and your team's core capabilities, identifying where you can best serve your clients, and where you have a competitive advantage. The next step is measuring the success of new services to determine further investment. Set clear qualitative and quantitative goals upon launching a service (e.g., target number of clients, revenue targets, profitability, referrals, positive client feedback, pipeline generated) and evaluate against those metrics quarterly. When building out new service lines, profit margin should be considered, but consistent margin across all service lines ought not to be the goal. Your core services might have a 30% profit margin whereas an emerging service only has a 5% profit margin but keeps out competition, opens the door to sell more profitable work, or helps develop junior team members. That new service line may still be worth pursuing. Regularly look back at the Venn diagram you made that tells you where you have the right to win. What new services might land squarely in the middle?

Be clear about these goals and their timelines to regularly assess whether to double down on your investment, adjust course, or discontinue the effort. Leading firms even go so far as to celebrate ideas or projects that failed, making an example of celebrating innovation while limiting wasted investment.

Buying New Services

Leading firms develop expertise in acquisitions and know when to build a new service line in-house or acquire the necessary skills externally, either through full firm acquisitions or "acqui-hires." Over the last few years, the increase in private equity

(continued)

(continued)

investment in professional services has driven a subsequent rise in M&A activity in the industry. This strategy makes sense, as investors recognize that acquiring firms in different geographies, sectors, or with different services can broaden a firm's opportunities. By combining firms, they increase the chances that clients will say, "I know them. I work with them. They are good, and I trust them."

Additionally, PE-backed firms can leverage scale to reduce delivery costs (optimizing labor costs across a large pool of consultants is easier than with a small pool) and gain access to new markets (e.g., "We can serve you, Ms. Transnational; we have offices everywhere!").

Referring to the increase in M&A activity in the legal space, law firm consultant Bruce MacEwan said in an interview with Thomson Reuters that law firms are responding to client preferences for larger firms with broader capabilities. "[Companies are] migrating towards shorter preferred provider lists" (Merken, 2024).

Take Womble Bond Dickinson's recent acquisition of Phoenix-based law firm Lewis Roca. In addition to overall geographic expansion, Womble Bond Dickinson (WMD) was focused on adding complementary services to better serve their clients. Said Caitlin McHugh, managing partner of Lewis Roca's Colorado office, "WBD had strengths in energy and IP, but it didn't have many litigators. Lewis Roca, on the other hand, has built a strong litigation practice in Denver over the past century. We are proud to be able to join WBD and add this missing piece to their wider set of services" (Rummel, 2024).

* * *

The Growth Engine

Jump 3: Leading to World-class

World-class firms build an engine around service development that involves client co-creation, and the development of a team that can effectively sell the full suite of services they offer.

1. Co-create highly responsive service offerings and innovate with clients.

The highest expression of an effective client advisory board (CAB) is when a hypothesis is jointly conceived around a service line that is both proprietary and able to propel clients – and the firm – forward. The firm leans into the project by running it at a loss while the client is willing to be a guinea pig in the hopes of achieving a competitive advantage in their industry.

If Leading firms establish CABs, World-class firms leverage them to their fullest potential. Prioritize integrated and ongoing client listening by running a third-party facilitated client advisory board to generate formal, consistent feedback from your clients on the direction of your practices and overall firm strategy. Establish additional listening programs (dinners, roundtables) that incorporate non-clients (*prospective* clients) to listen to the broader market and equip you with the information to adjust your strategy and service priorities based on the feedback you hear.

Walt recalls a very successful program that Accenture developed for their partnership with Cisco Systems to drive co-creation of relevant services:

> "Accenture developed a version of a venture capital fund to support new service development. For every $1 million Cisco spent with Accenture, $50,000 would be put into this 'discovery fund' to explore new projects. This was hugely beneficial to both Accenture and Cisco. Accenture was

55

Service Development and Expansion

well positioned to increase total account revenue while also deepening trust in the partnership by re-investing in the relationship. They were also able to get *real* direction into where they should be building new services based on the unmet needs of a key client. Cisco Systems benefitted by having an opportunity to dictate exactly where they needed help and were able to see these new services developed at no (or reduced) cost to them."

This arrangement worked because of strong client relationships and a scale of revenue that allowed for the "fund." Even if you're not Accenture, this is a great example of how to think about co-creation. Any size firm can and should have strong enough relationships to build a program in this vein. It may not be a well-funded "discovery fund," but even offering a few extra non-billed "discovery hours" could have a similar relative impact.

2. Position account leads as problem solvers and solutions developers, not sellers of one service.

Selling one core service to a discrete set of clients and ensuring the team is successful is a distinctly different job from managing a large, complex client relationship in which your firm is solving many problems with many service sets. As firms begin to offer more than one service to their clients, they recognize that this engagement has shifted and adjust relationships accordingly. The account lead relationship moves from one of delivery oversight to one of solutions architecture – a partner who can help identify broader client challenges and then pull in the right experts and resources from your firm to develop a plan for solving those problems with multiple solutions. In tandem with expanding your service set, be clear about this shift with your team and make adjustments to assignments where necessary.

3. Host an annual innovation competition.

World-class firms host innovation sprints and competitions internally to capture and capitalize on the plethora of ideas and opportunities for improvement that often fail to reach the surface due to a federated service model. An annual innovation competition creates the platform for these ideas to be shared, developed, tested, and scaled. It also allows employees who are working on the ground with clients to feed up solutions that may be less obvious to your traditional service line leaders. Be clear about parameters and next steps, and publicize the idea(s) that receive investment to show that this is more than just words. Here are a few tips to make it successful:

1. **Define ROI:** Clearly define the measurement criteria of the contest. Are we expecting to drive top-line growth or reduce expenses? What is the clear and objective view of these ideas that can help us force rank them effectively? Fuzzy metrics lead to project extensions for exceptional storytellers even if the business case clearly isn't there.

2. **Reward the behavior, not just the outcome.** It is not a "no holds barred; winner take all" contest. Design small incentives throughout the contest to reinforce the right behaviors and strategies. Specifics will depend on your firm's objectives, but several activities for consideration include:

   - Cross-team collaboration
   - Best alignment to client needs
   - Most achievable project based on existing skill sets
   - Greatest potential contribution margin
   - Failure – clearly, no team wants to fail, but the list of 100% batters on innovation projects is exactly zero people. Walt suggests that innovation teams should have "champagne

57

Service Development and Expansion

failure celebrations." When a team has explored an idea, tested it completely, and found the courage to cease investment in that idea, that is a moment worthy of celebration. This reinforces to the team that innovation is a team-based iterative process, not just writing great ideas on a whiteboard.

3. **Invite all seniority levels:** Make it easy for broad swaths of the organization to participate. When looking for manufacturing efficiency, Toyota emphasizes shop floor feedback as a cornerstone of its production system and overall management philosophy, viewing it as crucial for continuous improvement and rapid problem-solving. Utilizing the same philosophical underpinning, organizations should seek feedback from all levels in the organization. Frequently, the best ideas don't come from senior leaders with 25+ years of experience. Those leaders are often slightly jaded and blinded by the experience they have in the business heretofore. Great ideas often come from employees who are new enough to wonder, "Why in the world do we do it like this?"

Lastly, an innovation contest with no action is worse than no innovation contest at all. The project management of the outflow is incredibly important, and you must give employees the feeling that their feedback is valuable, and the business is going to improve because of this contest. Make certain that the plan ownership and communication are clear before the contest begins. If the team is sitting down after the contest and saying, "What should we do with all of this?" you're behind schedule.

4. Engage with alliance partners.

"A lot of people miss the Alliance bucket. That's one way to get incremental scale," argues Hap Brakeley, former Accenture Managing Partner and Chief Growth Officer for Merkle and Dentsu.

58

The Growth Engine

World-class firms strategically partner with other sales organizations to grow their rolodex, expand the menu of services they offer, and generate inbound referrals for work. Every large technology services provider is partnering with hyper-scalers and most firms partner with industry associations in the markets they're most keen to serve. Why? Partnering with those who serve the same audience in a complementary way without being competitive can speed up access to new markets and allow you to borrow that partner's trust and credibility to quicken your development with a new client. Alliance partners also expand a firm's capabilities to more wholistically serve clients and showcase the strength of their network to the marketplace.

* * *

While some of the best business ideas do in fact start as scribbles on a bar napkin, slightly damp from a downed bourbon, the path to World-class relies more on structured client collaboration than the right number of ice cubes. So, who are those clients to whom you're introducing your super-strengths? Let's dig into that next!

Part III

Clients

Chapter 5

Knowing Whom You Serve

In 1995, Mike Phillips led the effort to restore wolves to Yellowstone National Park. The project translocated 31 wolves from Canada to Montana and Wyoming, acclimating them in remote pens before releasing them into the wild. Acclimation attenuated the wolves' natural homing tendency. While the wolves were in captivity, Mike and his team provided food and water to ensure that the animals were healthy upon release, giving them the greatest chance of survival on their own.

Upon their release, the wolves no longer had food or water brought to them – they had to get back to hunting. Some of the wolves were quite young when they were flown to Yellowstone – pups just a few months old – so their parents, the Alpha Male and Alpha Female, had to quickly teach them how to hunt.

Wolves are fast, smart, capable hunters, and they hunt as a pack. Within days of release, one of the wolf packs – the Crystal Creek Pack – was successfully hunting elk in Yellowstone's Lamar Valley. The mother wolf would often initiate a hunt only to have her younger offspring quickly take over by targeting an elk that was predisposed to predation (for example, an elk with an arthritic leg). The average weight of a cow elk is 500 pounds. Gray wolves generally need to eat at least 5 pounds of meat a day, so this single elk – this single hunt – could feed the Crystal Creek Pack – a family of five – for at least two weeks. Contrast that with hunting mice, which weigh a fraction of a pound. If it chose to, a wolf could easily hunt field mice instead – but it doesn't do this. A mouse can't feed the family for a week; it can hardly satiate a wolf for an hour. The energy a wolf would need to expend to chase down 10+ mice a day could lead it to starvation.

One of the most important issues facing professional services firms is deciding which clients to serve and, perhaps more importantly, which ones to avoid. Determining an ideal client profile (ICP) is crucial for successful growth, but it requires discipline and intention, often overlooked as firms scale. In short, your ICP is that 500-pound elk that can feed the team for weeks, not a colony of field mice.

The first-order questions about whom to serve may seem straightforward – such as which industries or regions, and how to prioritize between new and existing clients. However, almost every firm serves too many clients. Those in professional services naturally want to help solve problems, making it difficult for partners to say "no" to potential clients, even when it's the better answer.

The more explicit a firm can be about whom they are serving – the firms and individuals most in need of and able to buy their services – the more effective they will be. A simple litmus test is to ask four people on your sales team to name four clients you want to serve and four you do not. In our experience, this is more likely to spark debate than show consensus.

Moving up the Maturity Curve

As firms mature, clarity around target clients becomes critical within each practice area, recognizing that different practices may have distinct target markets. Greg Callahan, partner and global head of the Software Practice at Bain, emphasizes, "A key piece of building a growth engine is creating clarity of targets. We spend a lot of time on this. If you say any target is a good target, it is like giving someone the Yellow Pages to find opportunities. It is really important to create clarity of mission here."

The most mature firms not only have a clear strategy about whom they serve but also communicate it so effectively that every team member, client, and even prospects can articulate who benefits from working with them (Figure 5.1).

STAGES OF MATURITY

FIRM CHARACTERISTICS

ENTREPRENEURIAL
- Sales are made to anyone willing to buy
- Reliance is placed on existing connections rather than a clear ICP and target list

TACTICAL
- ICP is clearly defined based on actual clients served, not ideal clients
- Ideal portfolio profile (IPP) is loosely defined, providing goals around client mix
- No formal account segmentation, but there is a general understanding of "top" accounts that get the most attention

LEADING
- The team is aligned around ICP to hunt together as a pack
- An ongoing review and refinement of ICP is in place
- IPP is clear and informs client expansion and new client acquisition goals
- A go/no-go strategy for accepting new clients has been established, and serving a client outside the ICP occurs only for strategic reasons
- Clarity exists on the conditions that must be met before adding adjacencies to the ICP
- Formal account segmentation is in place and helps drive important decisions around growth and budgeting

WORLD-CLASS
- New clients are brought in with high selectivity to align with the long-term vision
- Acquisition strategy is informed by the ICP

Figure 5.1 Firm characteristics at each stage of maturity – client discipline.

65

Knowing Whom You Serve

Jump 1: Entrepreneurial to Tactical

For most early-stage firms, their ideal client profile is not actually defined. Rather, it is the list of names that live in their rolodex (or cell phone), and whoever is willing to buy.

The move from the Entrepreneurial stage of "doing anything for anyone" into the Tactical stage of maturity is marked by this single critical action:

1. Define your ideal client profile (ICP) – as specifically as possible.

Emerging firms typically believe "the more clients, the better" and "there is no such thing as a bad client." In fact, the opposite is true. When you are just trying to build *something,* it is hard not to grab at whatever comes your way. Think mice versus elk. While client concentration can indeed be a key concern during these early days, hunting 100 mice isn't going to get you the growth you want. When your niche has been clearly defined, there exists a limited universe of high likelihood buyers with whom you should engage. It might be 50 or it might be 500, but it is not 50,000. Write this list down so the team can be clear and organized around whom you are trying to get in front of. The narrower the niche, the clearer the focus, the easier the list is to create.

For example, two accounting firms focused on healthcare could have two very different ICPs, as outlined in Figure 5.2.

When defining an ICP, consider the following dimensions:

- **Industry, sub-industry, and specialty/focus** – What industry (and sub-industry) do you serve? Your firm or practice may be targeting healthcare, but that is very broad. Do you serve hospitals, pharmaceuticals, the world of medical devices, clinics? Large companies might actually serve three or four subsectors but the number matters far less than the clear definition.

	ICP - FIRM A	ICP - FIRM B
INDUSTRY	Healthcare	Healthcare
SUB-INDUSTRY	Hospitals	Hospitals
SPECIALTY/FOCUS	General care	Leading regionals
SIZE	$5-$20M	$20-100M
OWNERSHIP	Private	Private, public
GEOGRAPHY	Rural, East of Mississippi	Major U.S. cities
CHARACTERISTICS	Underperforming	High growth and acquisitions
FUNCTIONAL BUYER	**Chief Financial Officer**	**Chief Tax Officer**

Figure 5.2 A example of two different ICP strategies.

- **Size and Ownership Structure** – What size company is too small or too big? The Fortune 500 ranges from about $7 billion to about $650 billion. What size client is the best fit for your firm? While serving the Fortune 100 might be an aspiration, these companies are on everyone's target list – and the Fortune 400–500 or even 500–1000 are often underserved.

  Additionally, what ownership structure is ideal for your work? Private or public companies? PE-held? Employee-owned companies? Non-profits?

- **Geography** – Will you target clients in a specific region? Will you focus regionally, nationally, internationally, or globally? Some sectors can be served very well in a limited geography. For example, Texas and Oklahoma have a very significant oil and gas business base, but if you elect to serve just the southwest region, you need to decide how you will respond when they ask for help in North Dakota, the Middle East, or Indonesia. Will expanding outside your target region add complication that undermines your ability to serve your current niche? Or is geographic expansion a natural move on the checkerboard?

- **Company characteristics and context** – Are there specific company contexts that fit your services profile especially well? For example, do you serve underperforming companies? High-growth companies? Are you exclusively focused on those with M&A activity? Would the U.S. subsidiary of a European or Asian parent company be a preferred target?

- **Functional Buyer: The Client** – A company is an account; a *client* is an individual person. Until you've defined *the individual* who has the ability to buy your services, your ICP is incomplete. This is where many practices run into the challenge of defining who they *actually* serve, versus who they wish they had relationships with. All too frequently, practices will be quick to say they want CFO or CEO relationships, when really the person signing off on their SOW sits two or three levels below their C-suite target. It is of course important to understand the key *influencers* in your engagements as well (perhaps that is indeed the CFO), but be clear on what these roles are and how they impact your sales process.

Specificity sets mature firms apart by enabling them to more efficiently and effectively serve clients. As Anne Callender, chief business development officer at Simpson, Thatcher & Bartlett, notes, "Clients want advisors who understand their business. It's getting more and more tailored and narrowed down every year. It used to be healthcare, then life sciences, and now it's a focus specifically on pharmaceuticals." Narrowing in on your ICP benefits your clients and gives your team clear focus on how to spend their time. Simply defining an ICP is step one; real maturity requires additional work. Leading firms add rigor and accountability to the process.

* * *

68

The Growth Engine

Strategies for Honing Your ICP

As firms look to move up the maturity curve and more clearly define their ICP, they are often tempted to start with an aspirational list of company names. Instead, consider the following set of questions about your current clients to inform who else you should or could serve:

1. Who are your best current clients and why?

    a. What are the most common characteristics of those clients? (Growing companies? Companies going through disruption?)

    b. What patterns do you observe?

    c. Who needs you?

    d. Whom are you most qualified to serve? Is it an entire sector or a more narrow subsector (i.e., healthcare or subsector of pharma, medical devices, hospitals, etc.).

2. Why are people calling you and what are they asking you to do?

    a. What are the problems or issues clients bring to you?

    b. Who else has this same issue that you can help solve?

3. What makes you unique, better, or different in the market?

    a. Where do you fit within the competitive landscape?

    b. What do your clients tell you differentiates you from competitors?

4. Who can afford you?

    a. What is the size range of your ICP? Floor? Ceiling?

(continued)

69

Knowing Whom You Serve

(continued)

5. Where is your win rate highest?

Winning is a lot like hunting elk. If you find a prime spot where elk are frequently passing through, stay there and keep hunting that area. Find your Lamar Valley and build a den.

* * *

Jump 2: Tactical to Leading

As we've outlined in the Services section, good strategy is often defined as much by what you choose *not* to do as it is by what you do. The same goes for clients. In addition to having a clear ICP and target list, Leading firms have a clear process for saying "no" to clients that fall outside of their ICP and employ the following tactics to move up the maturity curve.

1. Refine, review, and communicate your target client list.

The target list is not a static document that is made once and left unchanged for 10 years. New players come into the market that you may want to serve, M&A activity changes the dynamics of whom you may be targeting, and as you continue to get feedback from clients and see where you are really thriving, your focus areas may evolve. Michael Pittendrigh, national managing partner of Consulting and Private Business Advisory at Grant Thornton Australia, says, "Every partner has an ideal client profile, or ICP. This feeds into our firm's collective ICP, aligning across all teams including partners, marketing, and business development. We are focused on whom we serve, what we do, and what we want to be. This clarity has contributed to double digit growth over the last two years."

Clients may demand that you narrow your focus, or regulatory disruption might make it clear that you should double down on a sub-set of your target list in banking to be focused more on regional or digital banks. Regularly reviewing and updating your ICP and related target list guarantees a consistent and dynamic focus on the clients you are best equipped to serve and ensures every partner knows who falls within that ICP. Review your ICP as part of your annual planning and revisit it in the interim in conjunction with any major events (e.g., acquisition, major regulatory change).

2. Develop an ideal portfolio profile (IPP).

In addition to an ideal *client* profile, maturing firms also develop an ideal *portfolio* profile, outlining the desired mix of accounts. Consider the following questions to develop a target portfolio profile that aligns with your growth goals:

- How concentrated or diversified should your client base be? Are you more focused on bringing in new logos to offset client concentration, or more focused on expanding accounts to turn many mice into elk?

- Do you have the right mix of marquee clients (great to have on the roster but require very high-touch service) and easy-to-serve clients? Does this mix suit your team?

- What is your industry mix? Are you focused on adding more manufacturing clients because you only have a few clients there, with most others in pharma or retail?

- What is your regional mix? Are you hoping to win more work in APAC? Phase out of your work in LATAM due to loss of key talent there?

- What is your service mix? Are you primarily doing project-based or ongoing work? Do you want to do more or less of either, and is that best suited to certain accounts?

Getting clear about these questions will help bring direction to your team about whom you want to serve, how and where you want to serve them, and why that is best for your firm.

3. Develop a go/no-go process.

Saying yes to any new client who walks in the door is tempting. Without a clear ICP and a centralized approval process, each partner independently pursues new opportunities, making decisions based on personal or immediate interests. This can lead to smaller clients, higher cost of sales, increased risk exposure, short-term opportunistic decision-making, and lack of resources to pursue higher value opportunities. Say you are trying to build a reputation as the top accounting firm for Ohio retailers, and your old college friend from California calls you up and asks if they can hire you as the accountant for the summer camp they run. What's the right answer? As we learned with the "checkerboard" strategy for growth, *maybe* you reconsider their request when they open a summer camp in *Ohio*, or when they start looking to set up an associated commercial retail operation (who doesn't like to buy summer camp swag?). Until then, however, offering California summer camp accounting services would just create confusion in the market and take time away from winning that next big retail client.

Leading firms use a defined go/no-go process to inform engagement decisions with new accounts and clients that are aligned with practice- and firm-wide strategic priorities. Consider a two-stage approval process:

Stage 1 - Require Permission to Develop a Proposal: This step is used when a team believes there is a good opportunity and they want to begin to spend time and resources on the opportunity by writing proposals and estimating fees. As firms get larger, project pursuits can cost tens and hundreds of thousands of dollars. By requiring permission to develop a proposal, firms ensure time and money are spent wisely. Firms also protect against the risk of a negative experience for potential clients by pitching on work they can't realistically deliver. For large, established clients, this step may be cursory or skipped, especially for smaller projects. Some partners may even resist this step, as they view their time and their team's unbilled time as free; however, there is a real opportunity cost, given the expense of firm resources. Organizations can change behavior here by requiring sign-off on a proposal to gain access to firm resources, such as marketing and senior staff.

Stage 2 - Require Permission to Submit the Proposal: This last step in a pursuit occurs after significant resources have been spent developing the proposal. Before rainmakers can submit a proposal for new work, consider adding a final review of the proposal to evaluate pricing, proposal quality, staffing, risk, financial terms, and contract viability against your firm's ICP. While routine for existing client accounts and standard projects, this step is critical for new clients, new project types, large or high-risk projects, or work in new locations or countries. Approval to submit these proposals should consider the following criteria:

- Project size and scope
- Strategic fit within the industry sector

- Likelihood of winning the work
- Ability to perform the work at top quality
- Staff availability and client creditworthiness
- Reputation impacts (positive or negative) of taking on this new account

An effective go/no-go process integrates decision points within a firm's CRM for efficiency, streamlining the proposal consideration and submission process while avoiding unnecessary bureaucracy. Firms establish pre-determined approval levels based on project size and specific risk triggers, such as safety concerns (e.g., underwater inspections), geographic risks (e.g., operating in a new, highly-regulated market), and liability exposure (e.g., environmental projects). Although a more stringent go/no-go process may frustrate some senior partners, especially those used to independent decision-making, it is a critical framework for directing firm resources toward high-value, high-growth opportunities and investments and strategic client accounts essential for the firm's growth.

Finally, a productive go/no-go process also includes a strategy for approving exceptions. When would it make sense to say yes to a mouse? Perhaps you have a strong reason to believe that they are likely to grow into a bull elk soon. Perhaps the individual you're selling to is a long-standing client who has left to start her own firm and wants your help – she's well known in the industry so continuing to have her as a strong reference is important, and you know taking on this work will continue to pay off in referrals to larger accounts. Every firm and practice will have a few mice on their client roster – just make sure they are the *best* mice.

Those who sit in the seat of deciding whether and when to grant permission on these proposals should have a certain level of objectivity. An industry lead, for example, might be incentivized on new logos added or total revenue growth for their sector, and therefore lack objectivity in this decision. A firm's growth officer, or in some cases a committee of partners who are focused on the firm's overall strategy for growth, is better suited to decide.

4. Define an account segmentation strategy.

Leading firms segment their accounts to help guide internal activities. This usually includes three categories, for which nearly every firm has different names:

Account Group 1: Your biggest and best clients. They are still growing and represent critical relationships for the firm. They are engaged with the firm across multiple services and geographies. Loss of these accounts would be a big blow to the firm. (Often called *Core, Key, Diamond*, or *Top* accounts.)

Account Group 2: Important clients with high growth potential. Clients in this group might not yet generate a substantial relative proportion of revenue, but with the right resources and work, they could become a "Group 1" account. (Often called *Strategic, Developing*, or *Invest* accounts.)

Account Group 3: The rest of your clients. These are generally smaller accounts, or those that don't represent large growth opportunities and don't require as much high-touch service. They may fall outside of your ICP. (Often called *Opportunistic* or *Alliance* accounts.)

Client segmentation is important because it allows the firm to marshal resources appropriately. If a "Group 1" account is serviced across 15 geographies with four different service offerings, they will need very different account leadership and support roles than a "Group 3" account that will likely only ever buy a single service in a single geography. As outlined in Chapter 4 on service development, your "Group 1" accounts are those with whom it would be worth investing back into the partnership to drive co-creation of services.

"Group 2" accounts are where firms invest in alignment with strategic priorities. Perhaps you recently won a contract to do leadership trainings for McDonald's store managers across three countries in Europe, and you feel optimistic about your ability to unseat an incumbent and move into North America and Asia. If expanding your work in the consumer and retail sector is a key priority this year, you would put extra resources on this account to provide the highest likelihood of winning, and turning them into a "Group 1" account.

Jump 3: Leading to World-class

World-class firms and practices have built such clarity and rigor around their ICP that everyone in their marketplace – inside and outside the firm – knows exactly whom they serve. Companies *want* to be on their client list. This reputation has been built over time by continuing to be the best at what they do for a clearly defined set of client firms. World-class firms distinguish themselves with the following best practices:

1. Maintain a highly selective ICP and carefully manage the mice.

Like the White House State Dinner guest list, World-class firms have a highly selective list of target accounts they work with and pursue based on fit and growth potential. They focus 80% of their time and resources on that list. This selectivity ensures they avoid distraction by a long tail of client accounts that are neither profitable nor growth oriented – their tail of "mice." The cost and effort to drag in a mouse is often not worth the revenue generated from that sale. As firms mature and begin to track metrics like cost of sales, competitive win rate, and pipeline growth (more on this in Chapter 13), they will often discover that this client tail drags down overall firm profitability.

Shrinking this tail enables firms to commit more resources to more profitable areas of the business. While few Entrepreneurial or Tactical firms maintain the metrics or discipline to do this effectively, a good sign of maturity is both the ability to measure profitability by client and the courage to cut those clients hurting overall firm profitability.

* * *

How to break up with your mice ... And stay friends

We're all in the relationship business, so the idea of "breaking up with" or "firing" a client because they no longer fit your target profile can feel like the active destruction of a meaningful friendship. Just as in romantic relationships that are no longer working, staying in them out of fear or convenience is never a good choice. However, a breakup doesn't have to mean cutting ties completely. Staying friends with your exes is possible (well, *these* exes, at least). Once you've gone through the exercise of evaluating your current accounts against your ICP strategy, transition mice out of your portfolio over time while staying friends with them. Here are some considerations:

- Turn mice into elk – or at least into deer. Sometimes clients will fall out of your ICP because of their size, which may also mean they are unwilling to pay the same prices as your larger clients and may have little or no growth potential. Have a frank conversation with these clients. Let them know what fees you would in fact need to charge – or the amount of increased work you would need to see from them – in order to continue serving them. If they're open to evolving as a client, perhaps they can get a bit closer to your ICP and the relationship can stay intact, at least in the medium term.

(continued)

77

Knowing Whom You Serve

(continued)

- Introduce them to a new partner. Perhaps you started out doing individual tax returns for a few people in your community, but over time you've grown your firm and are now focused on serving mid-size businesses. You probably know another accountant in the area who is focused specifically on working with individual clients and would be happy to take on this work. The key is to make sure you're not sending them to a direct competitor who could take more business from you, but to someone who serves a different market (bonus: you earn gratitude from this other, non-competing firm who may return the favor one day).

- Make them self-sufficient mice. Say you've been engaging with a small non-profit client for the last few years to help organize and run their annual gala. You were happy to do this to get some reps and hone the services you now offer to large global NGOs. This small local organization is never going to be able to pay what you now charge, and you can't justify a team spending a full week offsite to prep with them every year. Rather than introducing them to a different events firm, you run a small engagement to train them on a few of your best practices, so they can run the event (not as well as you, but sufficiently) on their own.

- Keep them in your orbit. If you want to remain friends with your exes, think about what unique benefits you could continue to offer them even if you're no longer formally working together. Perhaps you allow them to maintain a free subscription to your quarterly newsletter, or keep them on the invite list for your annual conference that you know they've enjoyed each year. These actions likely won't cost you much (or anything), but will ensure they continue to consider you a friend, giving you positive referrals and being open to re-engage if they find themselves back on your ICP list in the future.

> While you should stop hunting mice today, the stash of mice you've built up already doesn't need to be thrown out overnight. The actions above are ideas for how, over time, you can increasingly ensure you're serving those you are best suited to serve.

* * *

2. Evaluate any potential acquisitions with ICP in mind.

World-class firms consider acquisitions that have a similar ICP (e.g., they serve the same client profile, just in a different geography). Acquisitions are likely to reflect adjacencies, either one jump forward or laterally on the proverbial checkerboard we illustrated in Chapter 4. Regardless, ICP should be a key consideration on the evaluative rubric when considering appropriate acquisitions.

The most fundamental step for a firm to be able to start hunting as a pack is getting sharp clarity on your ICP. Gray wolves overcome the challenges of big-game hunting by being doggedly determined and supremely social. As Rudyard Kipling opined, the strength of the pack is the wolf, and the strength of the wolf is the pack. Get your team to think like a wolf pack – first in identifying that 500-pound elk of a client, rather than getting distracted by field mice. Now that you know whom you want to target, we'll talk about how to work as a pack to tackle that elk that will feed the family.

Chapter 6

Double Down on Current Accounts

T hose beds.

Andi loved the historic house she bought in 2018 in downtown Bozeman, Montana. The original 1885 hardwood floors, the proximity to both Main Street and the local trail system, the big clawfoot tub in the first-floor bathroom – all of these brought her joy. What didn't bring her any particular joy were the multiple raised garden beds in the backyard. She'd barely even noticed them when she toured the house.

Indeed, her family and friends were much more excited about these garden beds than she was. Eventually, their enthusiasm increased her interest, and when summer arrived, Andi decided to dig into the farming life. She went to the local gardening store and bought seeds for all her favorite produce – carrots, zucchini, kale, lettuce, hot peppers, snap peas, and some tomato plants – ready for this new version of herself that was going to cook all her meals from home-grown veggies. She also bought a few garlic bulbs, having heard that garlic is easy to grow with little effort (and she LOVES garlic).

Andi has never had a green thumb; her office plants have been known to die without her notice. But she was determined to grow an amazing crop in her backyard.

During her first year with this new garden, Andi focused on filling the beds with brightly colored vegetables and fruits. Alas, the strawberries were eaten by bunnies, half of the greens went bad while Andi was traveling, and she completely forgot about the tomatoes she planted on the side of the house.

81

But, she'd planted a small section of garlic at the end of the summer, and when the snow melted the following spring, she was surprised to find a bountiful harvest of beautiful garlic.

It turns out that garlic needs very little attention. You plant the cloves in the fall, cover them with a layer of hay, and then leave them alone as they grow under the snow over the winter. No daily watering, no weeding, no fear of squirrels, rabbits, or birds taking it all. You just show back up the following summer and pull it out of the ground.

At the end of the second summer, after more bunny feeds and tomato neglect, Andi had an epiphany: She was great at growing garlic (and not much else ...). She also learned that none of her friends or family grew garlic even though they loved having it on hand for omelets and pasta.

Garlic was her niche.

Leaning in, the next year she planted all four beds with garlic, embracing her new identity as a garlic grower. She read up on garlic, planned the timing of her spring planting meticulously, drafted her husband, Nic, into what became an epic harvest day, and began to use the garlic scapes in salads and dips. Within her circle of friends, she earned renown as the local queen of garlic, and was appreciated for the beautiful bulbs she handed out to family and friends.

In professional services, we often find ourselves wanting to chase the shiny object – the *new logo* – even as we know the most straightforward growth path is to double down on our *current clients*. What happens if we put time, attention, and effort into our current clients? Into planting garlic? They will eventually become super-clients who advocate, partner, and even co-create with us. As Lori Langholz, principal and chief business development officer at BDO, states, "Investing the time to understand our current clients is critical. There may even be areas where they are unaware we can help. Adequately and effectively monetizing our existing accounts would likely feed almost all of our growth goals; imagine not needing to rely on new clients for growth!"

It might be great to say you can grow tomatoes and peppers – *and* green beans, *and* carrots *and* maybe even pumpkins – as soon as possible. But making sure you're doubling down on the places where you're already winning – your current clients – is how you build a growth engine. Firms too often under-invest in and under-celebrate current client expansion because it's much sexier to lock in that fancy new logo. But engines don't need to be sexy. They need to be reliable and get you where you're trying to go.

The Power of Planning – Diamonds Are Your Best Friend

The jump from Entrepreneurial to Tactical, to Leading, and, ultimately to World-class requires a shift in how teams plan and prepare for client growth to both optimize sellers' time and establish a flywheel for relationship development that goes beyond who you know right now.

In this chapter, we'll talk about what it looks like to lean into current client relationships, and how to put structure around account planning in a way that provides clear goals, involves a broader team, and sets you up to help your clients in as many ways as you can.

Let's revisit the Diamond of Opportunity, a model for current client expansion that Jacob wrote about in a previous book, *Never Say Sell*. The Diamond outlines how you leverage both trust and credibility to grow current client accounts and identify all of your opportunities for growth (Figure 6.1).

The easiest way to grow is by doing **More** – the same type of work with the same client who knows and trusts you. Think of an accounting firm that is hired to do a company's corporate tax filings. They're hired the next year to do this again – perhaps with slightly more hours as the company has grown.

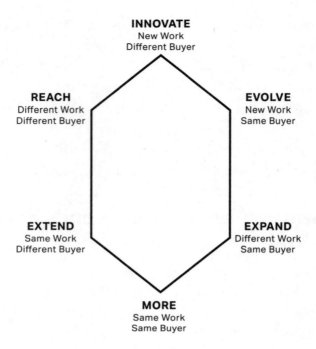

Figure 6.1 The Diamond of Opportunity.

As you move up the right side of the Diamond, to do **Expand** and **Evolve** work, you are scaling **credibility** (see Figure 6.2). You've built both trust and credibility with your current work, and while the trusted relationship remains, as this work is with the **same buyer**, you're relying on that trust to help scale your credibility into alternate services. They've seen you do corporate tax filings before, but only for federal U.S. returns. Now you're trying to win international tax work as they have expanded overseas. This is work your firm does and is good at, but you haven't done it for *them* so it's a big step. Even more challenging is **Evolve** work – this relies on incredibly strong trust, as it means selling work that you haven't done before – for them or anyone else. This same individual client trusts you and your firm enough that they're willing to be a guinea pig in testing a new product or service for you – likely something closely connected

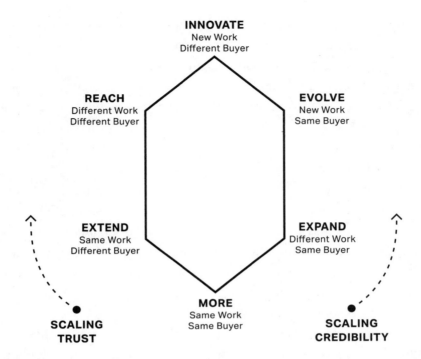

Figure 6.2 Scaling trust and credibility to move up the Diamond of Opportunity.

to your current work. For example, maybe they really want to see a monthly report of U.S. tax updates in their industry; perhaps you haven't developed and sold exactly this report before, but you are certainly capable and it's closely tied to the work you already do, and they are willing to pay you for it.

Moving up the left side of the curve, you are focused on scaling your **trust** across the client organization. Perhaps you've been doing the state and local tax preparation work for your client's Midwest locations, and now they are willing to introduce you to the Northeast regional lead for an opportunity to help them as well. While you need to build trust – build a new relationship with this Northeast lead – the credibility with the firm is there because you've done this exact same work before, just in a different place. This is **Extend** work.

Reach and **Innovate** work are the hardest because you are working to scale both trust and credibility simultaneously. Reach work is with a new buyer within the client organization doing work that you haven't done *for that account* before. You may have done this work regularly for another client and have great case studies, giving you credibility in the space, just not within this account and without a relationship with this buyer. Referrals from other happy clients become paramount. **Innovate** work is the hardest to win. It's when your client introduces you to their colleague in HR who wants to pay you to help review the job description of their open chief tax officer position and provide consultative input on a new team structure. Have you done this before? No. Have you worked with this particular buyer before? No. But are you confident in your ability to do it well based on your firm's core skill sets? Yes. If not, you would refer them to someone else who is better suited to help.

So, this is the Diamond – pretty, right? We will revisit it throughout the chapter as we move through the stages of maturity, looking at how you can set up your team to scale the Diamond across all of your accounts over time, turning those small but well-planted saplings into sturdy oaks (Figure 6.3).

Jump 1: Entrepreneurial to Tactical

Moving from Entrepreneurial to Tactical is marked by one key action: a shift from being reactive to inbound client requests, to being proactive about identifying how else you could be helping your clients. While this may seem simple, many firms struggle to make this shift. As Jennifer Anders, chief growth officer at Inframark, relates, "When you're already engaged with a client and they tell you about other needs that they have, it's easy to identify when you should be saying 'Oh yes, we can do that for you!' What's harder is proactively mapping that – to truly account plan."

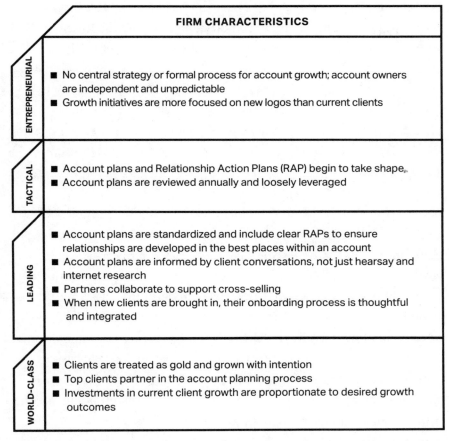

Figure 6.3 Firm characteristics at each stage of maturity – client expansion.

1. Start basic annual account planning.

The jump from Entrepreneurial to Tactical around current client account expansion comes with the single shift that Jennifer highlights – beginning **basic account planning.** In this stage, account plans aren't robust, but they do exist. You may rely a bit too much on Google or Yahoo Finance for company information, and

Double Down on Current Accounts

these "plans" may find themselves in the form of a piece of paper taped to a wall, forgotten about for months at a time. But the process of even creating one is a start. The first stage is to sit down with all relevant team members and think about the account, asking questions like:

- How happy is our client now?
- What other parts of the firm could we be helping in the same way, if only we knew the right people?
- What else does our client seem to be struggling with where we are well suited to help?

Tactical firms have these internal conversations on an annual or bi-annual basis, reviewing what needs to happen to retain and grow the account. Revenue goals for the account are set, but these are likely not based on any data, just a feeling that "I think we can grow this one 10% this year – it seems like they're happy, and we're already talking about next year!"

Given that, at this stage, you likely have just one or two core service offerings and you haven't yet built out a web of deep relationships across the organization, your plan will likely focus on the bottom half of the Diamond – thinking about how you can retain and renew the work you do have (perhaps increase prices?), maybe do the same kind of work for one or two others in the account, and perhaps discuss your one other core service offering with your wildly happy client (Figure 6.4).

Jump 2: Tactical to Leading

This is the big jump: realizing you don't need to grow apple trees and herbs because you can make great use of your garden by doubling-down on garlic.

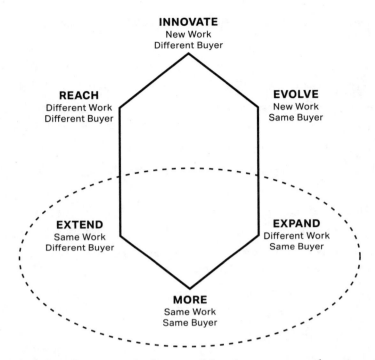

Figure 6.4 The growth focus of basic account planning for a Tactical firm.

You build a clear plan of action that includes not only the whole Diamond of Opportunity, but also layers in Relationship Action Planning (RAP). RAP is a concept originally coined by Keith Ferrazzi in his book *Never Eat Alone* that focuses squarely on the question of "who" rather than "what" – and making a *plan* to develop or nurture that relationship.

At this point, you've built enough relationships across the organization that you know who loves you, who loves your competitor, and who needs to understand that you exist. Making the jump from Tactical to Leading includes two major steps: leaning on account plans and leveraging robust RAPs.

1. Develop standardized, collaborative, comprehensive account plans.

Account plans at this stage are much more than some jotted-down ideas taped to the wall. Leading firms build clear plans with target revenue goals based on both top-down and bottom-up input – what the firm expects or needs from a given account, and a clear plan from that account partner that maps out how and where to generate that revenue. Leading account plans include the following:

- **Robust participation:** Everyone who is a key driver of account growth is in the room (account leads, account-based marketing [ABM] leads, relevant industry/practice/geo leads, critical account deliverers); meetings are taken seriously, brainstorming is productive, and any actions are assigned a clear owner.
- **A schedule:** The firm establishes clear checkpoints on the calendar to drive accountability and measure progress throughout the year, allowing the team to adjust the plan when needed.
- **Metrics:** Clarity on how you will measure progress and success; these should include KPIs around both client satisfaction as well as revenue retention and growth.
- **Robust customer knowledge:** Organization structure, financial performance, strategic priorities, industry and market trends, competition, and key stakeholders are well-known.
- **Diamond of Opportunity Map:** Understand the white space at a given account; what types of work do you currently do and with whom? Where else could you be doing work and offering additional services?

Dwight Hutchins has served clients at McKinsey and been a senior partner at Accenture and BCG. He underscores that really *measuring progress* on the plan is one of the key distinguishers for a Leading firm. "Sure, most of us are creating account plans. That's a process we can't avoid. But measuring performance against the plan? That's something great firms do: action and then accountability."

2. Build Relationship Action Plans (RAPs) into your account plans.

In the quest to drive sales, firms spend too much of their time focused on *what* they are selling and not enough time on *who* they are selling to – and not just the role, but the *person*. The Seattle-based dog lover who is gunning hard for promotion to CFO; the surprisingly introverted Marketing VP who is having some trouble adapting to the industry shift from healthcare to retail; the long-tenured CIO who is struggling with the fact that he's about to become an empty-nester. RAP (used by us as both a noun and a verb: Relationship Action "Plan" or "Planning") is a systematic and measurable way of establishing, growing, and strengthening the relationships most important to your business.

The objective of RAP is not short-term sales; it is a long-term investment in strategically building and growing *real* relationships with key clients and prospects over time. When Walt worked for Bill Green (then CEO) at Accenture, Bill used to call Walt out of the blue to check in on the business. His first question was often, "Where are you?" If the answer wasn't, "With a client," Bill would cut the conversation short with a quick, "Well that's where you should be!" … click. Known for his sometimes non-traditional but effective leadership tactics, Bill would occasionally cancel all the meetings on his calendar unexpectedly. He'd send out a quick note to the team saying something like, "You're spending too much time in internal meetings and not enough time with clients. This week's meetings are canceled." What Bill knew was that the success of a firm like Accenture depended on dedicated and systematic attention to client relationships. Spending time getting to know clients was the most powerful lever at his disposal when it came to driving growth, and RAP became the framework to guide and even incentivize this behavior. (Note: we know we're suggesting here that you *do* have an internal meeting to make this plan, but 99% of the work should be the *action* that comes next. The meeting isn't the goal, it's the setup for driving the right action. We're confident Bill would agree with this.)

It seems so obvious: keep in touch with your clients and get to know them as people. So why do so many growth leaders fail to do this? We believe they fall prey to a few common mistakes or misconceptions:

- We dramatically underestimate the access we have to clients. Clients want to meet with us more than we realize.

- We underestimate how much clients just want someone to listen to them, value a new perspective on what is happening around the industry, or want to hear what external people think about their business.

- We believe we must always have a specific answer or something new to sell if we reach out.

- We have a fear of rejection – concern that the client won't like us or will turn down a meeting.

- We don't really believe *anything* will happen – meeting clients before an RFP is a waste of time.

- We give up on the 5-yard line – we don't appreciate and recognize that a relationship has made progress.

In addition to identifying trusted relationships within an organization, Leading firms keep their fans, frenemies, and enemies close, identifying blockers and key strategies to win them over *or* win work outside of their purview. Understanding where your detractors reside is arguably as valuable as identifying your fans.

RAP enables teams to move beyond the myths and invest in both existing and new relationships across client accounts in a meaningful way. So, what does it look like to build a RAP? Let's dive in.

How to Create a Relationship Action Plan (RAP)

A basic RAP can apply to any account, large or small, and features seven steps (Figure 6.5).

Step 1: Form a RAP Team

A good RAP team includes a range of individuals who have responsibility, interest, or ability to help expand relationships with an account. Including partners alongside newer consultants creates fruitful opportunities for mentorship while also bringing in new ideas and perspectives. The team should meet regularly (ideally every 4-8 weeks) for quick check-ins to maintain momentum and accountability.

Step 2: Map the Organization

Map the broad reporting structure of the account to identify who you know, who you don't know, and who reports to whom. Think of

Figure 6.5 The seven steps of a basic Relationship Action Plan (RAP).

this step as creating a rough organizational chart for a client account to give greater visibility into how different teams and people work together and understand where your relationships sit. Start by mapping the areas of the organization that are most important and relevant to your firm's ability to help.

Step 3: Assign Relationship Statuses

How well do you know each person on the organization map? Are they aware of your firm? Are they an alumnus of your direct competitor and therefore a blocker when it comes to growth opportunities? Or are they a trusted advisor, someone who would feel comfortable dropping by your home for a drink to talk about their recent work frustrations? Use the chart (Figure 6.6) to assign a relationship status to each individual; this will help you prioritize relationships that need the most focus.

Step 4: Highlight Special Roles

Individuals in a client account often play important roles outside of their formal titles within an organization. Identifying special roles provides additional contextual clues for your list of top priority targets that can inform follow-up actions. Consider and note the following special roles:

- **Key Decision Maker:** Plays a key role in deciding when and where your firm gets work.

- **Active Coach:** Actively coaches your firm on how to improve relationships and position yourselves for success.

- **Major Influencer:** Doesn't directly make decisions but has significant influence on decisions around whether to engage your firm.

- **Advocate:** Advocates for your firm inside the client organization.
- **Disrupter:** Driving major change in the organization (could be good or bad for you, but important to have on your radar).
- **Competitor Advocate:** Advocates for your firm's competitor.

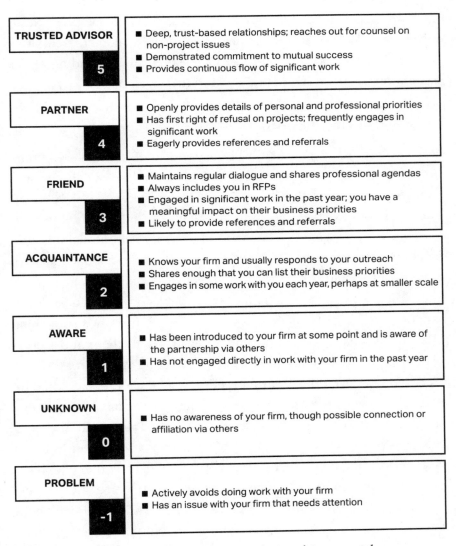

Figure 6.6 The spectrum of client relationship strength.

Step 5: Assign Relationship Action Leaders for Each Priority Executive

The relationship action leader is someone on the RAP team responsible for advancing the relationship with the target. This isn't to say they have exclusive or long-term ownership of that relationship, and they are not a gatekeeper. Instead, their focus should be on expanding and strengthening the relationship, pulling in others to help drive the relationship forward, and deepening their understanding of the issues and interests that matter most to that person.

Step 6: Develop Actions

Once you've assigned relationship action leaders, spend some time brainstorming actions, both big and small, to help move the priority executives up the relationship ladder. A good action plan should outline steps to introduce your firm and yourself, strengthen your relationship with the target account, and learn more about major issues, business challenges, professional aspirations, and personal goals. An action plan should not be focused directly on selling.

During workshops and trainings that we've led on business development, the biggest pushback on outreach often sounds something like, "I don't have something important to say to them and I don't want to just bother them." Kevin Legg, Managing Partner for SAGE, a learning and development firm based out of Singapore, has come up with an elegant exercise for this problem that he calls LEGITs. Legg says, "It stands for Legitimate Excuses to Get In Touch, and this really sets people free. LEGITs is just a big set of excuses to get in touch with people that won't seem lame. For example, something new was published or written, or you are in their building to see another customer of yours. Maybe you are leaving for travel and will be gone for three weeks, so in case they reach out to you, you won't be there, and you wanted to let them know (or get tips for your trip, if you're heading somewhere they've visited)."

Consider bringing colleagues together and take five minutes to try to come up with as many "legitimate" reasons to reach out to a client or prospect. There is some competition, there is some humor, and at the end of the five minutes, the team walks away with 30+ reasons to check in with their relationships. In an industry where perfection is expected, partners need nudging to not allow the perfect to be the enemy of the good. Remember, the outreach needs to be *legit*. As Jack Azagury, Group CEO, Consulting for Accenture puts it, "If the client thinks you're in it for yourself or to close a quarter with your target number, it's game over."

Below are a few examples of LEGITs:

- Send a note (e.g., note of congratulations) about recent company news or earnings reports and ask for their perspective on the news.
- Share relevant or unique observations based on something you've read or learned about their company or industry; this may be passing along a relevant article or blog post.
- Offer to help with small tasks (e.g., calendaring a meeting, reviewing a document).
- Ask for a favor (e.g., would they speak at your firm's upcoming all-hands meeting?).
- Catch up over lunch or coffee, chatting about both business and personal updates.
- Invite them to an event or conference, or meet up at a conference you'll both be attending.
- Ask for an internal introduction to a different part of the firm

Double Down on Current Accounts

- Help their family (e.g., share info about your alma mater with their daughter looking at colleges; make introductions for their spouse looking for a job).

- Show interest in their charitable priorities as appropriate and if they align with your interests (e.g., volunteer, donate, repost information).

Consider the type of actions and touchpoints in the same way an interior designer might consider decorating a new house. While each piece of furniture and accent light should tie together, they need not match. Interior designers often intentionally pair a unique antique table with more modern chairs and furnishings to create balance both in style and color. Touchpoints should similarly vary from short to in-depth and include a variety of mechanisms, from email and phone calls to engaging with LinkedIn updates, to sharing a drink or meal.

Step 7: Review and Update

Every four to eight weeks, the RAP team should meet (briefly, because you're busy with clients!) to review successes and failures, share insights and learnings, and brainstorm how to advance the plan forward. Regular reviews are also a good opportunity to switch relationship leaders, award prizes for major steps forward, and share creative strategies for connecting.

Jump 3: Leading to World-class

World-class firms grow their client accounts by living and breathing client relationships every day. Account planning is so engrained that it's part of the firm's DNA – and they invite their clients into the process, demonstrating the pinnacle of a trusted partnership. Two key actions move firms into World-class:

1. Integrate the five Ts into your account plans.

World-class firms add another layer to their account landscape analysis by integrating key trigger events, also known as the five Ts, into their planning:

- **Transition** – leadership or organizational change (e.g., new CEO, major reorg)
- **Transaction** – merger, acquisition, divestiture, new owner
- **Transgression** – major corporate wrongdoing (e.g., Exxon Valdez oil spill)
- **Technology** – industry/sector technology change; the company makes a decision to introduce major technology changes in a company (e.g., introducing a new ERP system)
- **Transformation** – corporate-wide change often signified by broad programs targeted to improve performance (e.g., multi-billion-dollar investment in AI practice), or new regulations that completely transform the way a company must do business (e.g., GDPR compliance)

The five Ts help identify clear timing for client outreach regarding potential opportunities and signal both opportunity and threat for professional services firms.

Typical consulting spend in companies is relatively stable year over year, and share of wallet tends to remain consistent. Breaking in can be difficult when incumbents have established trust and credibility, *and* have inside knowledge. Additionally, the cost of switching firms is typically high for clients and they are reticent to do so. Disrupting the status quo is often the result of a trigger event (see Figure 6.7) that can have a lagging, but important, impact on consulting spend, creating an opportunity for new players to enter the game and scoop up market share. An Accenture study found that business development time and expense typically pay off 20× during one of these five trigger events, offering a unique window of opportunity to establish new and deep relationships, capture consulting spend, and unseat competitors.

A trigger event might lead to incumbents losing out if they are identified as part of the problem while new consultants may be brought in and capture larger opportunities. Both before and during a trigger event, there is an important opportunity to position yourself as a part of the solution, not the problem. World-class firms pay attention to these trigger events in their account planning process, ensuring they don't lose ground when events hit, but rather are prepared to capture new opportunities.

The five Ts are most useful when the foundation of relationships across an organization has been established and properly cultivated prior to a trigger event.

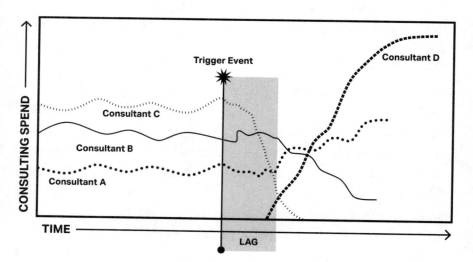

Figure 6.7 The impact of trigger events on consulting spend.

2. Engage your best clients directly in your account planning.

Client engagement and collaboration becomes the expectation at World-class firms. Rather than throwing ideas on a whiteboard of what you think a client wants and needs, the client sits in the room with you, trusting that what you recommend will be in their best interest. "Trusted advisor status means that you give and you give and you give. How can you be helpful to them – with whatever their current challenges are (whether those challenges have anything to do with your product or not)? And when your key customers are picking up your phone call on the first ring, why is that? It's not because they're thinking about you as a salesperson. It's because they're thinking about you as a trusted advisor who is going to help them," says David Popler, managing director and global head of the Technology Industry Division at JLL. Notably, the trusted advisor approach applies for both current clients as well as prospects. Showing up as a trusted advisor can be even more important when looking to establish a new relationship before you've demonstrated a track record of success. Once you reach trusted advisor status, you earn the right and the privilege to work alongside your client to map out how to best serve them over the next month, year, five years.

A World-class firm approaches account planning like brushing teeth – it is not an annual or quarterly "thing" you do and then forget about. It is an integrated routine woven into the everyday hygiene habits of the organization. **Account planning is a daily habit, not an annual exercise.**

* * *

101

Double Down on Current Accounts

Building Trust Internally

As firms move up the maturity curve, they often reach an inflection point where the expansion of existing accounts will either accelerate or slowly taper. The trajectory of this growth depends less on the accounts themselves and much more on the internal trust score between the firm's leading rainmakers.

The best ROI for business development happens when firms invest in building a strong internal network of trust. World-class firms intentionally create a culture where referrals, introductions, and account expansion are second nature and expected. Partners know and respect what their colleagues do best and are quick to bring them into client relationships. In contrast, firms where partners are unreasonably protective of their accounts, try to be all things to all clients, and ignore the power of the team will hit a ceiling with current client growth.

For a World-class firm, growth at existing accounts is easy because the partner down the hall, *who already has the trust of the people and accounts you want to serve*, need simply introduce you. So how do you build a culture of trust internally?

1. **Mentorship** – Create opportunities for senior rainmakers to show junior team members the way of the firm, making an example of providing introductions and prioritizing strong relationship-building internally to foster collaboration and cross-selling.

2. **Annual in-person gatherings** – Shared space, time, and experiences accelerate trust building. Before the COVID-19 pandemic, firms often took for granted the trust-building that

occurs through proximity. As work culture has shifted to more remote or hybrid formats, the natural trust that builds by seeing someone in the hall every day has disintegrated. World-class firms bring their teams together at least once a year in person to build a team mindset and enable the firm to go to market as a one firm.

3. **Share client stories** – When partners are gathered in person, use that time to not only build personal connections, but build deep understanding of each other's expertise and client work. If Molly learns about the three different accounts for whom Josh recently led leadership development trainings and got rave reviews, she won't think twice about pulling him in next time she hears that one of her clients needs help with this. Have partners ask each other: "How do you deliver value for your clients?"

4. **Study halls** – Like the camaraderie built while studying for finals with your college classmates, business development study halls carve out intentional time and shared space for sales teams to work collectively to drive growth. Even if 20% of an hour-long "study hall" is spent on growth-focused activities and 80% is spent chatting about the snow fort Cavin built for his daughter, the ramblings on best construction tools for a snow fort are the fibers of trust needed for a team to thrive. Study halls also eliminate the need to schedule a separate meeting or phone call to find out what your partner down the hall does for clients, instead driving organic knowledge sharing between areas of expertise and services.

* * *

103

Double Down on Current Accounts

World-class firms, like World-class gardeners, are excellent at focusing on where they are best set up to succeed, tending closely to their current clients – their beautiful bounty of garlic. They've created a system where the daily notes to clients, updates to organization charts, and client-centered actions have become as natural as grabbing a cup of coffee before digging into morning emails. The system enables good habits, but the culture of the organization drives the adoption of those habits and makes them norms. For World-class firms, clients sit at the center of culture.

Chapter 7

Winning New Clients

Bleeding green.

When seniors at Dartmouth College throw their hats in the air in front of Baker Hall on graduation day, they leave the small college on the hill with green running through their veins. As any college development director knows, alumni are the best avenue for future financial support – and Dartmouth College is known for having one of the strongest networks of happy former students. Those fundraisers are in luck.

The connection to the college begins even before matriculation (and in some cases before birth, if you happen to be the descendent of a parent bleeding green ...). Before the first day of classes, incoming freshmen spend three days rock climbing, canoeing, hiking, or biking with a fellow group of new students and upper-classmen leaders, immediately cementing the school's connection to the outdoors of New Hampshire. They build camaraderie and community tackling ridgelines in the White Mountains or, more often, hunkering in tents under a classic New England rainstorm. The shared experience (and sometimes shared suffering!) creates core memories that students carry with them long after graduation and good fodder for conversation when meeting fellow students of the Big Green.

Upon departure from the college, the Alumni Center invests heavily in creating events and pathways for continued engagement with their recently graduated students. They've established a series of exclusive giving societies with special recognition; they produce a monthly magazine shared with all former students, keeping alumni abreast of the accomplishments of students and staff both current and former; they offer a robust career and alumni directory to easily connect anyone with ties to the college. Annual reunions, volunteer opportunities, regional clubs, and mentorship structures strengthen the college's ability to create connective tissue, building a worldwide network of Dartmouth alumni and fans of the school. Dartmouth alumni are also given the opportunity to conduct interviews for promising applicants that live within their respective region. The conversation often marks the final piece of a robust application process and gives hopeful high schoolers the chance to hear firsthand about the college, while simultaneously connecting alumni with the future generation of Big Green fans. These alumni are busy people, but they see these interviews as an *opportunity* (not free labor for the school!) and are happy to give of their time, because they love and trust Dartmouth, and want to stay connected.

In 2023–2024, alumni contributions made up nearly 80% of the funds raised for the Dartmouth College Fund, which awards $149M in financial aid each year.

Dartmouth College is not the only higher education institution to effectively create raving fans and happy alumni. Princeton, Harvard, Stanford, Amherst, Northwestern, Texas A&M, and Notre Dame, to name a few, have similarly strong networks of alumni (but if you ask Erika, the Big Green is the strongest...). Each of these institutions recognizes the immense power of building strong relationships and continuing to follow, tend, and strengthen those relationships long after the easy connection of a shared campus is gone. They've found their fans, and they intend to follow them, even as they begin to develop new fans with every incoming class of bright-eyed freshman.

The world of professional services is no different, where relationships are the currency of choice. Similar to fundraising for a university, more than 80% of revenues at most consulting firms come from their fans – their current clients, former clients, former employees, and those they've brought into their circle of trust even before the sale (the excited high school students who have learned enough about Dartmouth that they bleed green even before showing up). World-class professional services firms have harnessed all these avenues to build and maintain trust with a broad network of target buyers. This is what drives new logo growth – the necessary supplement to current account expansion we discussed in the previous chapter.

While this chapter isn't about *how to sell* to new clients, it is about how to put the structures and programs in place that set you up to build and maintain the right relationships – get your whole target audience bleeding green – so that when any of them are *able and ready* to buy from you, all of the other prerequisites (awareness, understanding, trust, and credibility) are all firmly in place.

We call this "fan following" – the act of staying in touch with your raving fans the way Dartmouth keeps in touch with Erika, adding value before, during, and after an engagement. If you have a vast network of "fans" and can keep them that way until they (or their friends) need your help, new client acquisition will be cake. Forget the cold call.

What Is the Problem?

Staying close to your fans seems so obvious, right? So why is it a challenge? Why do we feel frustrated when we think about the amount of contact information and relationship capital that is lost when projects are completed or employees move on? The challenge is both logistical and behavioral. Hundreds of consultants working with multiple clients across various information systems and geographies naturally create a certain amount of information leakage. This treasure trove of relationships could generate business for firms indefinitely, but harnessing all of this goodwill is difficult. Proper follow-up with all of these contacts could eliminate the need for cold calls forever. So why don't firms do this well? We see a few common challenges:

1. **No system.** Fan following often relies on individuals to capture and enter data into a CRM system with the proper classifications. The most experienced people in a firm or practice are often the least proficient at this process, convinced their brain index is sufficient. Inevitably, relationships and connections are lost due to the lack of a well-utilized system by senior rainmakers, which gives the rest of the firm permission to skip the data entry process entirely. We all know mature professional services firms have outgrown the rolodex, but many haven't found, or learned to reliably use, a suitable technology-forward replacement.

2. **Too many disparate systems.** "We have 17 systems – it's a mess!" a chief growth officer exclaimed when asked about tracking key relationships. While some firms lack any fan following system, others have multiple, disconnected processes for tracking, tracing, and following their contacts. Due to acquisitions and poorly designed technology road maps, there is no single source of truth. Some data resides in a CRM, some in a marketing automation platform, and some in an industry-specific tool.

3. **Tunnel vision.** Too often, consultants ignore the entire universe of influential relationships on a project. Instead of treating all associated stakeholders as potential fans and future clients, consultants prioritize a handful of people they work with every day, forgetting those who are ancillary to the project. While individual relationships are key, a project is rarely, if ever, just for one stakeholder. There is a community of influence within the account that matters and should be treated as such if you want to add them to your future fanbase.

4. **Scared of spam.** Partners hesitate to enter "their relationships" into a central database if they believe those contacts will "just be spammed by marketing." While some marketing emails may seem frivolous, the absence of any outreach and total loss of relationships is worse. If you're not reaching out to your contacts, remember your competitor is.

5. **People are busy.** In good times, there is no time for business development (while in bad times, there is no money). The workload demands of a consultant can be exhausting, making the idea of spending extra time logging contact information or reaching out to someone not currently engaged feel overly burdensome. Even more problematic is that the payoff for this kind of initiative can take months or years, not weeks, so it falls to the bottom of the list.

What Should We Do?

Building a true growth engine requires meaningful and ongoing engagement with four specific cohorts of individuals: current clients, potential clients, past clients, and former employees. This chapter focuses on the latter three, emphasizing that past clients and former employees can also be potential clients! Moving from Entrepreneurial to World-class (see Figure 7.1) means developing a way to capture and continue to connect with the many people you've delighted, influenced, and employed over time, so they "bleed green" (or whatever color distinguishes your firm).

It goes without saying (but we'll say it) that this strategy must begin and end with doing good work and providing a great customer and employee experience. You need to have a quality of work and culture of which people can and should be fans.

STAGES OF MATURITY

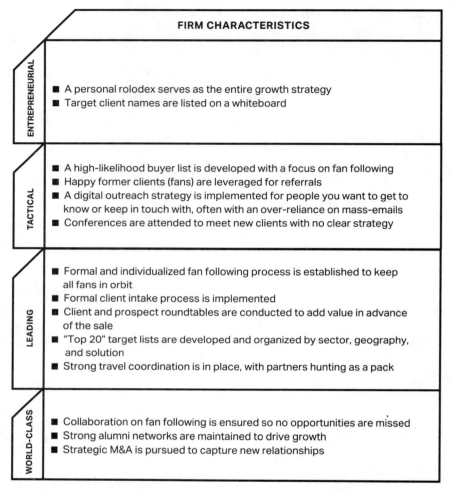

Figure 7.1 Firm characteristics at each stage of maturity – winning new clients.

Jump 1: Entrepreneurial to Tactical

Entrepreneurial firms in the early stages may actually be quite good at fan following. When there are only two clients and one moves to a new firm, it's clear that a call is necessary to keep the lights on.

However, relying solely on this is not sustainable, as two relationships cannot drive long-term, steady growth. Consequently, Entrepreneurial firms often resort to cold calling, hoping to turn strangers into fans with a quick sales pitch.

Firms transition into the Tactical phase when they realize that having two fans and two thousand strangers is not enough to secure their financial future. They begin dedicating resources to the highest payoff activities. This recognition leads these firms to the following activities:

1. Start basic fan following.

While likely not a formal program, Tactical firms recognize that keeping fans close leads to more work and lower sales costs. Instead of spending two years courting a prospect and convincing them of your value, engaging someone who already knows and trusts you is a much quicker and less resource-intensive sale. Tactical firms start to track former clients and employees who could become future clients, though likely in an uncoordinated way. Each partner might have their own spreadsheet, or they might check LinkedIn once a month for any role changes.

Sarah Clifford, former president of Seven2, has a simple system: "I've tasked our account managers and producers with a process that doesn't take much time but has a big impact: Connect with three people who are no longer our direct clients or who have moved into a different space. Maybe use LinkedIn, email, text, or social media, depending on the relationship. It doesn't matter how you get in touch with them; the goal is to check in and see how they're doing on a casual, organic level rather than asking for a sales call. In this way, we keep in touch with all the people we've worked with over the years, even if they move on to other roles or companies."

2. Leverage your existing biggest fans for referral.

Tactical firms recognize the value of transferred trust and credibility in the form of referrals. They've built some client relationships that are strong enough to make the ask of a "warm" introduction from clients, former employees, and other friends of the firm who are willing to use personal capital to make an introduction. Wondering who your biggest fans are? Think about those with whom you have what we call "fridge rights." When you've reached the pinnacle of a trusted client relationship, you could conceivably walk into their home and help yourself to a beer from their fridge. In an ideal world, you cultivate "fridge rights" with key stakeholders across your client portfolio. It's less about the cold beverage and more about how the level of trust and closeness will allow you to better and more broadly serve them.

3. Build up your online presence both as individuals and as a firm.

Use LinkedIn. It's free and it's vast. While specific platforms and tools will surely evolve, finding ways to keep in touch with your fans is evergreen. LinkedIn, personal emails, phone numbers, other social media platforms all create easy inroads for staying connected as circumstances change and new opportunities arise. A best practice is to connect with everyone you meet from a client account on LinkedIn immediately after the meeting while it's top of mind. Imagine how many people you've met who've fallen through the cracks. These people could be future clients, if you create an avenue to stay in touch.

* * *

The Mass-Email Mistake

In the hopes of turning a bunch of strangers into fans overnight, firms moving out of the Entrepreneurial stage often make the mistake of investing in tools for automated outreach that engage anyone with a valid email. The Hippocratic oath of business development is key here – do no harm. Strapped for time, a common misstep is to over-rely on automated touchpoints that should be personalized. Many of these marketing automation tools prioritize frequency of communication, not impact. As an example, sending a CFO a white paper on the benefits of going public as part of an email campaign when their company has recently been taken off the public market through a difficult private equity takeover misses the mark. While broad-based communications can certainly have a place in your brand-building strategy, far more important are the bespoke emails and touchpoints from the person who actually has the relationship. Don't confuse these two as having the same intended goals or outcomes.

* * *

4. Lean on your list of LEGITs

Central to finding success with this type of outreach is making certain your fans don't feel like you're peppering them with asks for a sales call, but rather you are demonstrating a genuine interest in the individual and your relationship. Lean on the list of "legit" actions that we outlined in the previous chapter, with the shift that the people you're reaching out to are not currently clients. The impact takes time to materialize, but it can truly become a flywheel if you do it consistently. Below is an example of a note that could be used when someone lands a new job:

> *Hi Theresa – I saw that you are taking over the procurement function at Heineken; they have gotten a good one! No need to reply to this as I'm sure you're getting inundated with notes from your network. I look forward to connecting again soon once you've settled. I have attached a document that a few of my partners pulled together called, "My first 90 days as a CPO." Basically, they interviewed CPOs, asking them what they would do differently if they had a fresh start at their role. Perhaps it will be helpful. P.S.: I saw that they gave the finals MVP to Brown instead of Tatum … Is that going to spell trouble in Boston?*

* * *

Jump 2: Tactical to Leading

The jump from Tactical to Leading builds on the foundation of strong client service and focused outreach to begin cultivating a broader "fan base" that paves the way to new logos. This evolution is marked by a few key actions:

1. Formalize fan following.

Leading firms leverage their CRM to track, manage, and stay connected with "fans" of the firm, enabling these organizations to skip much of the trust and credibility exercises required to win new logos and instead head straight to go. Long-tenured partners who have an expansive list of fans are supported in their keeping-in-touch efforts, both through administrative support and automatic alerts (e.g., from

LinkedIn or CRM) about job changes or promotions of people they know. They categorize this "fan following" list to prioritize those who represent the warmest opportunities. If you did great work for a controller at Target who has now taken the CFO role at Best Buy (an account you've been trying to break into), she goes to the top of your list. But the outreach isn't "let's have a sales call!" – it's a note of congratulations, and a suggestion that you'd welcome the chance to catch up and learn about her new role once she's settled in (see example earlier in this chapter). This aligns with the strategies we learned in Chapter 6 around creating Relationship Action Plans (RAP) and layering on the five Ts to an account landscape.

Every relationship owner in the organization has a "fan following" list and is actively focused on how they can use their networks of fans to drive growth. Leading firms move beyond individual spreadsheets and rely on a centralized CRM and other tools to track client movement and behavior in a seamless way, making sure people aren't stepping on each other's toes while simultaneously ensuring no fans are falling through the cracks.

2. Establish a formal client intake process, building more relationships within a new account.

A combination of enthusiasm and the looming deadline of a new project often causes firms to devalue the intake process, jumping right into delivery with the few people for whom they are directly working. Instead, firms should cast a wide net when signing a new client to begin building broader relationships. Map out the key players on the assignment along with any other relationships that should be developed to serve that client holistically. To whom do your key stakeholders report? Who is paying for the project? Who will be on the line if the project goes poorly? Who will be rewarded if it goes well?

This activity is beneficial for two reasons. First, it genuinely makes the project more successful. When you connect with any stakeholder who might be impacted (positively or negatively) by your work, you can help ensure any change management associated with your project goes smoothly. You also build a deeper partnership as you better understand the complexities (and perhaps the politics) of the account. Second, you expand your network! You may not become incredibly close to someone two degrees separated from your project, but if you spend time meeting them beforehand, you do a great job on the work, and then you follow up to ask for their feedback, you've built a real relationship. This means you'll have the right to reach out to them in the future, and they'll answer your call.

During the client intake process, capture all relevant stakeholders and associated contact, personal, and professional information. The better the data captured, the more useful it will be two to five years down the line.

3. Host value-first client and prospect executive roundtables – earning trust before the sale.

Building trust and credibility takes time, and Leading firms recognize they are playing the long game. While leaning on fan following to win new work as people move around in their careers is a strong strategy, you can't *only* rely on the people you've already worked for to drive new logo growth. So, how do you expand this universe? You put yourself in the position to develop "fans" *before* the sale. Leading firms find ways to add value while hanging around the hoop by convening their likely buyers to exchange ideas and insights with one another on an ongoing basis – they form a community of fans and future fans. Executive roundtables of true peers provide C-suite executives with an exclusive and helpful community while affording your firm a seat at the table with those you most want to serve, creating an organic opportunity to demonstrate expertise, build credibility and trust, and add value. These forums super-charge the "referrals" that Tactical firms rely on by bringing clients and prospects together; we all trust our peers more than we trust a sales pitch, so giving the prospect an opportunity to get to know you – and your clients – and hear their experience in an organic format is priceless. Community-based programs like this keep your firm top of mind so when they do need help, they know just who to call.

* * *

Hosting Roundtables That Win You Fans – and New Business

Many of PIE's clients hire us to develop executive communities on their behalf, hosting virtual and in-person roundtables for F500 executives. We've facilitated nearly 5,000 roundtables of C-suite executives since 2001. Here are a few tips from our 25 years of experience:

- Keep the group peer level – The COO of Starbucks wants to talk to the COO of Bank of America, not the operations manager of your regional bank.

- Join the conversation as an active participant, not a presenter – executives often exist in a silo; they want to talk to each other, not watch a sales pitch or a webinar.

- Invite participants to help shape the agenda – busy executives will only come if they are confident the discussion topics are relevant to them.

(continued)

(continued)

- Respect their busy calendars – start and end on time!

- Follow up – if you offer to help broker a 1:1 connection between members or say you'll send through the article you mentioned during the meeting, do it within 24 hours.

- Commit to a series, not "one-and-done" roundtables – relationships, trust, and credibility are won over time. Orient yourself at the center of an ongoing conversation so you stay proximate to the people who matter to your business.

- Consider hiring a third party – wrangling busy executive calendars and getting C-suite leaders to openly share their challenges is not a light lift; if you don't have the internal resources to do it well, enlist an experienced partner for help. A third-party partner also creates a layer of objectivity that positions you as the expert and encourages executive participation by guaranteeing a conversation rather than a sponsor pitch.

* * *

Jump 3: Leading to World-class

As part of their DNA, World-class firms have the ability to build *and maintain* relationships – with current, former, and prospective clients. This includes alumni of the firm, as associates and partners begin to transition to in house roles. These alumni retain a deep respect for the firm that developed them, likely becoming future buyers. Let's take a look at this key action:

1. Develop a strong alumni program.

How many Heads of Tax are former accountants at one of the Big 4? How many F500 General Counsels spent time at an Am Law 100 firm before making the move in-house somewhere? This world of former service providers moving into senior roles with budget authority is significant. World-class firms have a clear strategy for harnessing this as an avenue for growth. To the extent it's possible, extend resources of value from the firm to the individual. Create opportunities for them to interact, formally and informally, and look for opportunities to feature them on internal panels to highlight a success story that doesn't result in permanent partnership. Firms like McKinsey, Accenture, and Bain lead the way when it comes to engaging former employees and support robust alumni centers where those who have worked for the firm can connect with one another, find and post jobs, and stay connected with the firm. Once you've done all the hard work – through company culture and quality of work – to make your firm a place that alumni are proud of, take these steps to operationalize that network of alumni fans:

- Capture all former employee data in your CRM and review and update it annually.

- Conduct thoughtful exit interviews to give employees a great experience on the way out – ensuring they remain fans.

- If your firm has an "up-or-out" culture, HR should have a program to place departing employees in private industry with an eye toward growth opportunities. World-class firms never "fire" an associate, they promote each one to customer.

- Develop a steering committee to run the alumni program that includes business development, HR and marketing to ensure the alumni experience is consistent and thoughtful.

- Develop a series of alumni events – virtual and in-person – to keep your alumni connected to the firm and to each other.

- Map your alumni regionally and have current leaders host alumni events when in their area.

- Engage alumni regularly via digital communications (email, social media).

- Survey alumni regularly to ask what they want to hear and see from you.

- When possible (avoiding any competitive concerns), give alumni early access to research or other materials that might be of interest to them.

- Just like client fan following, develop a system through your CRM that flags changes in alumni roles that could be beneficial to the firm (e.g., if a former vice president in your digital strategy practice lands a CMO job at one of your target automotive accounts, reach out to congratulate her ... and find out if she needs a new digital strategy partner!).

Successful alumni programs require work, but, if harnessed appropriately, they pay for themselves over and over through referrals to new talent and new work.

Winning new logos in professional services is challenging. A new buyer must be aware of who you are, understand what you do, have a problem for which you have the solution, trust that you can deliver, believe you are credible and capable of solving their problem, have the budget to buy from you, and the timing must be right. The most critical elements are trust and credibility, which present a unique challenge in our industry. As Accenture's Jack Azagury underscores, "Trust starts with always being open, up-front, and direct – and having zero self-interest. Thinking about the clients first, second, and third is how you build trust. That's how you build relationships, and professional services are all about trusted relationships. You also need some intellect and good ideas, but if you don't have trusted relationships, there's no point."

As firms look to move up the maturity curve and rev the growth engine, they learn to win new logos at scale by building and capitalizing on an established network of fans – those with whom they have trusted relationships – and steadily expand that network. Excellent service paired with ongoing, meaningful engagement means those thousands of hats in the air during a graduation ceremony will eventually land as new logos for your firm.

Part IV

Talent and Performance Management

Chapter 8

Hiring and Harnessing Talent

As a kid, Andi dreamed of one day becoming a piano virtuoso.

She idolized her piano teacher, Liza, who had performed on global stages before settling down in Montana to raise a family and start sharing her gift with the next generation. In the beginning, Andi could only plunk out the melody to "Heart and Soul" with her right hand while her little legs swung from the bench, unable to reach the pedals.

Early in her piano-playing days, Andi focused on mastering those single-handed tunes. These songs came easily enough; Andi had a natural sense of rhythm, memorized the keys quickly, and could play most simple songs by ear after hearing Liza play them once or twice. As she practiced and improved, she moved on to more complex pieces and learned to play with both hands simultaneously. When she grew tall enough to reach the pedals, she incorporated those as well (sometimes a bit too dramatically …).

Then things started to get tricky. Andi wanted to play duets with her friends and was hungry to play more complex music – particularly the theme song to her favorite new movie, *Titanic*. Both of these goals required new skills: working in sync with a partner on a duet and reading music.

Initially, this felt like a step backwards in her development. Playing the music was fun! Staring at pieces of paper to understand what G sharp looked like in sheet music felt like homework. But without learning to read music, she could never accompany Celine Dion for

"My Heart Will Go On." So she buckled down, learned to read music, and got a standing ovation at her middle school recital.

In professional services, we all want to hire the virtuosos – the Mozarts who can play every instrument in an entire symphony by ear after one listen. But there is one Mozart in the world for every million great musicians out there with high potential. What we need to look for are people who have the innate attributes we need – rhythm, eagerness to learn, love for music – and can develop the skills required to perform complex arrangements alongside 100-piece orchestras at Lincoln Center.

We know it's not easy. Two factors make this hunt for talent uniquely challenging:

- **Great rainmakers take time to develop:** Your best growth drivers are also your best deliverers. Why? Because most professional services firms leverage a seller-doer model. The expertise that enables rainmakers to *sell solutions for client problems* has been built over time by *creating and executing those same solutions for client problems*. It can take years for a professional to develop the knowledge and language needed to identify and evaluate client needs and expertly communicate how they can help address those needs. Just as learning to play complex tunes on the piano takes time, so does developing deep domain expertise. The most successful business developers in professional services are those that can speak from experience. Handing a junior hire a cheat sheet on the business doesn't lead to the same outcomes as a senior partner having lunch with a prospective client and sharing how they personally improved benefits administration processes for three different franchisors last year. Building an effective growth engine depends on first identifying the right mix of talent and then creating a runway for them to develop into rainmakers (more on this in Chapter 9).

- **People hate failing:** Jose Bokhorst is CEO of the Benelux, France, Germany and Switzerland businesses for Robert Walters Group (RWG), a billion-dollar professional recruitment firm with offices in more than 30 countries. As Jose describes it, "Recruitment largely is a sales business – for us, as a global talent solutions provider, we're looking for people who can build strong relationships, excel at business development, and thrive in a high-performance culture." Not surprisingly, Jose has spent a lot of time honing her skills around hiring the right type of people for her firm – those who are not only capable of delivering on projects and winning new work, but who are additive to the overall culture she has worked hard to build. "We obviously want people who are great – people who want to win. But I'm more interested in how they handle losing." Jose explains what she has seen:

"You have two different types of people who really want to win. You have those who just want to win and score no matter what. That's not what I'm looking for. I'm looking for people who want to win and score but also have a human side. The three things we're really focused on when we're hiring people in sales are teamwork, ownership, and respect. You have to want to win, but you have to be able to really demonstrate these three characteristics whether you win or lose."

Part of what makes a great rainmaker is thick skin. Those driving growth at a firm need to be willing to take shots on goal and not feel deflated when only 1 out of 100 shots finds the back of the net.

Firms naturally go through different team compositions to drive growth as they ascend the maturity curve, often beginning with a small group of founder heroes, who then hire folks in their same image, before realizing true scale requires the identification and cultivation of a more diverse and dynamic team of business developers.

127

Hiring and Harnessing Talent

The culture of the firm is a natural outcome of the people you hire and the behavior they demonstrate. World-class firms embed growth in the DNA of their organization by carefully considering the composition of their team and then developing (Chapter 9), incentivizing (Chapter 10), and structuring (Chapter 11) that team to optimize business development outcomes. Any great team starts with the people, and that's what we're focused on in this chapter: how firms first identify the skills they need, then find and hire the right people with those skills, and, finally, keep them engaged over the long term to grow the firm (Figure 8.1).

Jump 1: Entrepreneurial to Tactical

Firms maturing from Entrepreneurial to Tactical begin to define the growth culture that will likely characterize the organization for years to come. This jump is an important one for that precise reason – the primary goal is to get clear on what you want that culture to look like and reinforce it with who you hire and how you engage them to embed growth in the company's ethos. In this phase, firms begin to think clearly about the skills they need to succeed and begin to look for those in hiring.

1. Expand your growth team.

If only a handful of senior leaders are responsible for BD in the Entrepreneurial stage, maturing into a Tactical firm requires those same leaders to find, hire, and enable additional growth leaders. The challenge is that not everyone in the company has the same capabilities and experiences as those who built the firm from nothing. But that's okay – not everyone needs to do everything! You can break down the distinct BD activities that drive a sale and assign responsibility for those activities based on level of seniority, experience, and capabilities. See Figure 8.2:

128

The Growth Engine

STAGES OF MATURITY

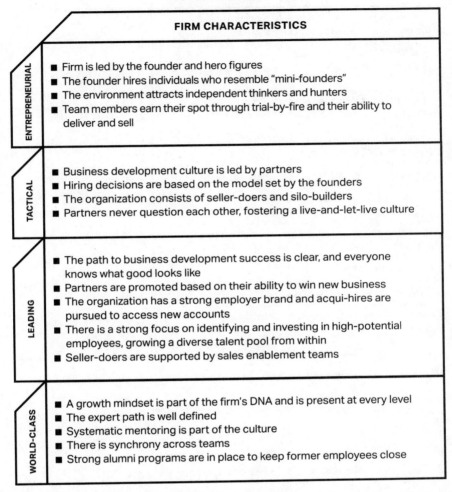

Figure 8.1 Firm characteristics at each stage of maturity – hiring and culture.

Engaging the broader team in business development achieves two things: First, it multiplies the reach of a few well-connected founders to grow the rolodex of possible clients. Second, it helps identify rainmaker potential that can be cultivated within the firm.

BUSINESS DEVELOPMENT ACTIVITY	RESPONSIBILITY
Researching 100 firms or practices that fall within your organization's ideal client profile (ICP)	Associate
Determining five individual targets for outreach within each of the firms identified above and sourcing contact information	Associate
Researching conferences where your firm should have a presence to build connections and securing speaking opportunities	Associate
Writing thought leadership	Partner
Drafting emails for partners or senior leaders to send to engage prospective clients	Associate
Scheduling (and rescheduling) BD meetings	Administrative support
Tracking contacts, meetings, and opportunity progress in a customer relationship management (CRM) tool	Administrative support
Meeting with prospective clients	Partner
Speaking at conferences	Partner
Developing follow-up plan for conference connections	Marketing Coordinator
Preparing decks and proposals	Associate

Figure 8.2   Business development activity responsibility.

We'll dig into these various roles and responsibilities and how firms build support around their business developers in Chapter 11.

2. Evaluate talent against a BD competency framework.

When looking at your current talent and considering hiring, evaluate both your team and candidates against baseline BD traits. Not everyone on the team needs to have a big personality or be the best proposal writer, but there are certain abilities that are harder to train and should always be at the top of the list of evaluation criteria when hiring.

One skills framework we really like can be seen in Figure 8.3. This framework was developed by Brandon Martin, president, chief

- ☐ **Easy to train**
- ▨ **Harder to train**
- ■ **Cannot train, should already have these abilities in hand**

EXTERNAL

	COMPETENCY	DEFINITION
Business Development	**Running Customer Meetings**	■ Demonstrates ability to organize and run effective meetings.
	Political Savvy	■ Aware of political factors and hidden agendas, and acts effectively with that awareness.
	Customer Focus	■ Monitors client satisfaction (internal or external). ■ Builds trusted partner relationship with clients. ■ Visible and accessible to clients.
	Resourcefulness & Initiative	■ Creative thinker with objectivity in decision-making. ■ Neither indecisive nor hip-shooter.
Pipeline Creation	**Intelligence**	■ Ability to acquire understanding and absorb information rapidly.
	Strategic Skills	■ Determines opportunities and threats through comprehensive analysis of trends. ■ Comprehends the big picture.
	Organization & Planning	■ Plans, schedules, and budgets in an efficient, organized manner. ■ Focuses on key priorities.
Relationship Management	**Enthusiasm & Passion**	■ Exhibits dynamism, excitement, and a positive can-do attitude.
	Oral Communication	■ Communicates well one-on-one, in small groups, and public speaking. ■ Fluent, quick on their feet, command of language. ■ Keeps people informed.
	Written Communication	■ Writes clear, precise, well-organized documents using appropriate vocabulary and grammar.
	Integrity	■ Does not ethically cut corners. ■ Earns trust of co-workers. ■ Puts organization above self-interest.
Value Messaging	**Negotiation**	■ Achieves favorable outcomes in win/win negotiations.
	Analysis Skills	■ Identifies significant problems and opportunities. ■ Analyzes problems and people in depth. ■ Sorts the wheat from the chaff, determining root causes.
	Vision	■ Provides clear, credible vision and strategy.
	Creativity	■ Generates new approaches to problems or innovations to establish best practices. ■ Shows imagination.
	Pragmatism	■ Generates realistic, practical solutions to problems.

131

Hiring and Harnessing Talent

INTERNAL	Relationships	Team Builder	■ Achieves cohesive, effective team spirit with staff. ■ Treats staff fairly. ■ Shares credit.
		Team Player	■ Reaches out to peers. ■ Approachable. ■ Leads peers to do what is best for the company.
		Likability	■ Puts people at ease. ■ Shows emotional intelligence and compassion. ■ Not arrogant; friendly, sense of humor, genuine.
		First Impression	■ Professional in demeanor. ■ Creates favorable first impression via body language, eye contact, posture, etc.
		Diversity	■ Embraces diversity and brings in diverse perspectives. ■ Creates environment of belonging for all.
	Coaching	Inspiring Followership	■ Inspires people to follow lead and creates motivation within team. ■ Minimizes intimidation. ■ Takes charge.
		Goal Setting	■ Sets fair stretch goals for self and others. ■ Encourages individual initiative.
		Performance Management	■ Fosters high level of accountability through fair performance management and frequent feedback. ■ Free with deserved praise and recognition. ■ Constructive in criticism.
		Training, Development & Coaching	■ Actively and successfully trains people. ■ Coaches and develops for promotion in positions where they succeed. ■ People builder.
	Problem-Solving	Leading Edge	■ Constantly benchmarks best practices and expects others to do the same.
		Conflict Management	■ Understands natural forces of conflict and acts to prevent or soften them. ■ Effectively resolves conflicts to optimize outcome. ■ Does not suppress, ignore, or deny conflicts.
	Drive Change	Change Leadership	■ Actively intervenes to create positive change. ■ Leads by example.
		Persuasion	■ Persuasive in change efforts, selling a vision. ■ Gets team excited about change.

Figure 8.3 Business development skills assessment framework.

revenue officer of Harmony Healthcare, with a few additions from us. The chart outlines the key abilities critical to consider and allows you to evaluate people against this rubric. It's helpful to focus on the black and gray for new hires, as those are the most difficult to build if not already in place. A basic sense of rhythm and love of music are needed to develop anyone into a World-class pianist.

* * *

Jump 2: Tactical to Leading

Hiring talent with a broader set of skills marks the jump from Tactical to Leading, shifting a monolithic sales culture to a more colorful one. As your sales team grows, so does the need to bring in different types of business development talent, specialists, and support. Honing your ability to identify – and attract – the talent you need is a critical step.

1. Hire for attitude, train for skills.

"I strongly believe you hire on attitude, and you train on skills," says Jose Bokhorst at Robert Walters Group. By the time candidates reach her desk, they have already undergone an intense vetting and interview process with her team. She knows that anyone she meets will be highly qualified for the job, so she focuses on assessing their character and attitude to ensure they will contribute positively to the team. In her final interviews, Jose asks questions that help her understand how candidates learn, how they embrace humility to engage with a team, and what ultimately drives them as individuals. Here are a few of her favorite questions to ask candidates:

- If you could wake up tomorrow and add one thing to your list of skills or capabilities, what would it be? What gift would you give yourself?
- What was a major failure or learning moment in your life and how did you handle it?
- What's one thing that has happened in your life that has defined where you are in this moment?

- What has been the most important phase in your life? Why?

- If you were president tomorrow, what's one thing you would immediately do or change? What keeps you awake at night in this world?

Ben Burke shared similar sentiments about the goals of hiring for attitude during his time at Point B Consulting:

"What Point B did really well was hire people who had an ownership mentality," he says. "We looked for those who demonstrated a feeling that they owned the fate and the outcomes of the company. This was very tied to having a consultative mindset versus just a 'doer' mindset, and this shift was really impactful – both inside the business and in how we showed up for clients. This evolution takes time. It requires shifts in how you hire, how you incent, and how you communicate what is important."

Stephanie Johnston, CEO of Transcend Strategy Group, has a specific approach to hiring people she calls, "curious and courageous." Most of her interviews are team-based, focusing on how candidates handle interacting with multiple people in real time and responding to different scenarios. For senior hires, the final meeting takes place in a client's office. "We do this to see how they handle meeting a client for the first time. It allows us to observe in real time whether they will show up as a curious and engaging individual."

2. Diversify your BD bench.

Leading firms broaden their BD talent pool to include a wider variety of selling styles and approaches to grow the company in new and different ways.

For Shobha Meera, who leads Group Sustainability Services for the Americas at Capgemini,

> "The most successful client partners are the ones who are right for a particular client – who truly understand the

unique culture of the client organization, the values and priorities that matter to key stakeholders, and intentionally act on these. If, for example, your client is focused on sustainability, you arrange a lakeside clean-up with the teams, or if they are innovation-focused, you carve out 1% of revenue for an innovation fund to co-create alongside them. The best client partners build those intangibles into their interactions, take a long-term view beyond business today, understand what really makes a difference for their client, and know how to navigate the resources needed internally to deliver. When you get the right person, it's magic."

Just as there can be different flavors of World-class pianists (Stevie Wonder doesn't play the same way Mozart played, but some people might find his music even more meaningful), so too can different flavors of talent drive growth. Consider the following BD strength grid from Vinson and Elkins (Figure 8.4) to help identify and evaluate the talent you have and where your gaps lie.

While this framework is specific to an individual firm – and specific to law – it is a helpful example of how you might think about the different profiles of people you need to drive your firm's growth. Do you have a lot of "social butterflies" but lack "connectors" to ensure the butterflies are meeting all the right people? Your current state and future goals will inform the talent you need, but step one is understanding what you have right now and how that talent pool is (or is not) driving the growth you want.

Jump 3: Leading to World-class

World-class firms are learning organisms that have developed the ability to strengthen their talent base every day – both through regular upskilling of their existing talent pool (more in the next chapter)

TYPE	DESCRIPTION
THE INFORMANT	This person serves their clients best through information sharing. Their most common touchpoint is sending articles and making clients aware of critical updates in the market or regulatory/legislative changes that might affect them. They have unique knowledge — or access to it — and they are generous in sharing it.
THE SOCIAL BUTTERFLY	This person loves going to social events with clients (dinner, trips, conferences, using client entertainment tickets, etc.). Their client relationships really thrive through face-to-face interaction. This type typically fosters more personal relationships with clients.
THE CONNECTOR	This person has a lot of relationships, but they don't necessarily serve as the contact attorney for a client. They're good at introducing their peers from other practice groups to their connections. This type is typically a good cross-seller and thinks of the client's needs in a holistic manner.
THE OPTIMIZER	This person's strength is taking advantage of what is right in front of them (i.e., the low-hanging fruit). They mine current clients (whether their own or their peers') for more work rather than going out and establishing new relationships. They utilize firm resources well to accomplish this (e.g., asking for top client lists, digging into our CRM system, tapping our alumni network, etc.).

Figure 8.4 Vinson & Elkins business development types.

and the addition of new talent to the firm across various roles and levels. Jumping from Leading to World-class requires the following:

1. Establish a growth path for experts.

World-class firms recognize the need for multiple differentiated roles to support growth. Professionals who develop deep domain expertise are critical to both winning and delivering work, even if they aren't great at managing people or originating deals and fall outside the traditional partner path. These are your "brain surgeons"; they may lack the skills to independently close new deals, but their specialized expertise makes them highly valuable in the sales process. They should be brought in throughout the sales process so potential clients can experience the thinking of the experts that will help them solve their problems. Law firms address this by having both a "partner" track and an "of-counsel" track. World-class firms manage these groups differently, pricing experts' time high enough to cover their costs three or four times over. Understanding the cost equation for "experts" enables World-class firms to evaluate when and where it makes sense to hire this type of talent, and how to best leverage them in the sales process.

2. Integrate lateral hires and acqui-hires while maintaining culture.

The criticism of private equity firms that invest with the intention of "rolling up" like businesses is that they infuse capital but leave the hard work of integration to others. Nowhere is this more evident than in the work of merging business development operations. Yes, all clients can now participate in a big annual conference and, yes, you now have an office in Austin. But enabling new and old partners to represent the expanded, fuller inventory of services resulting from an acquisition is much harder.

One Am Law 20 firm that recently experienced a large merger invests $6 million a year in partner-only conferences. Why all the flying and dinners? *Because partners don't refer work to partners they don't know.* World-class firms spend the money to ensure their internal referral engine operates at top efficiency. They understand that the acquisition cost won't make sense unless there are business development synergies. Similarly, when hiring laterals, World-class firms weigh a candidate's culture fit as heavily as their business development skills and the size of their rolodex.

Create an integration team focused on embedding new hires and team members to minimize tissue rejection and create cohesion more quickly. Integration should include cross-functional in-person

137

Hiring and Harnessing Talent

gatherings, training and development about service offerings and clients, and storytelling roleplay to equip new hires with a shared language to go to market. When you acquire a firm, one metric you should pay attention to is how much you are "paying" per employee when you break down the sale by FTE. For example, if you're paying $10 million for a firm with 25 FTE, that's $2 million walking out the door if five of their people decide the new firm isn't a fit. When you think of it that way, you spend more time on retention of the rainmakers.

3. Engage team members across the employee life cycle.

As we outlined in Chapter 5, World-class firms have happy alumni throughout the marketplace who refer both candidates and clients their way. They make meaningful investments in programs that keep alumni happy and close, knowing the advantages this can bring to the firm over time.

"McKinsey always managed this so well," recalls Walt. Each year, they would identify consultants who were not meeting expectations and have a clear conversation with them. They'd say, "We don't like the way you do XYZ, but we're going to give you one more year, okay?" That was the first conversation. If the following year wasn't stellar, the next conversation would be about which client might be a good new home for them. This approach was beneficial for both the unhappy employee and the company.

* * *

In professional services, people are the product we're putting into the marketplace. The right mix of talent looks different at every stage of maturity, but moving up the curve ultimately requires a shift from an individual to a team approach. "It simply has to be driven by intrinsic motivators," says David Popler, managing director at JLL, about great BD talent. "They need to be motivated by being the best at what they do, being obsessed with their customer's success, which then leads to their company's success. That's what makes them really great. Plus, they need to be passionate communicators and great team players." The teams that succeed are comprised of curious and driven high-achievers, ready to learn to read music and willing to share the bench for a duet. They've learned that playing their best depends on a team.

Chapter 9

Talent Development – Building Your BD Capability

Scribbled on a scrap of computer paper pinned to the wall were these words: "Smile, Listen, Add Value." Just beneath this Ted Lasso-esque sign sat Matt Ulrich, a man with a barrel chest (he filled a doorway) and even bigger heart. The shelf next to his desk proudly displayed his Super Bowl ring; he had played as an offensive lineman for the Indianapolis Colts when they won in 2006. The ring sat next to photos of his wife and four young sons and a few fidget spinners. Every morning during her first few months at PIE, Erika would sit down with Matt in his office and run through the previous day's drills before applying them in a back-and-forth role-play.

Matt was PIE's chief growth officer. Early in his tenure at PIE, before he'd joined the leadership ranks, Matt established PIE's first formal training for new hires. When he joined the firm, "training" had looked like being thrown in the ocean without a life raft. Matt didn't come from the world of professional services. He played football for Northwestern before signing with the Colts, where he played for two seasons. Following his football career, he co-founded a health-based fitness company called DexaFit Dx and ran high-end personal training in Chicago. He made his way to Montana – and to PIE – via his wife, who was raised on a farm outside of Bozeman and was itching to get back.

Matt never attended business school and had never been trained in business development. He certainly didn't identify as a "salesperson", but the same grittiness and drive that made him a football star served him well when being fed to the sharks during his first few months at PIE. The "survival of the fittest" mentality in PIE's early days forced new hires to step up to the task or step away from the firm. PIE's founder maintained that this was the only way to test for BD talent, and while it generated a few strong rainmakers, it failed to create a cohesive team that could drive growth at scale.

Coming from decades of sports training, Matt knew there was a better way. He established PIE's first iteration of business development training and called it Business Development University, or BDU. Matt ran every new consultant through his series of drills, stories, and best practices, breaking down the "magic" of business development into something concrete – something doable. When Erika was preparing for her first solo BD meeting with a large engineering firm in New York, Matt sat down with her, a pile of notecards in hand. On the front, he wrote the 10 most common questions that arise during such a meeting. On the back, Erika wrote down bullet points focused on how to respond, and she reviewed the cards during her flight to JFK. Not every consultant at PIE would go on to be a rainmaker, but BDU embedded celebration of growth into our culture, and people wanted to be part of it. Matt's key principles, the ones pinned above his desk, made business development simple: Smile, listen, add value.

PIE's business development training has evolved since those early days, but early on, Matt realized what so many firms (and successful rainmakers) fail to recognize – business development skills can be built, cultivated, and improved in the same way an offensive lineman can practice footwork drills and lift weights to improve their performance on the field. That's not to say creating a winning Super Bowl team, or a World-class growth engine, is easy. But it is possible.

The Challenge

As an industry, we underinvest in developing BD skills. Perhaps it's because we hate the word "sales," or perhaps because we wrongly believe "salespeople" are only born, not bred. Says Peter Braverman, formerly a partner and head of business development at a 1,200-person global accounting advisory firm, "I just think we're asking a lot of our doers to expect them to be able to sell without the proper training. The training needs to start early on, which we do not do other than a few trainings I conduct on an ad hoc basis. I do sales bootcamps with ten people per quarter, but that's not nearly enough."

Even when firms do invest in business development training, they are often met with skepticism at best. These professionals – who are trusted advisors to their clients – don't want to be trained to go door-to-door hawking encyclopedias. They are also used to being the smartest person in the room, which can make it difficult for them to show up with the humility and curiosity needed to make training effective.

Says Mary Rollman, Principal and Supply Chain Leader at KPMG,

> "I think the biggest transition period, and the hardest, is when people need to go from being really, really good at driving the day-to-day of a project or a program to selling and building pipeline, going out there and developing relationships, and then managing that pipeline. I don't think you can just take an online class and walk in front of a client and suddenly sell to them."

How, then, do leaders train domain experts to drive business development? Note that the word "training" is somewhat out of fashion given that it conjures images of recalcitrant dogs and shock

Talent Development – Building Your BD Capability

collars. In its place, companies talk about "upskilling," "learning and development," "continuing education," "coaching," "workshops," and "professional development." Let's speak of equipping, enabling, and empowering our professionals (Figure 9.1).

STAGES OF MATURITY

FIRM CHARACTERISTICS

ENTREPRENEURIAL
- No formal training; partners have a "watch and learn" mentality
- Sidewalk coaching is occasional and haphazard; feedback offered is limited
- The firm's culture agrees rainmakers are born, not made

TACTICAL
- Limited training is offered and is based around one partner's experiences or is external and cookie-cutter
- The firm rewards minders who become finders
- Business development tasks are occasionally delegated to junior professionals to build their experience
- Teams prioritize reading books on business development best practices

LEADING
- Training is based around the firm's skills gaps which are regularly reviewed and identified
- Training includes a role-play component as well as general sales tactics and techniques specific to professional services
- Programs formalize around coaching and mentoring

WORLD-CLASS
- Growth goals feed into training programs with clearly defined outcomes
- Trainings offered support various learning styles and are a mix of digital and in-person, led by both internal and external trainers
- Role-playing is systematic and expected
- Everyone is part of the training journey, not just newer consultants

Figure 9.1 Firm characteristics at each stage of maturity – talent development.

Jump 1: Entrepreneurial to Tactical

Entrepreneurial firms lean into an apprenticeship model. More junior consultants are thrown in the deep end and told to sink or swim. Those who take the initiative to shadow and learn from their more senior counterparts are rewarded, and those who don't reflect the style of the founders are exited.

Oddly, a kind of competition springs up where the success of the next generation makes the founders feel less god-like. Paul Boulanger, thirty-five-year veteran of the industry and former group operating officer of Strategy and Consulting at Accenture, calls it "survival of the fittest" where even the senior partners over-control work, fail to delegate, and as a result, fail to develop the junior professionals. He says, "We had a lot of partners who were in the military, and they have a term they used called 'eating your young.' It's not good. You don't give junior employees any responsibility. You don't bring them along. You don't bring them to the meetings. All you try and do is keep all the credit for yourself and as a result, the people underneath you don't develop."

The first jump a firm makes – from Entrepreneurial to Tactical – begins when a firm realizes that it cannot grow if the founders are "eaters." Instead, they communicate to junior professionals that to be promoted (or to make more money or have the firm's esteem), they have to bring in new business. But what worked for the founders – decades-in-the-making networks – works less well for the next generation, so junior professionals begin to get curious about how others drive business development. They buy books like *The Trusted Advisor*. They take courses like the ones offered by Sandler or Miller Heiman. They wonder if Dale Carnegie and Zig Ziglar are still relevant, and they begin to trade ideas on what works and what doesn't in search of an approach that brings in new clients and expands existing ones.

To develop these hungry junior professionals, Tactical firms make the following moves:

1. Begin to institutionalize your approach to business development.

Tactical firms supplement an accidental or informal apprenticeship model with intentional, albeit sometimes *ad-hoc*, training and development programs. Often, this starts as an internal initiative, conducted in fits and starts without consistency or accountability around outcomes. Ask partners to run the BD training, and develop a basic curriculum that includes simple role-plays or simulation activities.

2. Involve junior professionals in the growth process.

In the Entrepreneurial stage, junior members of an organization may come along with a more senior partner for a business development meeting to watch and learn. Their instructions are specific, "Don't say anything. And don't pick your nose." (Yes, someone really said these words to Walt at the start of his career.) Junior employees are meant to listen and learn but their involvement in moving a deal forward is zero. As firms move up the maturity curve, more senior partners should assign and delegate pieces of the sales cycle to other members of their team. Junior professionals might write up the first draft of a proposal, enter follow-up notes in a CRM, or prepare a deck to send to the client. They likely aren't driving the sale, but they begin to take on tasks that support the original rainmakers of the firm, and this gives them real-world BD experience that they can begin to build on (see Figure 8.2 in the previous chapter for an example).

3. Cultivate farmers.

For most professional services firms, as much as 80% of new work comes from current client accounts. That means your delivery teams are on the front lines for most growth opportunities. As Tactical firms look to identify and develop future rainmakers, they start by asking their best deliverers to not only deliver excellent work, but seek to understand where else a client may need help. Training itself becomes more focused on client listening.

In this phase, firms are good about asking questions of clients. There is a subtle shift in the business development *zeitgeist* from "What do we need to do to sell," which feels a little like objectifying the client and manipulating them, to "What questions can we ask that will get to the heart of their issues?"

Ross Hunter, founder of Copylab, leans into a similar reality:

> "We started doing these monthly gatherings where everyone comes together to just to talk about how things are going with their customers. Talk to us about your relationship with the people you deal with every day. We strip away that BS language that's attached to sales and take away the mystique. To get good client gossip, you have to be a good client listener. You need to be able to ask great questions."

Instruct your future farmers to ask clients questions not just about the current project, but about the business, about the industry, about priorities, and about threats. Paired with a news scan and stock review of the account, consider the following set of questions to better understand how you can serve your client:

- What is your strategy to grow? Where are you placing bets and what is gating you from making that happen?
- What is your strategy for driving the practice?
- What is the CEO telling the organization about where they want to put thier bets?

- What is most important to you as you step into this role?

- How can we be more helpful across different areas of the business?

These same questions also serve experienced rainmakers, but asking them of a current client feels much more natural for a junior partner than cold-calling the CFO of a new logo.

* * *

It's Not "My Way or the Highway"

As firms move from Entrepreneurial to Tactical, the firm learns one way to do business development – the way the founder does it. Too frequently, employees feel like they must match the founder's style – but gregarious, charming, and loud doesn't work for everybody. This can give rise to frustration and the idea that, "I wasn't born to be a salesperson." This strategy can also lead to scripts or written language for selling that others mimic. According to Kevin Legg at SAGE, this is like "sending your people out there like sheep among wolves, without the wisdom or shrewdness. They'll get destroyed after the first line of the script."

The reality is there are many sales styles that can be successful. Jeff Meyer at Catalant Technologies (a community of independent consultants and boutique firms) is a great business developer who earns his work through curiosity, introspection, and engagement. He speaks only when he has something truly relevant or helpful to share, asking thoughtful questions and actively listening so he can spot opportunities to add value. Loud does not always equal good.

Daniel Proietto, partner at Lander & Rogers, is similar to Jeff. Daniel worked closely with his group head early on in his career.

The Growth Engine

"He's a great salesperson," Proietto shares about his group leader. "I used to go to meetings with him, and I'd look at him and go, 'Wow, that's how you do it?' What was also clear was I was not him. I'm not a 'salesperson' in the sense of feeling good about asking people for work. It's just not my style. I just said that's fine. He can go out and win the work, and I'll do the work. I'm a strong technical lawyer and I will sit in the back office."

A few years into the role, Proietto's boss suggested he should be promoted to partner. Proietto reacted,

> "I was surprised because I knew partners have to win the work, and I didn't think I had the ability to do that. Still, I became a partner, and I didn't try to be a 'salesperson.' But the work started coming in and my message to all the juniors now is 'find your own style.' You still have to put yourself out there. I would go meet clients and do presentations. I found that me going into their place of work and presenting to their people was a great way to form connections and grow. I think if you do a fantastic job every time, you're responsive, you make them look good, you're a nice person, easy to talk to, and you stay connected to people, you can successfully grow a practice."

The identities we hold contribute to our business development voice – Erika's stories are different than Jacob's because, for one, Erika is a professional runner, and Jacob has been known to fall off the treadmill while listening to business podcasts. We need not try and sound like the most successful seller at our firm. It's more important to lean into our own authentic voice and trust our clients will meet us on common ground.

* * *

Talent Development – Building Your BD Capability

Jump 2: Tactical to Leading

As firms move from the Tactical stage to the Leading stage, business development becomes exponentially more difficult. The biggest danger to a Tactical firm is sudden extinction when their one large client changes course and fires them. The second biggest danger to a Tactical firm is the exit of their most successful rainmaker (perhaps the Founder), leaving a business development vacuum.

To guard against these threats, firms do two things:

1. Because growth at this stage is often based on the acquisition of new clients, firms focus on diversifying the logos they serve such that the loss of one large client is not fatal.

2. Because senior rainmakers might be getting itchy feet, because junior employees are hungry for more, or because the firm is quickly realizing that a growth strategy based on a handful of natural extroverts isn't sustainable, firms realize the imperative need for professional development around business development.

In Leading firms, this task is met with sophisticated training. Says Daniel Proietto of Lander & Rogers, "We put around ten partners through a BD program every year, helping them with how to develop their personal business development style, write a business plan, and get out and win work."

1. Create a standard sales methodology.

Scaling your growth function requires some level of standardization. As Hap Brakeley, former global chief growth officer for Merkle and managing partner at Accenture, says, "I need everybody talking the same language so that we know where we are in the lifecycle, we know the expectations, and we know what needs to be delivered at each point in the sales cycle. You want a common methodology, set of expectations and support structures."

Leading firms adopt a formal training framework and set of principles that are shared and reinforced across every level of the firm. Learning and development teams organize training based on the tenure and relative success of the talent they are charged with improving. Their curricula might look like this:

Focus of training for early-stage consultants:

- Delivering exceptional client work
- Writing, presenting to clients, and client engagement
- Identifying additional opportunities within current clients
- Developing curiosity and a more fulsome understanding of client priorities
- Crafting excellent online presence
- Networking/relationship development with peers
- Storytelling

Focus of training for pre-Partner stage consultants:

- Developing one's niche – emphasis on speaking, writing, and developing personal brand
- Learning how to lead a pitch presentation
- Working with the firm's RFP and proposal writing teams
- Collaborative selling with partners
- Account management and cross-selling
- Developing mentorship skills to train the next generation
- Learning how to leverage conferences effectively

Importantly, internal training workshops are now run by next-generation leaders, not the founders. From this emerges a firm point of view around best practices, which is often the founders' perspective minus all their idiosyncratic baggage, plus the next generation's consensus on what actually works.

2. Invest in storytelling.

According to David Popler, managing director and global head of the Technology Industry Division, at JLL:

> "Outstanding salespeople are great storytellers. I believe 100% that the way that you do this job is with stories because it's the form of communication that is memorable. How do young comedians develop their craft when they're not experienced at writing their own material yet? They listen to the best and then tell those jokes, right?"

In a real way, talking with clients is like comedy. Pros have "bits" that, like cards, are easy to pull out and play, vignettes that inform and make a point. The best firms share those "bits," which become firm stories that anyone can tell in their own voice with confidence, painting real pictures in their conversations with clients. They focus less on "I" and more on what "we" or "our firm" has done to bring success to clients, harnessing the full power of the many years of successful projects the *team* has delivered.

For example, rather than saying, "I think you should move your supply chain operations to the cloud using Oracle," Leading firms teach their team that the voice of the firm carries the most weight. Instead they say, "With our client from China, we dug in, and on the way to making their input sources more resilient, our client wanted to know more about what was happening in real time. In the end, we

The Growth Engine

put in Oracle to manage things and ended up decreasing their risk of plant shut down by 23% and lowered costs by 13%." This is a story of the firm, not an ego driven by commission. In Leading firms, every consultant has these stories in their back pocket, whether or not they actually served that specific client with that specific problem.

3. Use role-play regularly.

For Leading firms, role-plays are a training staple. Role-plays often focus on complex client scenarios that include managing shifting client expectations, staffing mismatches, client disappointment, pitching the next phase of work, managing differing expectations from multiple client stakeholders, and negotiation around pricing. For Leading firms, role-plays are full contact, emulating real-world scenarios as closely as possible.

Jennifer Anders, Chief Growth Officer at Inframark, says,

> "In this last round of sales training, we dedicated a full day to presentation training. We brought in experts who teach people how to present. They would videotape you, and then you would have to go back and watch yourself and critique yourself. It was horrible and wonderful all at the same time. It's shocking what you notice when you really have to see yourself do this – you get to see what a client would see, and it's helpful to drive improvements."

Role-play works because it gets you talking, not just thinking. It also bridges the gap between the classroom and being in the room with a client live. The consequence of failure is embarrassment, but it does not affect the firm's revenues. The jump from hearing how business development should be done by a talking head to having the right words come out of your mouth in the right way is as big as

153

Talent Development – Building Your BD Capability

the Danyang-Kushan Grand Bridge (102.4 miles to be exact). Making the leap is made easier by standing up a role-play island halfway.

4. Evaluate talent.

Leading firms assess talent both by outcomes and activity – are your rainmakers doing the right things? And are those things leading to the right outcomes? Take the 2x2 evaluation grid used by Chris Perry, president at Broadridge Financial Solutions, that evaluates activity (y-axis), dollars sold (x-axis), and size of pipeline (size of circle).

The chart in Figure 9.2 allows you to measure not only who does the most, but how effective that consultant is in both selling work and generating a pipeline. In this example, consultant B is your best seller even though consultant C is more active. Consultant B has sold more work and has built a bigger pipeline, meaning their activity generates more sales. Contrast that with seller A, who spends a lot of time "doing" without the results to match. Chris combines this evaluative model with historical performance to assess competency and determine to what degree each consultant is a pipeline

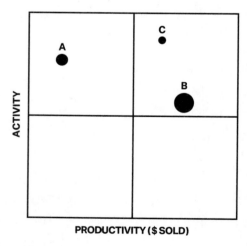

Figure 9.2 Sample sales team evaluation chart.

multiplier. This evaluative process mitigates learning and development department bloat that overemphasizes activity rather than growth outcomes. It also helps Leading firms organize their talent, direct training resources to those who are underperforming, or shift those employees to other areas of the business.

Jump 3: Leading to World-class

For World-class firms, business development training and improvement are embedded and welcome throughout the firm. Deb Resnick, VP and global director of Marketing and Business Development at Charles River Associates, ends every growth training by handing out red heart temporary tattoos that say, "BD Everyday." Culture matters. Does your firm think business development is a chore, or fun? Make it fun.

When World-class firms focus on business development training, they:

1. Build a training ecosystem.

World-class firms build best-in-breed growth teams by capturing the expertise of their top rainmakers and pairing it with external counsel and best practices to remain at the pointy end of what good looks like. Many mature firms run "academies" that feature curriculum for every stage of an employee's career at the firm, using proven best practices culled from years of experience. Paul Vinogradov, a Sales Excellence Leader at Deloitte, reports, "At Deloitte University in Texas we host a wide range of training tracks including Power Selling, The Art of Relationships, The Art of Negotiation, and the Art of the Sale." At Pearl Meyer, business development training is built in from day one, guiding new hires to first serve as trusted colleagues (meet deadlines and expectations, help peers), then develop into a trusted resource (become the go-to person for data, research, and answers), and finally, a trusted advisor (provide assistance and guidance beyond the data and numbers). Says Jannice Koors, senior managing director for the firm, "We have monthly training sessions and a series for each stage of the trusted advisor journey to teach fresh-out-of-college analysts to become helpful solvers, not sellers, for the firm." Investing in programs like this demonstrate to the team that these skills are important, and that the firm will support the team in developing them.

World-class firms build business development training into every role, no matter seniority or tenure. Consider hosting an annual or bi-annual partner training featuring a mix of successful internal BD leaders and external perspectives to equip partners with fresh ideas, tools, and industry perspective around how to grow the business.

2. Cultivate a growth culture.

World-class firms not only hire and train whip-smart growth agents; they retain the talent they need to grow. Dozens of factors, like compensation and advancement opportunity, impact an employee's decision to join – and stay with – a firm. However, in this people-driven business, culture is critical for retaining the best talent. Prioritizing mentorship – both for mentors and mentees – can make a huge difference in their experience. Matt found as much joy in mentoring Erika as she found in learning from him.

Kira Sandmann at Brown Gibbons Lang and Company would agree. She stipulates that, "Mentorship initiatives are critically important to helping ensure that every junior banker has a senior counterpart they can learn from with respect to business development. Mentorships act like training wheels for young professionals, enabling them to observe someone seasoned and successful in their role in all of the typical business scenarios, from lunches to conferences to pitch meetings, for example. Those inputs, combined with each junior banker's unique personality and strengths, really help them shape their own individual BD style over time. Along the way, our senior bankers reap the benefits of deepening the bench strength within their teams and establishing their relationships with the next generation of leaders. Mentorship programs lead to a culture of trust, which in turn leads to a culture of growth."

At World-class firms, the best rainmakers also find a lot of meaning and pride in being part of developing the next generation.

Finally, senior buy-in matter. Evan Tierce, chief sales officer at Baker Tilly says, "Tone at the top is critical, and it creates momentum. You can't operate without it. Once you have growth-minded leaders engaged, detractors can't slow down the progress." If the CEO personally opens every business development training session for new partners, they take note: BD is important to the firm.

* * *

Matt's legacy at PIE is one of humble leadership. Matt was good at BD because he was a smart, thoughtful storyteller, but he was great at BD because he was focused on making the whole team great. When he was talking about how PIE could help a company, it was never about him. It was always about the client's success. He wanted them to win, and they could feel it. He also wanted his whole team to win. Building a growth engine means building a team of people who want the ball, have the skills to grab it, are excited to toss it to their colleagues, and then are eager to toss it to their clients for the touchdown.

Chapter 10

Motivating the Team – Incentives and Rewards

Incentives are tricky little buggers.

Alberta has very few rats. Still, by the end of World War II, packs of rats found a home in cities and landfills across Canada. While the populations were not huge, in the 1950s, Alberta decided to eradicate rats because rats ate their farmers' grain production and because they were a public health nuisance.

First, the good people of Alberta passed a law making it the duty of every Albertan to destroy or report rats to the authorities. Second, they required every town to appoint a pest control inspector, known thereafter as "Rat Patrols." They established a Rat Control Zone (RCZ) along the eastern border with Saskatchewan where most of the rats were coming from. They toured community halls and 4-H clubs to educate citizens about rats and their control. Since most Albertans had never seen a rat, they sent taxidermied rats to the regional Alberta agriculture offices, so folks would know what to be on the lookout for. They also hung menacing posters in schools and hardware stores and distributed arsenic trioxide in bulk to farmers. Finally, they made it a fineable offense not to do your part to rid the land of rats.

There are virtually no rats in Alberta to this day.

Hanoi, Vietnam, in 1902, had a similar problem: too many rats. In response, the French civic authorities stood up a squad of professional rat hunters. At first, they were successful, but then labor strikes diminished their effectiveness; rat hunters stayed home on the principle that a good rat hunter shouldn't be undervalued. So, Hanoi decided to turn all citizens into rat hunters and put a bounty on each rat killed. Officials said they would pay for every rat killed upon being presented with a severed rat tail as proof. It worked, and populations went down, but after a while, the rat office noticed that there was a rise in tailless rats scurrying around sewers and back alleys. Seems that non-professional rat hunters had realized that actually killing the rats would eventually mean fewer tails to be sold, so they would catch the rats, cut off their tails, and then free them, wishing them well in their efforts to start large rat families.

Even seemingly simple carrots and sticks are complicated and need to evolve with changing landscapes and reactions. That said, World-class firms do something a bit different. They develop a culture of people who want to kill the rats for their own sake – because they enjoy being part of a rat-free city and trust that those leading the city will make the right decisions and investments to keep the city beautiful.

What Makes Something an *Incentive*?

Firm leaders use a lot of different language to talk about how they pay people for doing good work and growing the firm. Compensation is incredibly complex – it can include monetary and non-monetary rewards, it can include current compensation and future compensation in the form of stock options, equity, or bonuses. We'd like to highlight a few key distinctions here.

Incentive plans can be made up of any form of compensation outlined above, but they have a very specific goal – to drive a particular behavior or outcome. A commission for current account expansion with new service lines may be put in place to *incent* account leads to bring in other partners who can help introduce new solutions to their clients. An announcement that the top 10 revenue generators for the year will get an all-expenses paid trip to Bora-Bora is put in place to *incent* new revenue growth. Incentives have a clear definition of what behaviors or outcomes will be awarded, who is eligible, and a time frame for achieving success. Individuals or teams have a clear level of control over their success and know what to expect.

Bonuses can take a somewhat different shape. Firms often use these words interchangeably; we view them as distinct. Often, leaders award "spot bonuses" to people after-the-fact for exceptional performance. This is not an "incentive" – the consultant didn't take a certain action *in order to get the bonus*. It is a way to recognize good behaviors with money. Bonuses may also take the form of a company-wide profit-share at the end of the year, for example. While everyone has a hand in making the company successful, this is different than an *incentive,* in that a single individual's behaviors or results likely won't be the only factor contributing to their bonus.

Variable compensation is tricky, and *no one* we spoke with claims to have a perfect system. However, as firms mature, they begin to evolve in the way they consider their options for using monetary and non-monetary rewards to motivate their teams. Figure 10.1 shows how firms mature in their approach to incentives over time.

Jump 1: Entrepreneurial to Tactical

A founder's first hires are likely a ragtag team of work horses. They might be young people who, fresh out of university or with just a few years under their belt, are eager for experience; maybe they're mid-career and willing to sacrifice a higher salary for the chance to apprentice under known domain experts; maybe they're at a stable point in their career, can afford to take a risk, and are ready for a leap into a new venture. Early joiners are often game to stay up all

STAGES OF MATURITY

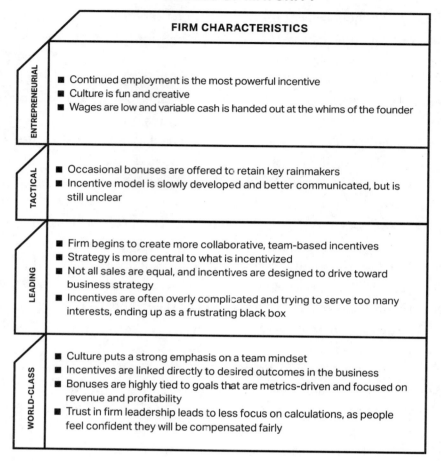

Figure 10.1 Firm characteristics at each stage of maturity – incentives and performance management.

night to beat a deadline. Trust is abundant because of the collective and shared experience of being part of something "new" that they're building together, and there's nowhere for underperformers to hide.

When times are good, founders are often generous, paying out extra (variable) compensation to the team. Sometimes, this looks like spot bonuses; other times, payouts are offered based on pre-announced goals to individuals or groups. Importantly, an Entrepreneurial firm's bonuses are unpredictable – even to the founder herself. To move into the Tactical stage, firms do two things:

1. Implement a simple incentive system.

The creation of a formal incentive system communicated across the company marks the shift from Entrepreneurial to Tactical. This system will surely be imperfect, but it brings needed structure to compensate and motivate those helping grow the firm. A basic incentive system aims to do one or more of the following:

- **Change Behavior:** Incentives are offered to steer employees to do something they wouldn't do if just paid a salary. In this case that might be "Stay an extra day in Boston away from your family to cultivate possible new clients," or "Work Sunday nights on a blogpost series to be posted on LinkedIn that will raise your profile as a subject matter expert." Note that the individual incentive does not reward the changed behavior, *per se*; it rewards the presumed outcome (new sales) of that increased activity. Smart firms look at that causal link closely. If incentives are meant to change behavior, then the firm should be pretty clear that the behavior they are changing obtains the growth they want.

- **Reward Rainmakers:** Here the firm is agnostic about effort. There is a simple *quid pro quo* between the firm and the professional – you give us more revenues and we will give you more money. It doesn't matter to us if you spent all night writing follow-up notes to people you met at a conference or invited a high-flyer that happened to go to your high school to the Knicks game or if you're just plain lucky. The firm is much less prescriptive about how you get the job done. Do what you have to do and you will be rewarded.

163

Motivating the Team – Incentives and Rewards

- **Retain Key Employees:** Incentives can help firms retain star performers and compete with other companies who offer incentives or bonuses for their high-flyers. Whether you believe incentives cause your employees to sell more or not, incentives are table stakes for professionals.

- **Add Variability to Pay:** Founders can't afford high salaries so they pump up offers by adding the possibility of earning variable pay. This pads the offer number so they can compete with bigger firms and costs them nothing unless the company grows.

Simple systems typically work best for incenting new logo work (hunting) but are less effective when the goal is to boost same-client revenue (farming). This is because there is often a team that is doing the good work for the client that eventually begets new work. Who gets the money in that case? Some shops choose to just reward hunters, but that can engender internal conflict. Harmonizing incentives prompts many questions:

- How will you handle hunter credit when there have been multiple touchpoints with the new client? Jennessa from the hyperscaler implementation practice met a key stakeholder at a conference. Bob went to college with a board member. Sundar stopped by the offices and asked for the sale that brought in the contract. But he was introduced by Bob. Will you share the credit?

- Under what conditions would you pay commissions for existing client growth? Would the whole delivery team get it or only the senior partner on the project?

- Does it have to be proactive outreach to earn commission or do you reward "order-taking"?

- Are you trying to roll out new services to existing clients? If so, should there be a fund to drive that activity?

- Is there a seniority level for incentives? Would we pay someone's assistant if they helped rope in a big deal by going the extra mile to set up the first meetings?

- Can you imagine a situation in which, under this structure, you would be angry paying a commission to someone based on a completed process?

- Is there a tail on newly won work if the work renews or does the incentive only apply to the first pilot amount sold?

- When do you pay? When the contract is signed or when the work is done? Would you pay someone for work they won even after they had left the company?

There are a million ways to answer these questions and so, a million possible incentive schemes. Here is how Steven Castino, chief growth officer at the advisory firm Rehmann, thinks about the challenge:

> "It's important to create an incentive program where your salespeople, and all of your people for that matter, are incented to originate work. The hardest thing to do in professional services is to originate work, and we need to make sure that people are compensated accordingly for that. That being said, we also have to create that culture in a team atmosphere, which is the difficult part. There's a balance there that you want people operating on what is best for the team and at the same time what is best for the firm. I'm a believer that there needs to be both individual accountability and team accountability, and you need a structure set up to do that. And it's not easy."

2. Introduce non-monetary incentives.

Non-monetary incentives offer a powerful tool for driving behavior that can complement a strong compensation structure. Rainmakers are often gold star seekers: they love the chase of the sale, namely because they thrive on the jolt of excitement and the proverbial gold star that comes with a win. We love non-monetary incentives. For years at PIE, the team vied for the coveted "rainmaker windbreaker," a raggedy old brown jacket that signified excellence among peers, covered in autographs of its prior years' winners.

Performance can be rewarded with a prestigious opportunity to present at a conference in front of clients, by sharing positive client notes with a larger group of peers or senior leaders, or even by the CEO picking up the phone to just say thank you. Gold-star seekers are often motivated by specialized trainings or leadership development courses – a win-win for firms looking to develop key talent. There are a few other key non-monetary incentives to consider:

- **Access:** Invite high-performing junior team members to attend exclusive events with other senior partners, giving them additional exposure to firm decision makers and leadership. Consider an innovation competition where the winner presents their idea to the C-suite.

- **Passion projects:** Provide opportunities for strong-performing team members to take on pursuits that are personally meaningful, whether that be pro-bono work or a special research project. Although the pursuit may not have a direct monetary value to the firm, it adds value for the individual in the same way a monetary bonus might add value.

- **Trips:** Reward your team by bringing them on an invite-only trip paid for by the firm for meeting an objective or sales goal.

One thing that leaders in growth companies agree on is the importance of being clear and simple. As Allan Platt, the CEO of Clareo says, "Our colleagues have to be able to understand the incentive clearly. A black box doesn't work. A simple principle we have is that if anybody brings us a client, we pay them a commission. You should see how excited they are when they get an email from a classmate that turns into a project that then turns into a bonus. It also builds trust when they introduce us, and we close a deal. It's incentivizing a good network *and* driving cross-selling, both behaviors we always want to encourage." Allan recognizes that this system is easier to manage in a smaller firm (where 100 different people wouldn't potentially have their hands on a new account), but it's been a meaningful step for his Chicago-based firm.

Adds Murray Joslin, executive vice president and global head of Creative Services for Integreon, "Simple is better. I've always said if you read a company's sales compensation plan, one can gain a clear understanding of the exact company strategy. Too often leaders try to solve for too many hypothetical situations in the incentive plan, simply because managers want to avoid refereeing conflict on commissions or incentives. I think that's a mistake; let the strategy guide the comp plan and be a motivator to sell more."

* * *

Jump 2: Tactical to Leading

As companies mature, their goals around growth and EBITDA targets, industry strategies, business unit objectives, and geographic expansion become increasingly complex, and incentive systems follow suit. Leading firms pivot from pure commission to "points-driven" compensation. Points are given to partners in proportion to their contribution to the firm in the form of new work, collaboration with other partners, mentorship, margin, account planning, and firm leadership.

Leading firms have highly engineered compensation systems that directly reflect leadership's strategic vision. There is talk of the "algorithm" because the incentive designers treat the task of creating a compensation system as a math problem, solving for what will produce certain outcomes and the relative weight of numerous growth dimensions. Leading firms lean into their incentive structure to:

1. Build a wolf pack – orient your compensation around collaboration.

Because Leading firms begin to shift their emphasis from winning new logos to expanding their remits within current clients, the solo roadshows tend to fall out of fashion in favor of rewarding those who hunt as a pack. Clareo's Allan Platt puts it this way, "You have to identify the behaviors you want and then design the comp system to reward them. For example, we wanted more team selling. We changed it from a 'zero-sum' system rewarding the lead partner, usually 'winner-take-all,' to a system which pays for co-selling partners without diluting the lead. That has helped encourage teamwork and diversify account management, resulting in much greater value to the firm, far above the additional cost of those co-selling rewards." To encourage hunting as a pack, firms begin to think in terms of collaboration credit.

2. Take off the "new logo" blinders and recognize cross-selling.

Leading firms find creative ways to incent current client growth in addition to new logos. Accenture's Paul Boulanger tells us, "There is a natural tendency to pivot away from a client that you have grown to pursue a big new logo. There is status in landing a major new client. To mitigate this problem, Accenture would publicly praise individuals who could go in and drive year-over-year double digit growth in an account, guaranteeing their compensation for two years. They celebrated those partners as 'account explosion specialists.' All the sudden, the culture pivoted, and people wanted to be known as account penetrators who could grow existing clients, which is how the firm wanted to grow." The simple act of recognizing current client growth on par with new logo acquisition helped shift firm behavior to focus on current client expansion.

Cross-selling inherently introduces risk (i.e., what if you introduce another partner who does a bad job and ruins the relationship with the account?). To overcome that risk, Leading firms align incentives to encourage and even mandate teamwork that drives account growth.

Greg Callahan, partner and global head of the Software Practice at Bain explains, "We spend the time every year to evaluate how much you actually contributed, the scale of your network, the power of your network, and then on top of that, how you treat our teams in the process. The one rule is that if you try to do everything solo and go out and source, sell, and serve and you're the *wrong* person to sell it or serve it, we will pay you less *even if you use fewer resources, the ROI is better, and that kind of stuff*. We want you to actually do the right thing and create the right teams. It's all about the team. We don't care if you bring two people or four people. It's about getting to the right answer for the client."

3. Customize incentive systems.

In Leading firms, compensation systems begin to splinter for the better. Leading firms realize a one-size-fits-all approach fails to consider that different groups within a firm need to optimize on different priorities. If the firm is asking a few key players to go open an office in a new geography and drum up business, they should be incented differently than those staying in the home office focused on slow, steady growth of current accounts. Michael Restivo, former vice president, Security and Resiliency Sales at Kyndryl, argues that, "Compensation drives activity. It should be very specific, and it should shift with the needs of the business and the needs of the customer." Leading firms drive toward an ever more perfect formula that achieves all the ends the company hopes to obtain.

But....

The problem is that on the way to driving to this perfection, inevitably, the unintended happens, leaving you with a basket of rat tails *and* a growing population of rats.

This train of unintended consequences that bears down on you when you are a Leading firm is what we call the "Black Box Problem." A black box is where the electronics that power a system are hidden from view. In the case of professional services incentives, it means there are so many incentives and edge cases and rules and exceptions that no one in the organization really understands the algorithm, which leads quickly to the incentive scheme not changing behavior. For incentives to work, sellers must understand what they are being asked to do. When professionals in a firm start talking about their point-based compensation system as a black box, it is a sure sign they aren't exactly sure what goes into the calculation, eroding trust and stripping the system of its power to incent.

* * *

Making Complexity Work – The Power of Chalk Talks

Trying to create a simple and perfectly equitable incentive system is like trying to map out the exact play that will score a winning touchdown in an NFL game seven weeks from today. We can put all sorts of Xs and Os on paper, trying to imagine exactly how a game will unfold, but the exercise becomes more of a guidebook than a step-by-step checklist for winning. The best coaches and players adapt their plans based on what actually happens in the game. They don't throw out the playbook completely, but sometimes they call an audible because that is how you win.

When Walt was at Accenture, he would host a "chalk talk" with his team on a quarterly basis to help bring clarity to the incentive playbook while also explicitly calling out the exceptions. During the chalk talk, Walt would explain the results of the past quarter: "Last quarter, 10% of partners (about 50 of you) got bonuses greater than $300,000; another 10% of you got no bonuses at all. There were also 50 of you that didn't get paid enough and 50 of you that made more than you should have."

By breaking down the incentive pool, partners were able to compare their performance against their peers. After running the numbers, Walt would also share a few case studies highlighting what those in the top 10% did to land themselves there. The goal was to help people understand what was working and how to get there. And, if needed, he could call an audible to correct the bonus of someone who was "underpaid," ensuring the team remained focused on the right things. Sometimes you need to change the rules to reward the right behavior.

* * *

Jump 3: Leading to World-class

A kind of revolution against incentives occurs in World-class firms. Given complexities and dynamic strategic initiatives, leaders in these firms have lived through the wars of unequal credit and misaligned action, of hero egos that slayed dragons and resentful experts who straightened out the mess and delivered value.

Leaders at World-class firms tend to start letting go of the need to understand their incentive system and return to their instincts as professionals who do good work for clients while stewarding the firm as a whole. On any given day, a consultant at a World-class firm isn't asking if a task or a project will result in more pay. Rather, they're interested in the simple challenge of the work at hand and growing the firm.

Most critically, this shift is underpinned by firmwide trust that everyone will be compensated well and fairly. It's less about a formula, and more about understanding that leadership wants to grow the business, retain great people, and recognize success – and that they will. This trust comes from seeing that happen, time and time again. When high-performers end the year with a fraction of the pay of their not-so-hard-working peer because of a technicality in the equation or a bit of dumb luck, that trust is eroded.

So how is a culture like this built?

1. Link incentives directly to long-term business outcomes.

A shift toward "long-term wealth" and away from "get rich quick" happens in World-class firms. Incentives are less focused on current compensation and more focused on increasing equity upside for partners. Litigation around incentives and who gets what for doing which activities decreases. As Walt says, "No one at Accenture ever got crazy rich from incentive pay. They got rich when their options in the public company went from $14 a share to $400 a share." That kind of growth is motivating. To achieve this, base compensation has to be fair and competitive – no reasonable expert professional would work at a below-market rate, but if base compensation and benefits are already strong, and the firm has a culture and reputation that they are proud of, then the "variable" part of pay can be more long-term focused, rather than prioritizing tomorrow's bonus.

World-class firms leverage their capital structure to encourage the growth they want. They go public, they take on private equity money, they issue options. Even in the case of partnerships, they look to drive as much upside as possible for partners, whether that's reissuing options on a down year or offering end-of-year dividends in an up year.

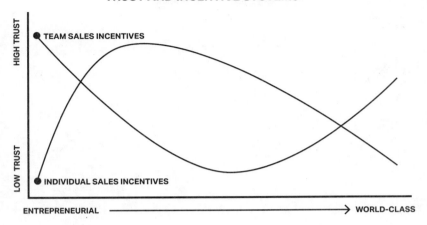

Figure 10.2 The relationship between trust and incentive systems as firms mature.

In some sense, all that is old is new. A firm that started with five people hustling in someone's basement, creating their company on the fly and sharing in the bounty when it came, moves toward and then away from incentive-based pay-for-performance, only to reembrace a more global conception of value sharing (Figure 10.2).

In World-class firms, the more the firm is rewarded as a whole in both short-and-long-term value, the more they succeed at collaborating and better serving clients. This causes the firm to move away from simple but crude individual incentives and toward rewards for doing great work and building a great firm.

Think of it this way: World-class firms experience a rat-free culture by doing the right things for clients over and over again. They value perpetually clean streets and subways more than the $1,000 they earn from delivering a pile of rat tails to their boss's door, investing in the long-range strategy for a pest-free community.

Part V

Operating Model

Chapter 11

Structure for Scale – Supporting Growth Leaders

When you think of some of the best soccer players in the world – Messi, Maradona, Pele, Ronaldo – you also immediately think of the teams and countries they played for – Argentina, Brazil, Portugal. Even the best players do not play just *for* themselves, or just *by* themselves. They did not win World Cup titles alone. They are part of something larger, and they are surrounded by people – arranged in a certain way – who get the ball on their foot in the right place at the right time so they can score the goal. In Messi's case, it's *109 goals* to date for Argentina (and hundreds more for his league teams).

Lionel Scaloni, manager of the Argentina national team for the 2022 World Cup, had a plan. He did not just haphazardly throw people onto the field, wish them luck, and assume that Messi would win the day with his skill alone. "Scaloni's man-management has helped this version of Argentina gel and develop positive momentum before the World Cup," said a *New York Times* article leading up to the tournament (Cardenas, 2022). "Argentina plays in a 4-3-2-1 formation, dominating possession through their technically gifted three-man midfield. The key difference between this team and past Argentina sides is the way in which Messi is utilized. Instead of just playing through him, Messi's midfield partners work *for* him."

There is no question that star players – those extraordinary story-tellers who seem "born" to make new friends and win new work – are key to a firm's successful growth. But they alone do not a growth engine make. They need to be organized the right way, and with the right people around them, to set the *firm* up for long-term success. Getting this right – or at least making steady progress over time – is the only way to scale your business development efforts. There is too much risk in relying on the showmanship of a few stars. "Sales is not an individual sport," says Mary Rollman, principal and supply chain leader at KPMG. "I make it really clear to my team that it's a *team* sport. You need to have your lead, your amazing storyteller. But you've also got to have some supporting actors." Mary is spot on – business development is a team sport, even when teams have clear stars.

In this chapter, we will explore the ways in which firms begin to add structure to their business development function, and the choices available to firms as they grow in both size and maturity. While there is not a one-size-fits-all approach for every services firm (firms can be Leading and World-class while pursuing different structures), there are some key learnings and best practices that should be considered when deciding what structure of support is best suited to enable your firm's growth engine. While you want today's Messi to score that 110th goal, you ultimately want to build a team that will win another World Cup after Messi retires – a structure that creates space and support for all future stars to succeed.

To BDR or Not to BDR?

A key question in professional services firms when it comes to structuring for business development is whether firms should focus on a seller-doer model (where those responsible for driving growth are generally senior client partners) or a model that relies on a true "sales" team, often in the form of Business Development Representatives (BDRs) who are doing cold outreach to prospects. Our research and experience lead us to be strongly in favor of a seller-doer model for professional services firms that rely on trust and credibility to win new work, while developing necessary support structures to enable seller-doers to scale and be successful. This direction is consistent with the evolution we outlined in the previous section on clients; being targeted about your buyers and building substantive relationships (rather than cold-calling thousands of prospects) is how you grow a practice that sells knowledge and experience.

We understand that the world of professional services is broad, and no two firms are exactly the same. Indeed, we often see an inverted relationship between the success of BDRs and the complexity of the sale (see Figure 11.1). Firms that are completely focused on efficiency and that sell more commoditized services (e.g., staff augmentation or off-the-shelf Salesforce integrations) can have success with BDRs. For firms leaning more toward Experience, and certainly for those selling Expertise (really selling their individual "rocket scientist" brains), expecting BDRs to drive growth is exceedingly challenging – if not impossible. The way clients think about

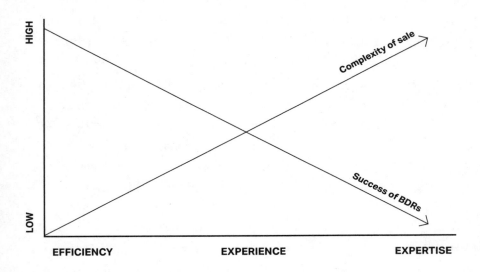

Figure 11.1 The inverse relationship between the complexity of a sale and the usefulness of business development representatives (BDRs).

buying these types of services is different: when a company needs urgent staffing for one of their call centers, they are thinking about considerations like price and speed-to-delivery. These are easy selling points for a BDR to have on hand and use to lock in a meeting with a new lead (let's reach out to the 1,000 largest companies with call centers and give them our pitch!). When a F500 company is looking for the best attorneys in the world to help them defend against a hostile takeover, they want to talk to the best in the world – part of the sale is being able to discuss the details of a complex legal strategy and demonstrate the skills that you will deliver. You can't expect a high school JV midfielder to get the ball on Messi's foot.

KPMG's Mary Rollman wants to protect others from the challenge she experienced:

> "Do not create an internal team of people hired specifically to generate demand. I have seen this done many times and then watched it be completely scrapped. I've never seen it be successful in professional services. This is typically a fruitless effort because companies do not buy consulting services based on a cold call or messaging that isn't specific to them, their function and their organization. The best way to sell services like ours is with good client teams that have strong relationships with decision makers in an organization. The ability to understand client issues and engage in rich dialogue on those issues leads to strong relationships that are critical to success in this business."

For those firms that land more in the Experience or Expertise corners and *do* opt to house a dedicated sales team, those team members can be in for an uphill battle. Daniel Proietto, partner at Australian law firm Lander & Rogers shares, "I think it can be hard

STAGES OF MATURITY

	FIRM CHARACTERISTICS
ENTREPRENEURIAL	■ Firm takes a *doer*-seller approach ■ Independent, loosely connected affiliation of sellers ■ A few founder-partners do all the selling
TACTICAL	■ Firm takes a *seller*-doer approach ■ A matrix begins to develop as the firm expands services offered, industries served, and geographic presence; teams start to organize around geography ■ Some support structures are built around top sellers ■ Partners run their own practice/P&L and drive BD in their own ways
LEADING	■ Firm takes a seller-doer approach, with a high-level of support provided to top sellers ■ Firm's structure and roles support growth strategy and goals for both client expansion and new logos ■ A formal matrix is used to guide organization's growth, providing clarity around go-to-market efforts by industry, geography, and service line ■ A strong focus is placed on client experience with smooth handoff from sales to delivery ■ Use of centers of excellence to respond to RFPs
WORLD-CLASS	■ Client-driven sales model that is organized around primary accounts and industries ■ Go-to-market efforts are centrally-led and industry-implemented ■ Structure supports a culture of growth ■ Firm has a well-respected revenue operations team that includes finance professionals ■ Revenue operations team leverages data and analytics to support team and direction ■ Sales and marketing are closely aligned with shared KPIs

Figure 11.2   Firm characteristics at each stage of maturity – structure.

Structure for Scale – Supporting Growth Leaders

to succeed in a centralized BD role, even in a firm like ours, which is a really great place to work. At the two extremes you have some partners who feel like 'Well, we've got a BD team, so shouldn't they be winning my work for me?' and other partners who think, 'This is fully my responsibility – why are they interfering? I don't need any help at all.' So, I've got a lot of sympathy for people in internal BD roles. There is definitely the need for a central BD function, but with 100 partners, you're going to have a lot of different views about how things should be done." Clarity on structure, roles, and responsibilities is key to maturing your team (Figure 11.2).

*   *   *

Jump 1: Entrepreneurial to Tactical

While firms can grow relatively large while retaining an Entrepreneurial structure, they will eventually hit a ceiling. In the Entrepreneurial phase, sales are important, but there is no clear organization around how it's getting done, and business developers are left to their own devices. There is a shared understanding of who the "rainmakers" are, with perhaps less understanding of exactly how they got there, how they get their work done, or what one would do to become a rainmaker. Moving into the Tactical stage requires two key structural support actions; think of this as doing the minimum work to put a goalie in place – a baseline for ensuring a win is even possible:

1. Shift the rainmaker mentality from "*doer*-seller" to "*seller*-doer."

Create an explicit business development mandate for those who are expected to grow the firm. Rather than having "doer-sellers" (rainmakers who are great at client work and also *happen* to drag in big new contracts in their spare time), move toward an explicit *seller*-doer model: identifying people responsible for driving firm growth who *also* manage client relationships, enabling them to retain a deep understanding of the market and client needs as they continue to focus on winning new work. Define a clear expectation of the amount of time these team members should put toward business development and what their expected results are, so they can be measured. This provides clarity for everyone at the firm about who is responsible for its growth and how the firm will know if it is being successful.

As highlighted earlier in this chapter, for firms selling Experience or Expertise, it is incredibly important to have those who most deeply understand the content involved in the sale. Judith van Schie, managing director at the European legal and public affairs consultancy Considerati, shares, "Translating the problems of a client into help that we can provide them – that is the bottom line of these sales conversations. In my eyes, only experienced people at the firm who have been in the trenches can really understand what the client is saying – or not saying. That is how work is won." Similar to Mary at KPMG, Judith's firm tested out hiring sales reps. While Judith's firm is far smaller in scale, she, too, quickly realized, "It didn't work. They just didn't speak the language of a client."

Keeping the "doer" half of the seller-doer role is what Mary and Judith – and dozens of others we spoke to – feel is necessary to retain the ability to win in a marketplace of expertise. We agree.

2. Invest in basic support for business developers.

It can take firms a surprisingly long time to recognize something very simple: it is not a great use of resources to have their most valuable (and most expensive) people chasing up clients and prospects, scheduling – and rescheduling – meetings, and putting together a bunch of follow-up materials (you wouldn't have Messi put together the training schedule or clean the team's jerseys). While many firms will not make use (or significant use) of BDRs, they still need to be conscious of the time their most expensive people spend on BD. An important step for firms moving out of the Entrepreneurial phase is to make the first real investments into support for their growth team. This can take a few different forms. Most often, it begins with an administrative support role – someone who can stay on top of scheduling, help track opportunities in a CRM, and ensure opportunities are not lost because of logistical balls being dropped. Sometimes this takes the form of delegating explicit tasks to junior associates (as suggested in Chapter 8) who are supporting growth. Either way, clearly delegating responsibility around administrative sales tasks is a key step to allowing your growth drivers to scale their time and focus on conversations about new work.

Roberto Jiménez, managing director of Puerto Rico–based V2A Consulting, also tried out the idea of hiring a small team of salespeople after recognizing this burden of time on their senior people. Can you guess the result? "Our senior team needs to be the ones selling, but we needed to find time to do that effectively," reflects Roberto. The firm has worked hard to shift their senior team to a lower amount of billable time to allow for focus on business development while remaining close to client work. Shifting the bulk of client delivery work down a level – to the senior engagement managers – has been successful so far. Roberto also recognized that for their top sellers to be consistent rainmakers, they needed some support. "We hired an admin person to help support our senior team leading business development. In addition to scheduling and admin support, she sets 30 minutes with the leaders each week and it's amazing how much pressure it puts on you as a seller. She'll sit with you and say 'Hey, so you were going to have coffee with Mr. Smith – did that happen? Is there a next meeting we need to set?' And if you didn't have the coffee, you are immediately thinking – 'I've got to reach out to him right now!'" As V2A is building up this structure and support, they've taken the first important step, and it is paying off. "It has been magical," says Roberto.

Jump 2: Tactical to Leading

As firms move into a Leading phase of how they think about their structure, they begin to put more than just administrative support around their sales teams. They surround their Messis with other A-players on the field and invest in top-notch trainers and coaches to ensure fitness and readiness. Leading firms also become increasingly client-centered in the way they organize and manage themselves. To move into the Leading stage, focus on the following developments:

1. Create an exceptional sales-to-delivery process that delights your clients.

When asked about the world record for the 400-meters, track experts will highlight the time of Wayde van Niekerk of South Africa, who set a time of 43.03 seconds at the Rio de Janeiro Olympics in 2016. However, the fastest time ever recorded for a single lap around the 400-meter track is actually 36.84 seconds. That time was set by the men's Jamaican 4×100 m relay team at the 2012 London Olympic Games. Why is it that the relay record is nearly 15% faster than the individual time? The relay pulls together a team of people who are best at the individual legs of each portion of the relay and includes three seamless baton handoffs that allow each of those individuals to maximize their 100 m time. While the individual efforts are impressive, a smooth handoff is critical. Fumbling the handoff can be devastating for medal contenders (just ask the 2024 U.S. men's 4×100 m Olympic relay team). In a perfect world, the sales-to-delivery process functions more like the Jamaican relay team than an individual 400 m runner, resulting in a faster, more efficient, and more seamless process that gets the client experience off to a roaring start. Just like in a relay race, this should include a period of brief but coordinated and practiced overlap between the teams.

Walt recalls that at one firm, this internal handoff meeting was often referred to as the "Good luck!" meeting (or sometime an even less friendly version of this) – the message being, "we sold it, now go figure it out!" When this is the tone, clients can feel it. The transition from the "sales" phase to the "delivery" of a project sets the tone for an entire client relationship.

People with deep client knowledge and experience are best at telling stories – at winning new work – and their new clients fall in love with them. Leading firms set themselves apart by developing structures and processes to support an excellent client experience through this transition to the delivery team, without requiring that the sellers remain on the project for the long term. "Clean handoffs from post-sale to implementation demonstrate, to me, a lot of maturity," shares Mike Greto, president at Aperian. "Having a strong connection between the business development team and the folks who are going to do the work is key."

Says Centric Consulting's Michael McNeal, "You must have the maturity to look like you've done this before,". As firms grow in size and begin to distinguish between those selling the projects and those delivering them Michael continues, "You can hit those breaking points where you start to look disjointed. You have sales and delivery teams bumping into each other. This especially happened when we tried to outsource some sales – they were calling on clients, messaging wasn't consistent – it wasn't a good look for us." McNeal underscores here the fact that making this handoff is hard enough, but adding an outsourced sales team into the mix makes it even more challenging. Getting the structure right first is important to ensure this handoff process can thrive.

One option to solve this challenge is to assign a role specifically to project implementation (we'll dig into this more later in this chapter). Another is to clearly map out the baton handoffs – ensuring that

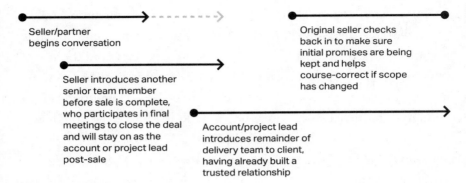

Figure 11.3 Optimal overlap in the sales to delivery handoff.

overlapping time is sufficient and with the right people. It could look like the following outline in Figure 11.3:

2. Align marketing with business development.

Our next chapter will expand on this, but Leading firms have figured out how to manage through the friction that can exist between business development and marketing. They drive success by getting the teams rowing seamlessly in the same direction. Firm structure is a key piece of this, and our research demonstrates that to drive this alignment, marketing and BD should be on the same team, reporting up through a Chief Growth Officer (CGO) or a Chief Marketing & Business Development Officer (CMBDO) with shared KPIs.

3. Create clearly defined sales enablement roles – build your engine room.

At this point, firms have moved beyond basic administrative and scheduling support to develop teams that can really boost the effectiveness of rainmakers. As EY's Managing Partner of Americas, Mark Hawn, put its: "They might be giving up a bit of independence in how they operate, but the tradeoff is that they get access to Navy

Seals on their team. That's what I help them understand." While business developers may now be given more direction and accountability, they receive excellent support structures to make them successful. Often this means hiring specific positions, but sometimes it is as simple as giving a clear role or mandate to someone on the team that defines the activities they will do to enable overall growth efforts – it could be just 25% of their time.

Hap Brakeley, former global chief growth officer for Merkle and managing partner at Accenture, calls this *The Engine Room*. "You can't shoot the moose from the lodge. If you are a hunter but you spend all your time in the lodge doing proposals or RFPs, you aren't selling. If you are going to get more productivity out of your sales team, you need to build an Engine Room that helps the sales team be more effective. Your Engine Room manages market analytics, identifies target clients and best opportunities, and creates use cases and proposals so the sellers can spend more time in the field, and in the right field, because it has been informed by where the moose are gathering, what they are eating, and when they will be there. This is how you get leverage."

Your "Engine Room" should include some combination of the following, depending on your firm strategy and priorities:

- **Account planning support:** As we emphasized in Chapter 6 on client expansion, formalized account planning is key to building a growth engine. This may or may not be a full-time "role," but someone on the team needs to be responsible for making sure account planning is getting done and executed consistently across the firm. In many cases, the practice or industry leader will sit in as the accountability partner, while the administrative tasks of setting meetings, updating opportunities, and tracking account developments will sit with a marketing or BD administrator.

- **Project implementation/handoff support:** Some firms have gone further than creating a sales-to-delivery processes (mentioned earlier in this chapter) and have created specific roles to ensure this handoff is successful. Franklin Covey's managing director charged with growth, Jeff Downs, identified this as a key area for improvement and took action: "We created a critical role called the implementation strategist. After we've landed a client, they work with the client partner to ensure that we're meeting the needs of this particular client. This role is key to ensuring we're renewing that work – getting off to a good start so we can keep working with that client again and again and again and again." The perfect fit for this role is hard to find, Downs says. "You want someone incredibly detail-oriented, but you also need them to be flexible and strategic – to know that client satisfaction is their number one priority." While this person is measured against project-based metrics and hitting deadlines, they are also client-facing and measured on client satisfaction – not just on implementation, but on client longevity. Did the project launch so well that they are a client 6 or 12 or 24 months later? This is what dictates success.

- **Accountability support:** At leading Dutch law firm Houthoff, this accountability role is called a BOP – business opportunity partner. The idea is that this BOP will sit down with each partner regularly and ask questions like, "What are you busy with? What are you focused on? Why? Where? Have you spoken with XYZ? What are you doing to grow the firm right now?" At Houthoff, this role is shared by the managing partner and the head of business development, who are working together to drive this accountability. At other firms, like Roberto Jiménez's firm V2A mentioned previously, this role is played by a more junior person who asks the questions and then produces reports to share with more senior leaders.

- **Pipeline management:** As we will discuss in Chapter 13, Leading firms make meaningful use of CRM systems that enable strong visibility around client work and growth across the organization. While the best firms have built habits and expectations around CRM use that lead to partners all putting excellent data into the CRM, this is a global challenge. Making progress here brings you to Leading; getting it perfect will help move you to World-class. Therefore, having a single person or team who is responsible for constantly looking at the CRM, auditing the opportunities, and making sure pipeline integrity is intact sets the overall team up for long-term success.

- **Research and prospecting:** As firms focus on defining (and refining) their niche and deeply understanding their target client profile, some firms will invest in roles (or portions of roles) that are focused on building out the specific target list of likely buyers, unearthing details about previous engagements with competitors, shifts in prospective client strategy, budgeting processes and timelines, and unique characteristics that would support the seller's outreach and engagement strategy. This background research is immensely helpful to senior folks whose time is best spent on relationships – not on Google.

- **Proposal development:** Developing custom proposals can take an enormous amount of time. Dwight Hutchins has been a senior partner at Accenture and BCG. He shares, "There is a huge amount of value in actually having a dedicated proposal development center." This is an area that gets far more support at scale (large firms have full teams within BD and marketing developing proposals), but it is a less obvious investment for smaller firms. While this may take different shapes, the idea is the same: just as senior storytellers aren't spending time

Googling details on prospects, they can also avoid spending their evenings pulling together creative decks and proposals, hunting through old materials for good content, or creating new materials that struggle to follow brand guidelines. Better, they relay what needs to be done, and others are producing drafts for them. "I'd say it's been a huge win," says Lori Langholz, principal and chief business development officer, on centralizing BDO's proposal team. "We've seen a major increase in quality since we centralized this team. You're not running the risk of someone messing up a 'find and replace' with the wrong client's name – you have a professional doing it. And it matters." As Langholz underscores, this role can be extremely helpful but also requires skilled people who understand the nuances of what is being proposed.

For certain types of work, having a proposal team is non-negotiable. "In large-scale transformation work, when we're getting into $200M proposals for big outsourcing or big technology deals, the selection process is very intensive," says Accenture's Paul Boulanger. "You need professional sales roles where they do nothing but manage the sales process. When you're submitting RFPs that are 10 binders-worth of content – that's a whole different ballgame. The public service group at Accenture was excellent at this – every tender was enormous. It would take months – if not years – and a lot of it was very formulaic, so there was an industrialized way to approach it. In these situations, you need to have very formal sales roles that are never going to touch the project once it's sold, but their whole reason for existence is managing the process."

* * *

Structure for Scale – Supporting Growth Leaders

When Going "Less Mature" Makes You More Mature

Six years ago, Elisabeth Houtman took over as Head of Business Development and Marketing at Houthoff, a leading full-service Dutch law firm based in Amsterdam and Rotterdam that has 300 attorneys and another 300 in business services. "I noticed there was a lot of frustration," Elisabeth reflects, upon stepping into the role. "We had a couple of senior business developers at the time. We have three levels in business services: execution, specialist, and advisory. The idea is that people in the senior advisory roles in business development are giving advice to our partnership on how to grow the business. So I had a mature business development team, but they were frustrated, and the partners were frustrated."

After trying some new team structures and ways of working, Elisabeth realized there was a clear mismatch in expectations. The BD folks were not getting the time or attention they needed from partners to pursue their ideas and provide guidance, and the partners were not readily accepting help from the BD team. "So I talked to the partners, and I asked them, 'What are your expectations from my team? What do you want them to provide for you?' They said, 'We simply seek prompt and efficient support for our BD initiatives.'" The reality, as Elisabeth describes it, is that there was no way her team *could* have succeeded in the advisory role – with one BD advisor assigned to 10 partners, that advisor is never going to know their clients, or their market, *better* than the partners do.

"Who are the business developers here? It's the partnership," says Elisabeth, who sees her team clearly as enablers and accountability drivers. After the feedback from the partnership, Elisabeth made some key changes. She rebuilt her team – with more junior team members. She mirrors the business where lawyers start after university and are "home-grown" within a firm.

192

The Growth Engine

These new hires also come from universities starting in their first real job; they fall into the "execution" level. They are focused on providing quick, friendly, and high quality service to the partners' requests, helping with commercial documents and other support activities. "My team members love their internal clients – the partners. They are excited about what they are asked to do." Elisabeth "focuses on *making clients and people successful*, so the development of these young professionals is super important. And the partnership is happy because they are serviced in a better way." Elisabeth's managing partner at Houthoff, Alexander Kaarls, concurs: "Previously, there was a credibility issue with the BD team. They wanted to be advisors, but they'd come to us with ideas that we often did not think made sense for our accounts. They also didn't want to get hands-on and help us with things that felt important to us, like submissions to the legal guides or quick one-pagers on what we learned from previous pitches to a client. Now, we have smart, good doers."

Just as Elisabeth did, identifying the specific kinds of support that your partners both need and *want* is critical to ensuring your growth engine hums along smoothly, with clearly matched skills and expectations for each role.

* * *

Jump 3: Leading to World-class

The jump from Leading to World-class is not marked by significant alterations in structure, but rather by a deepening sense of clarity and conviction both internally and externally around the purpose of each role on the team and how they all interact to optimize growth. The World Cup title is all but guaranteed because everyone is clear about their roles, on and off the field; the team is completely in sync; and Messi feels supported. The lineup has been named; now it's all about maintaining focus and trust through practice. The hallmarks of World-class are:

1. Develop a go-to-market model that supports your client needs and growth strategy.

World-class firms do not go to market with an industry focus *because* they are structured that way; they structure themselves with industry P&Ls and growth targets *because* that best supports their defined strategy of supporting clients. "You need people who know the industry and region and they need to be out there with clients all the time to understand how to put together big deals," says Mike McDaniel, EVP group president for Commercial Solutions at Conduent and former president of Modern Workplace at DXC. "Then you need the more consultative sellers – the specialists inside the practice areas – who are well known and can be brought in by account folks to help attack a really specific problem."

The growth strategy (which in turn defines your organizational model) is built based on what makes sense for clients. If your clients tend to be smaller regional or national banks that require completely different types of regulatory and risk service based on their location, a growth strategy driven by geography and underpinned by deep knowledge of industry and services would support your goals. In this example, the P&L (profit and loss) might sit with each regional director. The location of the P&L determines who ultimately has decision-making power in the firm.

As firms grow and expand beyond three or four service lines, orienting the firm based on industry, and even key account, becomes best practice. At scale, World-class firms build teams around specific industries. This model allows World-class firms to set themselves apart by developing deep industry expertise, hiring partners or resources with broad industry knowledge, and building service teams that create proposals and deliver work specific to that industry.

Eventually, the growth of key accounts may warrant a further evolution of the model tailored to serve each of those accounts with their own set of experts. "At first, most firms align by region or geography, service model or industry," says Jason Delles, CGO at Eide Bailly. "What people aren't doing is aligning by an account model. What I care about most is that client account and solving problems, and we're going to get the best outcome when we serve the account the right way." Because the firm is structured with a client-first approach, the friction among geography, practice, and industry dissolves, replaced by client-centric pathways to collaboration. Everyone knows exactly who to call for what type of question because roles and priorities are clear, resulting in an excellent client experience.

2. Engage everyone in growth.

World-class firms have developed a *culture* of growth. Not only are the partners and BD and marketing support roles focused on winning new work, but everyone – from CEO down to the newest intern – feels the importance of their involvement in providing the firm's services to those who can benefit from them. "The most important part of success is what everyone across the organization thinks their role is," reflects Nortal's Ben Burke. "Business development has a lot more to do with the role that every single person plays in the firm – not just the sales function. Everyone should feel like they have a responsibility for understanding their clients' pains, problems, needs – and then knowing what to do inside the firm when they touch on something important." This mentality around growth is a key driver of our point of view around retaining a seller-doer model and not fully separating BD from those delivering client work. The minute even one person in a professional services firm starts to feel like growth is "not my job" is the same minute your growth machine's check-engine light starts flashing.

3. Build a sophisticated, data-driven revenue operations team.

While the specific roles that support top sellers may vary, World-class firms *must* have excellent revenue operations team members – those looking and working across BD, marketing, and client experience to optimize systems and processes that drive revenue growth. This team drives the backend operations around growth, and ensures successful delivery of data analysis, software implementation, CRM management, reporting, process design, and cross-departmental communication and collaboration.

As we'll dig into further in the next section, World-class firms have moved beyond gut feel. Decisions – both internal and external – are data-driven, and roles and teams are developed around that. Leadership has perfect visibility into the performance of those driving growth across the organization because of the (accurate!) data at their fingertips. "If you have a large organization, you've got to have a team that is running all your analytics," says Accenture's Paul Boulanger. "If you've got 200, 300 managing directors, you need analytics to understand how everyone is doing. You need to understand how to set targets and manage the team against those – when you get to this scale, this is a big job, this isn't a client-facing role. It's more adjacent to finance, and in some firms, it probably does sit in finance. Sales management, sales administration, sales enablement – whatever you want to call it – you've got to have that analytics engine." Walt has seen this work best when someone with a finance background is moved directly into a sales operations role. Their tendency to be realists – not optimists, as most salespeople are – adds an element of clarity that is hugely beneficial.

World-class firms build data and analytics roles into their structure to ensure the goals they are setting make sense and everyone's time is optimized.

The 2022 World Cup final was close – at full time Argentina and France had three goals apiece, and Argentina took the win in penalties. France had their own star closer – Kylian Mbappe, who scored all three of their goals – and their own structure: a 4-2-3-1 formation. There is not one perfect structure that suits every organization to ensure the ball hits the back of the net. Your industry and target market, your people and culture – these will all likely have an impact on the exact structure you choose. But absolutely necessary are the people and roles surrounding your closers – your Messis and Mbappes – that will set them up to score. They cannot play coach, goalkeeper, defense, outside midfield, and center forward all at once. They might score one goal, but they would be lucky, and then they would burn out. They need direction from their coach, great training from their physio, solid delivery from the back of the field, and a great assist from their teammate right in front of the goal. That creates a winning team.

Structure for Scale – Supporting Growth Leaders

Chapter 12

Aligning Marketing and Business Development

When Jon Batiste set out to compose *American Symphony,* he intentionally brought together sounds and styles traditionally housed in their own distinct silos. Batiste spent seven years leading the house band on *The Late Show with Stephen Colbert*, his music and improvisation combining with Colbert's comical crooning. He is a five-time Grammy Award winner and renowned musician, composer, and musical artist.

Reviewers and critics have struggled to place Batiste's music in a single genre. His work intentionally collects disparate types of music to create something unique through the power of collaboration. American Symphony is the most recent culmination of his "social music" philosophy – the idea the "we as humans can use music as a part of our lives to create community." Combining traditional orchestra with the loud power of a marching band, Batiste has a talent for bridging the gap between different genres, styles, instruments, and people to create a mesmerizing symphony of sounds all in concert with one another. The final composition includes police sirens, Indigenous vocalists, banjos, steel drums, piano, and a full classical orchestra. On their own, each piece may not strike harmony in listeners' ears, but the collective outcome is powerful.

A World-class growth engine draws on the same principles of collaboration as a World-class symphony – each individual, department, and role has an important part to play in the final outcome. While we spent the last chapter reviewing a variety of roles that play a part in success, no collaboration is more critical to drive growth than that of business development and marketing – the focus of this chapter. But simply combining many different instruments does not a symphony create. In fact, many professional services organizations struggle to get beyond the cringe-worthy screeches of a pre-teen garage band. Why? Because the guitarist can't stop obsessing over the new riff he made up while the lead singer wants to pivot to a 1990s-era grunge vibe and the violist is confused as to why they were added to the band in the first place. If you've ever found yourself in a sub-optimal BD or marketing role, this feeling of friction will seem familiar. If the lead singer is BD, the lead guitarist is most certainly marketing, and until those roles are playing in sync, world-class fame, fortune, and professional success will elude even the most talented musicians. As Kira Sandmann at BGL shares, "Our firm has been in a high-growth stage over the past couple of years, which has brought so many new voices into the conversations we have regarding identity and strategy. It's both a challenge and an exciting opportunity to determine how best to leverage that collective experience and intelligence as we move into this next chapter." Her goal is to make those voices sing in harmony.

What is the problem?

Marketing professional services (i.e., professionals) is different from marketing Diet Coke:

"We are not selling Diet Coke and French fries on the street corner," says Sarah McHugh, former corporate vice president and chief marketing officer of Huron Consulting. "We are selling an individual mind's ability to solve a significant challenge, or a group of minds to do that, and that requires something far different in terms of sales."

Professional services organizations rely on both business development and marketing to drive growth, but the nature of professional services itself makes creating harmony and coordination between the two hard. BGL's Kira Sandmann notes, "What we are ultimately selling is an answer to the question of how our professionals' unique expertise and networks, when backed by the broader resources and reputation of our organization, can add up to the right solution for our potential clients. Promoting that messaging at the firm level is our marketing effort, and enabling our professionals to relay it individually or in small groups falls into the category of business development. At the leadership level, our job is to ensure that those efforts are aligned and complementary to one another, from the awareness stage through to engagement."

Too often, marketing and business development find themselves at odds in this effort, and firms confuse the two. Marketing centers around brand awareness and recognition, brand prominence, brand equity, and collateral. Marketing creates the bridge for business development but is less focused on fostering one-to-one relationships off which new work is scoped. That is BD, and is most often the responsibility of the partners or practice leads. Problems come up when marketing builds bridges to the wrong destinations, or when they build the right bridges, but their business development counterparts fail to use them. Marketing gets frustrated because they built the beautiful Brooklyn Bridge and then the sellers hopped on a ferry instead, and sellers are frustrated because they actually wanted a bridge to Hoboken.

The biggest challenge for any firm in moving from Entrepreneurial to Tactical to Leading and, finally, to World-class is creating synergy between these two teams, building the best bridges to the right people at the right time and place, and then making sure traffic on those bridges is steady and smooth.

201

Aligning Marketing and Business Development

Ill-defined roles and responsibilities:

Marketing professionals want to bring their experience and point of view to the table to help grow the firm, but they are often missing the seat at the table that they want. "A successful BD and marketing organization is inclusive and they're teaming together," says Christine Conforti, former global marketing director for FTI Consulting's Forensic & Litigation practice. "The challenge is the client-serving professional will come to the marketing organization with a completely different point of view about what they need as a marketing tool to bring their knowledge and expertise to the market. They'll say, 'I really need a thought leadership piece around this topic that I can send to my client.' We want to say 'yes, we have that,' but we also want to understand what the client's needs are and why now? We want to ensure we have a full go-to-market plan around this as a priority vs. just a one-off tactic." Both teams feel they should be in charge of knowing what messages and materials to bring to market, and disagreement can cause deep frustration. Sellers want to be enabled by marketing with the exact materials, events, and activities they want, and marketing wants their expertise and knowledge of that tactic, tool, or channel to be respected – not just be an order-taker.

Overlapping ownership:

Let's revisit the Seven Elements of the client buying journey that we discussed in Chapter 1, from *How Clients Buy*. The first three Elements in the buying journey – **awareness, understanding,** and **interest** – are where we often lean most heavily on marketing to help grow the firm, and where we often think about the "marketing" activities that create the bridges for sales to stroll across (Figure 12.1). We need a strong brand in the market that tells good stories about exactly what we do and how we're different, and we need this to be with the right audience – the individuals who have an abiding *interest* in what we do and could benefit from our services.

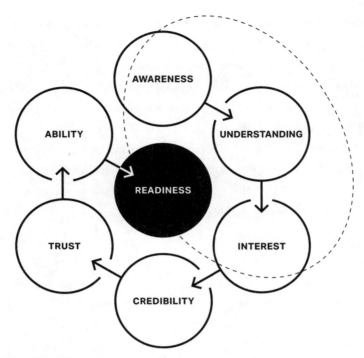

Figure 12.1 Marketing's primary zone of influence on the buyer journey.

Strong storytelling and case studies presented by marketing can certainly contribute to building credibility, but ultimately the partners/experts are going to take the baton when it comes to building **credibility** and **trust** with a potential client – the two most important pieces to winning new work in expert services.

Bain's Greg Callahan describes his expectation of having marketing help get Bain on the "day one" list of his target audience: "We did a study with Google, and what we found is that every person who is going to buy services has a 'day-one' list. This is a list of two or three players that is based on the research that they've done, and more importantly the people they've talked to who have shared good references. Ninety percent of the time – ninety stinking percent of the time – they ultimately buy from one of those three players. If you missed being on that day-one list, your odds of being the final winner are very, very, very, very low. The mission is just to create awareness and activation; create a community of the right people who know your brand, so when the time comes, you can be a selling machine."

Let's take a look at the actions needed to build that perfect harmony between the teams – that harmony that will make you a "selling machine" – helping to build your growth engine (Figure 12.2).

Jump 1: Entrepreneurial to Tactical

Marketing for Entrepreneurial firms is 80% logo and name and 20% fun ideas from the founder. Dedicated marketing efforts are often an afterthought, perhaps rightly so, for early-stage firms focusing most of their efforts on building out their book of business based on existing connections and referrals. Entrepreneurial firms rarely invest time and money to cast a wider net because they don't yet need to – work coming in the door keeps them busy and the early rainmakers of the firm bring in most of the new business based on past experience and personal charisma. However, a waning rolodex will often be the spark needed for a firm to ignite more formal marketing efforts to reach new audiences and support long-term business development. While Entrepreneurial marketing efforts may include sponsorship of a local softball team, the shift to Tactical brings a focus on getting your brand in front of the right audience – those who have an actual *interest* in your offerings. Once you've taken the following four actions, you'll be well into the Tactical phase and ready to continue up the curve:

1. Create a marketing role or team.

As firms move up the maturity curve, they establish an individual or small team charged with "marketing" the firm. This team doesn't sit at the leadership level and likely has a small budget – often a marketing

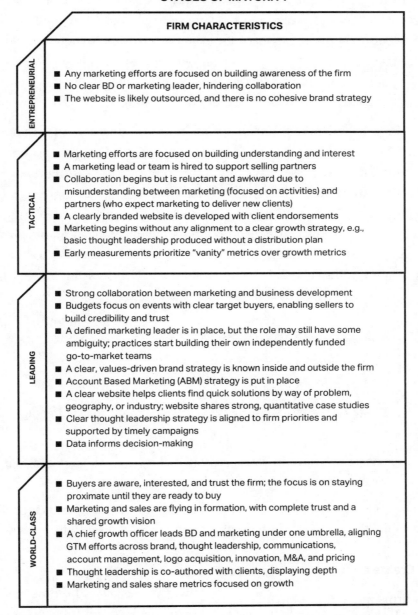

Figure 12.2 Firm characteristics at each stage of maturity – BD and marketing alignment.

manager or marketing coordinator. They may become the receptacle for lots of one-off projects from client delivery and leadership teams intended to support the growth of the company. Still, there is now a clear person or group to go to with marketing-related requests.

2. Build a clear website that supports your brand.

When Jacob joined PIE, the firm's website consisted of a single "homepage" with a request for clients to log in. That's it. No background about what services they offered, the team, or their clients. These days, such a rudimentary online presence is rare given easy access to website-building tools, but it's still a critical step of jumping out of the Entrepreneurial phase – having a clear brand presence via your website that can allow potential clients to get to know you quickly. Table stakes for a professional services firm's website include:

- A description of your services
- Firm background/history
- Bios of firm leadership
- A quick and easy way to get in touch (either with individuals or to set up a time to connect)
- Consistent branding throughout – logos, look and feel, language used
- Most importantly – client endorsements and case studies demonstrating that you have done this work successfully for other others

Fortunately, a very basic website was in place by the time Andi was thinking about joining PIE. She was able to see a brief description of the firm's main service offering, bios of the firm's leaders,

206

The Growth Engine

and a lengthy overview of the firm's history. When Andi came in for her first interview, she recognized the firm's (old) logo hand-painted on the wall. PIE has taken some major steps forward in its branding since then, but at least *something* was in place!

3. Produce basic but substantive thought leadership – don't publish just to publish.

Gone are the days of the ad-hoc blog posts and LinkedIn ramblings from the founder. Tactical firms recognize the value in publishing thought leadership on a regular basis and make efforts to do so even if the resulting publications fail to bring in new leads. The firm has a point of view (a great start), but it likely lacks the rigor or research of more mature firms and almost never includes the client point of view in publication. "I see firms pump out a lot of content, thought leadership and webinars. But the mistake often made is to call that lead generation," warns Evan Tierce, chief sales officer at Baker Tilly. Producing consistent thought leadership is step one. Embedding thought leadership into a dedicated and personalized sales process will move you into the Leading stage.

4. Establish *some* metrics and start measuring success.

The number of followers or "likes" on social media, downloads of thought leadership, attendees on webinars, and media mentions often dictate marketing success for Tactical firms. Measuring *anything* at this point marks a level of maturity not realized for Entrepreneurial firms, and watching the number of LinkedIn followers increase often feels good for emerging marketing teams! However, until the firm understands *why* this matters and can track the impact of these numbers on true relationship development and revenue generation, the value of these vanity metrics will remain limited.

207

Aligning Marketing and Business Development

Firms in the Tactical stage often suffer the most friction between their teams. The emergence of dual functions is exciting, but without a broader, connected strategy these teams rarely play in harmony. Aaron Smith at L.E.K knows this problem well. He says, "Historically, we had marketing reporting to and executing instructions from individual Partners. That had some success but missed the opportunity to learn and leverage best practices across the practice or firm through a more integrated approach."

As the rolodex dries up and cold calling fails to deliver results, sales points the finger at marketing, asking "where are the leads?" Marketing points the finger back at sales for not following up with the new subscribers to the firm newsletter and asks for budget to get new leads. There may also be a sense that the new marketing leader is too focused on what they personally want to do (e.g., Conferences! Social media! Rebrand!) and partners can feel like the tail is wagging the dog. Because marketing doesn't have senior internal support, in this phase it is often cut dramatically during downturns. The duel persists until firms invest in a more comprehensive and collaborative marketing and business development strategy to align teams, roles, goals, and, importantly, outcomes. Which brings us to our next jump.

Jump 2: Tactical to Leading

Marketing and sales teams in Leading organizations demonstrate strong collaboration, with marketing initiatives integrated into growth plans. They work together toward shared objectives and outcomes closely tied to company strategy. While BD and marketing still have independent leaders and may bump into each other, they tend to work synergistically. Marketing has been successfully integrated into the growth team, if not yet 100% aligned. Marketing initiatives have moved beyond creating brand awareness, and instead are focused on building the small, sturdy bridges to a select target audience where trust and credibility can be more readily developed. This jump from Tactical to Leading is the most significant, and therefore requires more actions:

1. Use data to inform metrics and decision-making to drive ROI.

At Leading firms, all marketing activity feeds into the organization's CRM, enabling data to drive decision-making around how to spend marketing dollars most effectively going forward. Every marketing activity demonstrates a clear return on investment closely tied to company goals. Gone are the days of "we reached 100 people at this conference." Instead, marketing can track exactly how many of those 100 people comprise the firm's ICP for business development and show established contact nurture plans to convert a warm introduction into a new client. This ability to measure impact breeds deeper trust in marketing from the sellers, because they can see that the strategies pursued by marketing are allowing them to expand their clients or win new ones.

At Harbor Global, a legal consulting firm based out of Chicago, marketing is directly responsible for revenue creation. "We create attribution for every marketing event," explains Kevin Clem the firm's chief growth officer – Corporations and Community. "For example, marketing has a specific revenue goal tied to our community and insights program. In our CRM there is a dropdown that asks 'what were the marketing assets that helped contribute to this opportunity? A specific thought leadership piece? Invite to a sounding board? Did we meet them at an event?' We are trying to instill in both the sales and marketing teams that we're all driving revenue together, not just making beautiful things. We now have empirical data that shows quantifiable improvement in revenue associated with prospects who participate in our Legal Lab event, for example, to demonstrate the ROI for that specific marketing motion, which helps us determine how much to spend on it year over year."

2. Create a senior marketing role.

At this stage of maturity in a firm's life, marketing initiatives demand the creation of a senior marketing role (likely a CMO or a VP of marketing). As the firm expands to serve different geographies and industries with a variety of services, marketing organizes itself around the go-to-market strategy while benefiting from a central leader to ensure consistency of brand and client experience and alignment with firm goals at a senior level.

3. Build a clear brand strategy to tell the firm story.

BD and marketing are "working in tandem, asking, 'What is the story we want to tell?'" describes Arjun Davda, director of Market Growth & Business Development for one of the Big Four in Canada. Telling a clear and consistent story – to the right audience of potential buyers – is the key opportunity for marketing to help set up sales teams to develop the credibility and trust needed to win new work. Ben Burke, SVP North America at Nortal, concurs, "I think marketing is important because it helps you tell stories. What matters most are referrals – that one-on-one storytelling – and that story has more credibility if it's backed up with the same story and the same look and feel everywhere. Marketing plays a very strong supporting role to make sure that this one-on-one storytelling has the most impact." A few key components include:

- **Best-in-class website:** Beyond providing the "table stakes" elements outlined for Tactical firm websites, Leading firms demonstrate their story through this critical online presence. The website is organized the way the firm is organized, allowing potential clients to easily navigate through the services most relevant to them based on their industry and geography. There is also a clear and consistent brand presence that is underscored by firm values, which are made clear on the website. Mike McDaniel of Conduent shares, "Getting your story into the marketplace has to be in 'kitchen English.' As technologists, we always want to talk about how we crack atoms, but nobody actually cares how the atoms crack. What they really want to hear is a story that elicits some emotion and that is what I rely on my marketing team to do."

- **Strong, quantitative case studies:** Client case studies (both on the website and in other materials) bolster the firm's credibility and reputation. Your best clients in your most important services and industries are happy to be named in a case study, cementing your expertise in the areas where you say you are best. Case studies are both qualitative and quantitative, providing clear examples of ROI for clients.

According to Evan Allen, co-founder at start-up accelerator 9point8 Collective, companies often overlook the importance of brand. He says, "A good brand is paying for a shorter sales cycle and a higher conversion rate. It helps suspend or reduce the due diligence a prospect conducts on you. A strong brand is a major accelerant."

* * *

211

Aligning Marketing and Business Development

When Awareness Works

Targeted sports marketing is often a hallmark of large firms; this can serve as either a powerful client development tool or a complete waste of precious marketing dollars (are your 50 target chief operating officers all seeing the logo you spent tens of millions on to place on the side of that F1 car?). Firms typically invest in sports for two main reasons: to increase brand prominence (lots of people watch the World Cup, why not let them know who you are?), or to enable a unique client experience (being able to invite your Denver-based clients to sit courtside at a Nuggets game will cement that relationship, right?). Firms ensure a return on investment for sports events or sponsorships by establishing a clear "why" for the investment, determining metrics to evaluate ROI, and aligning the investment with their target market. The key is being targeted and thoughtful – not just throwing money at it because it feels flashy and fun.

During the 2024 Paris Olympics, Grant Thornton Australia partnered with a canoer by the name of Jessica Fox. While the firm had not historically invested large dollars in this kind of sponsorship, the timing felt uniquely ripe. The Big 4 accounting firms were under extra scrutiny in Australia in the wake of some widely publicized conflict of interest issues with the Australian government. As one of the largest accounting firms in the world, trailing the Big 4, Grant Thornton saw an opportunity to make themselves more widely known as an alternative to the Big 4. The bet paid off when Fox went on to win two gold medals and was named the Olympic flag bearer for Australia. The name Grant Thornton was quickly known by many Australians, and associated with excellence. National Managing Partner of Consulting and Private Business Advisory at Grant Thornton Australia, Michael Pittendrigh, also noted the campaign's impact on the importance of alignment between sales and marketing. He says, "We have more clarity end-to-end and the trust equation with the market has increased exponentially. Marketing activities and messaging are aligned to our purpose, values, and brand promise, Reach for Remarkable, and are backed by purposeful business development and sales support. As a professional services firm, we're stepping outside the traditional industry comfort zone to strategically focus on top of funnel brand awareness – which has had a tangible impact from the inside out."

While it's an assumed challenge to measure the success of an investment like an athlete sponsorship, it doesn't mean it isn't worthwhile; it simply means higher stakes marketing investments should be made thoughtfully, with clear objectives aligned to firm strategy and backed by research and reporting against agreed upon success criteria.

* * *

4. Develop a clear content strategy with multi-channel distribution.

For Leading firms, thought leadership becomes a vehicle for effective storytelling that refines and reinforces brand while also demonstrating expertise in targeted areas. What separates Leading firms is the clear strategy they have around what they produce and what they do with it. Anne Callender, chief business development officer at law firm Simpson, Thatcher & Bartlett, explains the challenge: "Sometimes it can feel reactive – like we need to put out thought leadership so that our clients don't call us and say, 'I just got memos

213

Aligning Marketing and Business Development

from 17 firms; where is the Simpson memo?' But there needs to be a bigger focus on people and tailored client engagement activities. We need to really focus on who we're trying to get to know, how we can communicate our unique expertise that could help them and draw that connection." Leading thought leadership strategies are incredibly targeted to key audiences and focused on actually saying something new. These strategies have a few key elements:

- **Topics are defined based on interests of current and potential clients,** and gaps in the market that need to be addressed, not just based on what partners think is interesting or feel like they know. A plan and publication calendar is mapped out in advance in alignment with firm strategy.

- **Perspectives are differentiated from competitors** to help clients understand how your firm uniquely approaches challenges or issues.

- **Thought leadership is part of an overall strategy,** aligned with speaking engagements, customer forums, and digital marketing campaigns, to ensure that target audiences are hearing a consistent story across channels. For example, a new research report may be presented at a conference, shared in detail in a small-group customer forum, discussed on industry podcasts, highlighted across social channels with a summarization of key findings, and provides an avenue for 1:1 deep-dive conversations to review with interested clients and prospects.

Marketing at leading firms goes beyond monthly blog posts or LinkedIn blurbs and capitalizes on a coordinated multichannel approach that includes in-person events, community-based marketing, email, LinkedIn, websites, social media and additional digital

214

The Growth Engine

and physical assets created in close partnership with clients and business development team input. "We are rigorous about the execution of our marketing plan," says Stephanie Johnston, CEO of Transcend Strategy Group. "We have discipline when it comes to podcasting. We have discipline when it comes to presenting at conferences and then doing the associated social media and marketing. It's a surround sound communication model that is about laser pointing to your target audience. Our written content tends to impact the influencers, who inform the purchase decision. Our presence at very select conferences and events is where we make sure we get 1:1 C-suite time, which is the most impactful strategy to nail. Everything else we do is about surrounding that target audience with education and information."

5. Implement account-based marketing (ABM):

"There's broad reach marketing, and then there's ABM," says Bain's Greg Callahan. "There is a finite number of customers that I know are target for my market, and I am going to cover them with things that are truly relevant to them at this moment. We make sure that our marketing is very targeted towards those key accounts, whether it be invitations to small roundtables, or creating specific reports on the state of the market that are insightful for those accounts." Greg is spot on. In professional services, account expansion is the key driver of growth, and that growth can be broader and faster when supported by strong ABM programs. Leading firms (or practices) shrink their ponds to focus on the small universe of accounts they need to be targeting, and exactly what the individuals within those accounts want and need. Marketing efforts are tailored for each key account, with ABM team members working hand-in-glove with the client account teams to plan and drive growth.

6. Invest in a targeted event strategy.

Meeting clients and prospects in person to break bread and build human relationships is critical in professional services. Leading firms have deep alignment between account teams and marketing teams about the type of events that are worthwhile – and those that aren't. Dollars are spent only in places where relationships can flourish, and the firm's unique brand and expertise can be displayed. While some presence at industry conferences is likely table stakes for most firms, the bigger focus is on the spaces where you can gather with 20 people – instead of 20,000 – to move the needle on individual buyer relationships. Jules Stott, partner and head of Marketing & Business Development, EMEA, at consulting firm AlixPartners concurs, "Our job in marketing and BD is to get our people in front of our true target clients. Sometimes it means sponsoring the right conference or creating the right content, but what we really need to be prioritizing is organizing roundtable dinners where we have the 20 people in the room that matter most – and then we need to *follow up*."

Leading firms have marketing teams that set business developers up to succeed at events. They know exactly who will be there and what they should talk to them about, and they will develop an immediate plan for follow-up at the conclusion of the conference. And the follow-up is not "I'll see them at the conference next year" – it's a clear set of action steps for how you will stay in touch with them in the coming months (e.g., sharing thought leadership, meeting up for coffee to continue a conversation, connecting them with another client around a shared topic of interest).

These more intimate conversations can and should be a launching ground for thought leadership; when you are at the center of these conversations, you gather deep insights and learn what *really* matters to this audience. Roberto Jiménez at V2A Consulting hosts an ongoing breakfast series with 30 C-level executives (a mix of clients and non-clients) around specific topics in which they've shared their interest. The content discussed during those small group sessions is then packaged and shared more broadly by marketing to draw broader interest in V2A and in the breakfast series, which is where relationships (and business!) develop.

*　*　*

Getting Creative – Events and Experiences

Our experience at PIE leads us to be unequivocal in our view that the best client and prospect events are focused on substance – generally small-group peer discussions where you can demonstrate your expertise through conversation with the exact right people who need to hear from you. Within this framework, though, you have the opportunity to make an experience truly memorable.

Walt recalls an event he hosted in partnership with PIE for a dozen F500 chief operating officers when he was serving as Accenture's North America managing director overseeing the Management Consulting Practice. The event included a full day of roundtable discussions and was kicked off the night before with a dinner held at Walt's home outside of Washington, D.C. The meal was prepared by former White House chef Frank Ruta, who was a participant in the evening and shared both an amazing meal as well as personal stories of his experience serving First Families. Many of the following day's roundtable discussion topics were based around a recent presidential election and potential legislative changes, so a dinner with a former White House chef was fun, memorable, and timely. And there is nothing more intimate than

(continued)

Aligning Marketing and Business Development

(continued)

hosting people in your home – Walt had invited his clients and prospects to get to know him on a deeper level by inviting them into his house for the evening. This greatly moved the needle on each of those relationships.

In another example, Andi recently hosted a roundtable dinner with a client who was focused on deepening relationships with women executives at their largest customer accounts. The discussion topic was around developing women leaders, and the dinner was held at a popular woman-owned restaurant in Toronto. The restaurant owner (who is a bit of a local celebrity) joined the group for dinner as an active participant, providing a very memorable experience for those who attended (one participant's husband was such a big fan of the restauranteur that he was jealous not to be invited!).

The number one priority at events like this is substance – it *has* to be a valuable conversation for all involved. Creating a unique setting or experience to surround the dialogue will make the gathering – and you as the host – even more memorable.

* * *

Jump 3: Leading to World-class

"There's marketing integration, and then there's marketing *alignment* ... and there's a big difference," observes Jason Delles, chief growth officer at Eide Bailly. "Most firms get to marketing integration, where they get along and work well together, but it's very hard to get to the point where you're fully aligned. You can go in a lot of directions, but we want to be aligned to a North Star." While Leading firms are *integrated,* World-class firms have clearly defined their North Star, and they are truly *aligned* in how they are powering toward it.

This alignment comes with formal structure, shared metrics, and a culture underpinned by the importance of client input and firmwide growth. World-class firms:

1. Align reporting structure with shared goals and metrics.

For World-class firms, sales and marketing work seamlessly together to define and align on shared metrics and priorities. World-class firms have broken down the silos between BD and marketing, with all growth efforts formally rolling up to a single chief growth officer (or equivalent). Murray Joslin at Integreon describes World-class firms as ones that, "Recognize the need for both sales and marketing, where nobody worries about the credit." The groups operate in a kind of symbiotic relationship, trusting each other's judgment to make decisions aligned to a shared growth strategy. When the full team is working toward shared metrics (such as topline revenue growth, pipeline growth, profitability, customer retention, or account expansion), the practice or firm succeeds together.

2. Embed a client-service mindset across the team.

As a marketing and client capability consultant at Accenture, Danielle Tenconi never saw the separation between marketing and sales. "We were all brand stewards," she recalls, "I never actually felt like I was selling." Now, as CMO at McChrystal Group, Tenconi has everyone in her marketing team do some client work to ensure they know the client well and are connected to the sales side of the business. Tenconi's connectedness with clients has its roots in her first job in marketing at Mars just out of college. "I expected this glamourous job, and then during my first week, they had me stocking shelves in supermarkets. The idea was that if I couldn't see customers buy Mars candy bars or dog food or Uncle Ben's rice, then I couldn't truly understand the company and help lead it into the future. It reinforced that whether

219

Aligning Marketing and Business Development

in marketing or sales, who we serve – our clients – are real human beings. We can't forget that." The underlying and connected ethos around client service is the foundation of a truly integrated sales and marketing function.

At Harbor Global, client listening is key to this alignment. Kevin Clem, chief growth officer for Corporations and Community, explains that marketing sits within the broader go-to-market function alongside Client Engagement, Client Operations (i.e., Sales Ops), Alliances, and Corporate Development. Marketing leaders participate alongside client owners and growth leaders in their Client Sounding Board series, so teams are working hand-in-glove with a focus on direct response to client needs.

3. Co-author thought leadership with clients.

World-class-firms have a thought leadership strategy not only focused on exactly what the market is asking for but they also use publication as an opportunity to deepen their best relationships by co-authoring content with clients. This ensures that thought leadership is strictly focused on topics that matter most to clients, it highlights the strength of client service and relationships to the rest of the market, and it elevates their clients while also elevating their firm, cementing their role as a true partner and providing extra visibility for their client in tandem.

* * *

At the top of the maturity curve, BD and marketing play in perfect in harmony, reading the same piece of music, creating and building off the same score, and playing in the same key. They can riff off one another and improvise when needed but ultimately generate a sound that is a consistent and powerful symphony of aligned team members and actions.

Part VI

Data and Measurement

Chapter 13

Measuring What Matters

Erika had a steaming cup of hot cocoa in hand as she walked door to door on a chilly October afternoon. She had a goal of knocking on 30 doors for the upcoming election. She had rallied her friends to join her and could see a friend in a puffy coat two houses down the block from her knocking on a bright yellow door.

Erika knocked on the dark wooden door in front of her. No answer. She checked the house off on her tracker and made her way to the next address thinking about the bipartisan voter information session she was holding in a few days – she needed to finish her slides.

Her friend came up behind her and spooked her (maybe it was all the early Halloween decorations on lawns – gravestones and massive spiders). "So, the residents in that house are college students. They'd love a stack of 20 fliers to hang on campus."

Erika smiled – another small step.

Politicians running for office are looking for one end of a binary outcome – to win. But there are numerous small, measurable actions needed to get to that outcome. Doors need to be knocked, information sessions held, fliers distributed, calls made, polls conducted. There needs to be focus on high turnout for locked-in voters, and unearthing the priorities of swing voters. The data from all the regional campaign offices needs to be pulled together to make sure candidate teams can view the complete election landscape – who has increased their polling numbers and how? Who has forgotten about the youth voter turnout? What can the primary results tell us about what voter activists should do next?

In professional services BD, we are also looking for a binary outcome – you win the work, or you don't. But, in order to achieve that outcome, there are many small steps to get there that need to be taken and measured. *How many doors were knocked? How many business development meetings happened?* In order to have a humming World-class growth engine, a firm needs to measure what matters and what they can manage – the things they know will drive their desired outcomes. They also need to provide visibility into growth data to ensure smooth business operations.

Outcome Goals versus Process Goals

In political campaigns, individual successes don't win elections on their own. Things like improving turnout in two districts by knocking on twice as many doors as your opponent nationwide, or broadening your donor base by hosting more donor events, or shifting the majority of the college vote into your camp by recruiting more university campaign managers are individual pieces of a campaign. They are measurable goals that matter. *Collectively,* these are the metrics that lead to a win. Herein lies the difference between process goals and outcome goals. A process goal is the activity or discrete action, often improved through repetition, that enables a specific outcome. For example, a process goal for losing weight might be to walk every day for 30 minutes. An outcome goal is the desired end result, say, to lose 15 pounds. The trap many fall into is putting undue emphasis on the outcome goal (I'm focused on losing 15 pounds!) and not enough time into the process goals (to lose 15 pounds I need to walk regularly, eat three servings of vegetables a day, and cut out processed snacks), the things you can actually *manage* to reach the intended outcome.

In professional services sales, the same is often true. Firms spend a lot of their time focused on outcome (backward-looking) metrics like top-line growth, while not looking enough at leading metrics – ones they can actually manage – such as cost of sales or number of sales meetings. This decision around what KPIs matter most is a constant challenge. Why?

1. **Too many metrics** – "You can't possibly pay attention to all that stuff and hold people accountable – it's just unrealistic," says Paul Boulanger, former group operating officer of Strategy and Consulting at Accenture, reflecting on the challenge of the "25-metric" scorecard. The explosion of data, reports, and dashboards means everything from the number of sales calls made in a year, to pipeline, to website clicks, to new opportunities, to time-to-close, to trends over time across all of these, can be measured and tracked. Many of the people we talked to have sales reports with 15–25 different metrics. The problem is not a lack of things to measure. The problem is that firms have too many metrics to weed through and lack clarity around which are the most important and why.

2. **Too many data sources** – The marketing team has a set of numbers it measures quarter over quarter, and that number is different than the industry group which pulled a report from four weeks ago that looks different from the Excel sheet used by the infrastructure services practice that was pulled on Monday. When people come to a meeting with different spreadsheets, credibility and clarity around what is happening in the business decreases. Meetings are spent debating data accuracy rather than making decisions around how to impact those numbers.

Measuring What Matters

3. **Bad data** – The metrics and measurements used to evaluate progress and inform decisions are only as good as the inputs informing those numbers. Many professional services firms suffer from bad data – either a lack of data being put into CRM, data that is out-of-date, or data that is simply inaccurate.

4. **No visibility** – Without making performance visible, teams can hide behind their individual spreadsheets, slicing and dicing the data in their favor. One of the fastest ways to motivate salespeople is through peer pressure – everyone wants to be a leader among their peer group, and no one wants to be publicly behind. Making data more broadly visible will also drive better quality data, holding teams and individuals to public account for what is shared with the broader firm.

When leveraged appropriately, metrics can be a powerful tool to guide the firm and make decisions, but good data requires discipline and the consistent and *accurate* input of data into a widely used CRM. World-class firms don't just measure progress, they measure what they can manage – metrics that give them directional visibility, hopefully up and to the right.

The Perfect Balance: Utilization

Three minutes a year.

When Walt was running Accenture's North America business, he said it was a well-known joke that "we were perfectly staffed for about *three minutes* a year." Utilization is the holy grail in professional services, as firms look to drive EBITDA margin. But getting this right is a challenge. In professional services, sales cycles are longer and less predictable than in other industries, and your main input of expert labor hours are harder to scale up and down quickly. The line between being overstaffed (and losing money) and understaffed (and eroding quality of delivery) is often paper thin. At small firms, the timing of landing just one or two contracts might make the difference between a great year and closing your doors. At large firms, having an overflowing bench that is eroding margins will make for unhappy shareholders, while having zero bench and an inability to take on key projects will drive potential clients to competitors. Firms cannot grow without the resources and visibility to do so.

This is why firms need to measure growth metrics that will ultimately impact utilization. Growth cannot happen if firms don't have the resources to deliver quality work, allowing them to build their community of raving fans. And firms cannot prepare for growth and ensure they have the right resources without visibility into performance and likely outcomes.

Predictability is hard – and it is really hard at scale. But getting *closer* to accurate is not impossible, and it is what will set you free in ensuring margin while driving growth. Turn those three minutes a year of utilization perfection into three months, and you've got the golden ticket. In this chapter, we'll talk about the critical forward-looking metrics that can help move the needle on predicting the future.

* * *

Love-Hate Relationship: The CRM

A new associate at PIE once asked Jacob about the biggest professional mistake he's ever made. Jacob's response was, "Forgetting to put everything I know into the CRM." CRM (customer relationship management) tools are some of the most important technology tools in a professional services firm – and also cause the most frustration and eye rolling among partners. Having up-to-date information in one place across the firm about current projects,

(continued)

(continued)

whom you're working with, what's in the pipeline, timing and likelihood of renewals, wins, and losses – this is what can really lead a firm to *far* more than three minutes a year of predictability. There are a number of reasons CRM input doesn't happen as readily as we'd like:

- **Not enough time:** It's laborious in a seller-doer model; tracking sales activity feels like a waste of time for a busy partner who has all the information in their head. They have the next meeting set, they know the person well – why does anyone else care? Can't they just share the good news once the new work is locked in?

- **Loss of control:** It gives some control of the relationship to marketing. As we've outlined in previous chapters, we often hear something along the lines of, "I am not putting any information into CRM because I'm not about to let marketing spam my contact with pointless newsletters." This is, of course, an adoption and change management issue, as well as evidence of the need for clearer alignment between sales and marketing. It is not a system problem, because controlled outflow of information to a client is easily adjustable in any CRM system that has been updated in the last few decades.

- **No clear value:** The value is not clearly understood by practitioners. CRM systems are often sold internally as, "We need to track all of our information." That feels pedantic and wasteful. Consider what is actually on the line: dynamic pricing based on competitive win rate, reduced cost of sales by properly tracking former customers, mapping opportunities for cross-selling, and dramatically improved ability to manage the business in a profitable way when taking into account realization and utilization data. Done properly, it's a crystal ball for your business that allows specific levers to be pulled in order to run a profitable, growing business. That is often the right place to start: communicating that proper implementation will make you more money as a partner in this firm. Too frequently, firms spend time talking about *what* needs to be done, not what *impact* it will have if done properly.

- **Troglodyte leadership:** If leaders in the firm don't support the implementation and utilization of this technology, it will fail. Secure leadership buy-in, identify Return on Objective (ROO), and measure relentlessly. ROO is a helpful mechanism to identify all of the value streams of a technology, not just a hard dollars and cents evaluation.

* * *

Jump 1 – Entrepreneurial to Tactical

Early-stage firms manage most of their firms' growth metrics in their heads, spending time and attention primarily on outcome metrics – namely, revenue and profit margin. As these firms mature, so must the metrics by which they measure themselves (Figure 13.1). There are three key actions firms must take to begin the journey toward World-class in their use of metrics to drive better decision-making:

1. Invest in a CRM tool.

At the Tactical stage, firms are (often reluctantly) investing in a CRM system. It's a simple equation for most entrepreneurs, how in the world can this system that just tracks the people I already know drive ROI anywhere near the cost of the system? Too often, it's the other side of the coin that creates the burning platform: the team misses a huge opportunity because they don't have data. All of a sudden the

STAGES OF MATURITY

FIRM CHARACTERISTICS

ENTREPRENEURIAL
- No real CRM; client and prospect information held in individual spreadsheets
- No formal metrics or goals; firm led by gut feel, with leadership just thinking about: Are y/y sales up? Are we profitable?
- Lack of predictability; firm is as likely to have a down year as a windfall year
- Use of technology is not standardized; everyone uses different tools without any major technology investment

TACTICAL
- Measure lagging indicators (e.g. revenue, renewal rates, EBITDA margin, revenue/partner, win rates)
- Firm makes an investment in CRM technology; rudimentary, input standards aren't clear, and adoption is mediocre
- Decentralized goal-setting and metrics, with no central visibility
- Pipeline tracked, but with poor data; it cannot be used to drive hiring and utilization decisions
- A few investments are made in tools to help BD, but they aren't well adopted so no one can really tell what works
- Unsuccessful testing of tools to do "sales" for you (e.g., mass AI-generated emails ignoring ICP)

LEADING
- Clear expectations are set around the use of the firm's CRM and there is consistent use by the whole team (if sometimes begrudgingly)
- CRM ensures pipeline visibility for forecasting and seamless reporting
- Firm measures leading indicators (e.g. real-time utilization, sales capacity-to-revenue goals, trends in meetings, and time-to-close)
- Metrics are aligned to firm goals
- Centralized and shared data provides visible metrics and accountability
- Technology is leveraged for internal efficiency and skills development

WORLD-CLASS
- The CRM is a powerful source of data for decision-making across the business; companywide adoption and consistent use are an expectation
- Firm is managed with data and CRM is used as the basis for all key decisions, including investments in growth
- Metrics enable leadership to accurately predict what will happen and manage behavior to impact the outcome
- A dynamic dashboard is the single source of truth that aggregates all relevant firm data
- A continuous improvement mindset ensures data is captured and is measuring the right things
- New technologies are tested, adopted, and evangelized by leadership in a thoughtful and consistent way, ensuring the firm is ahead of the curve and only using tools that will benefit the whole growth team

Figure 13.1 Firm characteristics at each stage of maturity – data, metrics, and technology.

$10K CRM investment is irrelevant in the face of fumbling that $2M opportunity. For one reason or another, firms start to utilize a CRM, though imperfectly. They realize they can now answer some basic questions (though with only moderate accuracy):

- Who are our clients?
- Who are we targeting to be our next round of clients?
- At what stage are our existing opportunities?

That's it. That's the list, and it is an actual game changer in terms of your business. This is what moves firms into the Tactical stage of maturity.

2. Begin to develop metric visibility and accountability.

Making the jump to Tactical means first having clear metrics to track and then checking in on those metrics on a regular basis. When done well, metrics are clearly aligned to company strategy. Leadership will work with practice leads to identify what to track, and then revisit those metrics annually. The proliferation of spreadsheets and metrics reporting is often a hallmark of a Tactical firm that discovers both the power (and the problems) with measuring what matters. A few examples of key metrics firms begin to track include:

- Average project price
- Most successful revenue generator
- Pipeline
- Average sales cycle
- Sales by industry or service line
- Win/loss rates

Many of these metrics are lagging, meaning they show what *has* happened rather than helping predict what *will* happen. They are also hard to manage. While it is interesting to know that the average project price is $100K, that metric tells you nothing about why that is the case or what types of projects sell for more than that, or how much it costs the firm to sell a project more than $100K, or what you might change to increase that number. But this is a starting point of learning about your business and will enable you to make decisions and move toward more useful metrics as you mature.

3. Set pipeline goals and track your progress.

Nothing (or, at most, a random smatterings of things) is measured in the Entrepreneurial phase. This results in a pipeline that is neither accurate nor helpful for predicting revenue. Moving up the maturity curve requires firms to implement greater discipline around what goes into their pipeline in CRM, what qualifies each stage of the pipeline, and perhaps most importantly, what eliminates something from the pipeline. Tactical firms begin to recognize the power of a good pipeline and invest time and resources to ensure it accurately reflects the opportunity landscape as much as possible. Critically, they begin to understand what the pipeline should look like in order for them to meet their goals around realized revenue growth. For Camille Clemons at Cohen & Co, a strong pipeline is one that is at least 3X your revenue goal based on understanding her firm's close rates and growth targets. This forces business development leaders to not only enter opportunities into their pipeline but ensures the pipeline can power realistic revenue growth for the firm. Michael Restivo shares from his experience at Kyndryl, this number might be as large as 5X or 10X – it depends on your firm's sales cycle. As firms move up the maturity curve, they begin to track what this multiplier *needs* to be in order to hit or exceed expectations.

* * *

232

The Growth Engine

Avoid the Easy Button – The Tech Temptation Trap

The Tactical stage is when many firms make this mistake. They now have a CRM with a bunch of client and prospect data – why not get after it in the most efficient way, by blasting out mass emails? They try to take advice from the old Staples commercial and smash the "easy button." AI-driven outreach tools have given us the ability to broadcast (efficiently reach out to a big audience) while making it feel somewhat like an individual email. The problem is that it doesn't *truly* feel like personalized communication. Says Wade Dokken, CEO of WealthVest, "For new folks, I struggle with a lack of appreciation for relationship building and their reliance or dependence on non-relationship marketing activity. They often use pre-templated emails and do everything by the book. But we are in the friend building business and that needs to precede everything else. If you don't establish trust and relationship, then you are swimming upstream."

Most executives can recognize a mass email when it lands in their inbox, even if it includes a paltry attempt at personalization. Take the last three cold outreach emails that Jacob received:

1. Jacob, your take on professional services really resonated with me...

2. Jacob, your take on professional services really resonated with me...

3. Jacob, your take on professional services really resonated with me...

Three different messages in a row that started with the EXACT same AI prompt, never mind the irony that resides in those 10 words. If you believed in Jacob's "take" on professional services

(continued)

(continued)

sales, you would never send an AI-written message that barely scraped the web for any information. The appeal is clear: send out 10,000 messages, get 100 replies, 30 meetings, and three projects. That's a low-cost outreach strategy that could work, but it erodes an advisor's ability to become trusted. It should only be applied to commoditized services with a large target market. In no way should this be an approach toward winning "bet-the-company" projects or building meaningful relationships. If a person is selling cleaning services for your office building, great technique; if a person is selling a strategic overhaul of your business, it looks flippant at best, obtuse at worst.

* * *

Jump 2 – Tactical to Leading

The move to Leading goes well beyond the procurement of a CRM tool; a culture of performance measurement and firm-wide visibility begins to emerge, with a focus on leading metrics that drive accountability, profitability, and decision-making. Here are the key actions to move toward Leading:

1. Set the tone at the top.

The firm has technology-savvy leaders who talk the talk but also walk the walk. Rainmakers use the CRM system and highlight this best practice by utilizing the CRM's reporting features in public facing meetings. One comment from a leader or senior rainmaker saying, "Oh, I don't use the system, let me pull up my personal notes" and you've lost any chance of getting the team onboard.

2. Demonstrate CRM wins.

It only takes a few. "Did you hear about Frank and Teresa? Apparently, they had both been talking to a few people at Occidental Petroleum. They noticed this via the new CRM tool, and they were able to link the opportunities and present a cohesive strategy case to the entire leadership team. Those two are going to be receiving a nice bonus on this opportunity." Granted, it never happens exactly like that; it's usually much more of a slow burn. That's why it's hard. But the wins do exist, and they need to be celebrated and broadly shared to drive widespread adoption of the CRM. Find your rainmakers who can evangelize the tool to their peers, who will be eager not to be left behind.

3. Align metrics with firm goals.

Leading firms allow strategy to dictate metrics, not the other way around. "Every practice group, every CEO, every leader, has a different way to look at it," says Koree Khongphand-Buckman at Foley & Lardner. "For example, my former firm focused on realization and hitting somewhere above 83%. At Foley this year, the thing we're focused on is growing practice groups. How many more practice groups have we introduced to the client with billable hours of 100 or more? We measure how many practice groups we have added to a client and track the increase in collections; this tells us we're expanding across our clients in a different way. We have thousands of clients, and our goal is to really concentrate on growing relationships and adding more practice groups rather than spraying all over the place." Metrics should directly reflect the strategic goals of the firm and should be shared broadly so everyone can see how the company is performing against what you've said matters most.

4. Begin tracking leading metrics.

In addition to unique metrics aligned specifically to your strategy, as outlined above, Leading firms shift from tracking lagging metrics (did we grow last year?) to looking at leading indicators that can help predict future revenues and profitability. Here are the **six leading metrics** that teams should have on their dashboard. While each metric may not be extremely meaningful on its own, the combination can help you understand where you have room to improve your business development strategy:

1. **Cost of Sales:** Any management consulting firm would recommend to clients that they understand their cost structure in detail, yet many firms fail to measure or manage the second largest cost in their business – business development. What we're describing as cost of sales is the dollar equivalent of time and resources required to drive business development for the company. It is the single most valuable metric, and it is also the least used by most professional services firms. Understanding the cost of sales helps firms determine how much is being spent on service development, how much work is being given away (rather than billed), how much work goes into marketing materials, and where to direct business development resources most effectively and efficiently. One of the key reasons current client expansion is such an efficient (and prevalent) avenue to growth is that the cost of sales is lower – you generally need a fraction of the number of meetings to lock in work, as you're not trying to scale both trust and credibility in an unknown account.

   Capturing a true cost of sales number can be challenging. There is often a lag between the initial business development investment and the return on that investment. However, a

236

The Growth Engine

robust understanding is often worthwhile in shaping a firm's long-term growth strategy and better understanding around the profitability of various efforts. Consider a firm pursuing work in the utility sector. The firm allocates two partners to drive growth in this sector; however, only 30% of the work they are doing is billable. Twenty percent of their time is spent developing newer services, and half of their time is focused on client development. Say this cost of sales for two partners equates to $150,000 per partner per year. The initial cost of sales is high, given the average contract for a new utility client is less than $500K annually. However, once a new utility account becomes a client, that client continues to renew work year over year for the next 10 years, thereby reducing the relative cost of sales via renewal. After reviewing this data, the firm determines the cost of sales for a utility client is actually quite low and therefore can plan to double its dedicated sales resources to capitalize on growth opportunities in the utility space. While it might barely break even in year one, the years that follow can be immensely profitable.

Clarity around cost of sales also enables firms to rearrange resources more effectively. For example, a firm might discover that partners are only billing 30% of their time because 20% of their time is spent putting together proposals and preparing SOWs. A firm would be wise to allocate lower cost resources at a rate of $50/hour rather than $500/hour to manage those more administrative tasks, thus freeing partners up for more billable work. Without a clear understanding around how much a firm is spending on all its business development inputs – particularly time of its partners – resource decisions like this become a guessing game.

237

Measuring What Matters

Michael McNeal emphasizes his focus on improving cost of sales tracking at Centric Consulting. He notes, "We haven't historically done a good enough job of measuring time spent on deals. We're starting to focus on how to capture all that BD time, not only by BD people but by the supporting team members and understand how much time we put into each pursuit and the stage at which it closed. This will help us truly understand the cost to close." As firms mature, the ability to accurately track this "cost to close" enables them to make smarter decisions around where to place their business development bets and how to more effectively allocate their growth resources.

2. **Competitive Win Rate (CWR):** Competitive win rate is the percent of competitive work a firm actually wins, based on dollars won rather than number of projects won. Ideally, for Leading firms, this number should land somewhere between 60% and 80%. If it's below 60%, a firm is likely spending an outsized amount of money and time on proposals that don't make sense or that the firm is unlikely to win. On the flip side, if the number is above 80%, it could be an indication that the firm is not pricing high enough.

When Walt was working for Accenture in the ASPAC region, he noticed an interesting trend in CWR over the course of six months. His region covered eight different markets including Thailand, Vietnam, and Singapore, and the firm had a consistent win rate across those regions of about 70%. However, that number started to drop, eventually falling to 40% despite teams feeling like they were working harder than ever. After some digging, Walt and his team discovered that someone had made a mistake in the pricing tool teams were using to price proposals, adding in a double tax that increased the pricing on a standard proposal by 10–12%. Teams had inadvertently been pricing proposals too high, which had led to a decrease in projects won. Clarity on CWR helped fix the pricing tool to reverse the downward trend. Better visibility around competitive win rate not only ensures firms make good decisions around pricing but also informs where firms should focus their growth strategy (i.e., where are we winning vs. not) and target resources to drive profitability.

3. **Percent of sales sole source:** We all love sole source work – a procurement method where a single entity is the only one that can provide a service or product. It's great to avoid competing when we don't have to! But, if sole source work is 100% of your work, that is likely an indicator that you're not tapping into places you could be. Few, if any, *growing* firms truly have zero competition. If you're never competing for any work, you're likely either choosing not to grow or growing very slowly. For a top – and growing – professional service firm, a good goal is to have 40–60% of work be sole source. If the percentage is higher than 60%, this often indicates that a firm is missing an opportunity to sell more work because they are failing to compete in another area.

4. **Number of sales meetings:** Number of sales meetings is often a strong leading indicator for growth, and it is a number that firms can manage much more effectively than pure sales numbers. If you're not having conversations, you're not going to win work. If you're not knocking on doors, you're not getting to know voters. While results matter most, number of sales calls creates more opportunity for luck and can be an indicator of the health of a sales team. A partner might have one big win and "outperform" their peers, but if that was the only conversation they were pursuing, they won't sustain that

growth success long term. On the flip side, if another partner had 100 sales meetings in the last six months but sold nothing, it would be a flag to dig into why they have been unable to progress or close deals.

5. **Weighted and dated pipeline:** Clarity around what is in a firm's pipeline and the percentage of that pipeline that is likely to convert into sales based on stage enables growth leaders to better target business development efforts. Most CRM tools utilize stages for sales pipeline. For example, perhaps a firm has $2M in stage three opportunities and knows that typically 60% of stage three opportunities convert into won work within six months. This allows them to predict and manage the resources needed to best deliver that work and when it will be needed. However, the same firm may notice an anemic set of stage one opportunities, with only $1M in the pipeline. If only 15% of stage one opportunities typically move through stages two, three, and four to closed won within six months, the firm can use this information to focus partner energy around filling the pipeline and increasing meetings to ensure new work coming in six months from now equates to more than $150,000.

6. **Percentage of business from biggest clients:** New logos are exciting, but as emphasized throughout this book, existing clients present the greatest growth opportunity and often have a much lower cost of sales, making them significantly more profitable targets for growth. Mature firms capitalize on this growth potential much more effectively than Entrepreneurial firms and realize an increase over time in the percentage of work from key clients. Tracking this year over year helps guide firms to direct more resources to existing clients until 60–80% of business is generated through existing client work.

5. Use win-loss metrics to fine-tune business development efficiency.

When building a World-class growth engine, firms teach partners that not all growth is created equal. Growth is good, but high-margin, low-cost-of-acquisition growth is better. The best firms teach partners that winning every bid might mean you are charging too little. Losing every bid might mean you are just throwing Hail Marys without regard to where your practice has relationships and the right to win. World-class firms teach their partners how to use pipeline analysis to drive profitable growth.

6. Use shared data to drive behavior.

Rather than every practice lead showing up to quarterly meetings with their own deck or spreadsheet, Leading firms use one source of truth – a centralized, shared dashboard – to ensure teams can access the same, up-to-date data concurrently. Shared data also ensures accountability around data accuracy and inputs. If a partner often shows up to meetings bragging about the $10 million in their pipeline but none of that is reflected on the shared dashboard, their partners will let them know that the firm won't be ready to staff that work when it comes in as there's been no visibility – if indeed the pipeline is real.

Mike McDaniel, now at Conduent, recognized this problem when he moved from Accenture to DXC. "What I found in our sales operations at DXC was many different types of platforms, and that led to inconsistencies around how different practice leads were measured and our ability to drive things like win rates," said McDaniel. "What I wanted to get to was three things: the processes, the systems, and a consistent way to measure overall performance of our salespeople. We put controls in place around all three of those and then had a roadmap for technology in terms of how we were going to improve overall sales operations in order to get win rates up to where they should be."

241

Measuring What Matters

Shared, consistent data ensures leadership has better information off of which to make decisions to drive outcomes, and partners are held accountable when it comes to data entry. A simple solution to separate smoke from true sales fire? If the data to support things like win rates or sales meetings isn't in the CRM, then partners do not get credit for it.

And it's not just visibility for visibility's sake – shared data drives behavior change (more on this in Chapter 14). Michael Restivo has found that data shared across peers is critical to driving behavior. He argues that sales leaders should regularly be measured against their peers. "We have a report that comes out and it's a stack ranking. Here's your top 25%. Here's your top 50%. Here's your top 75%, and then you've got the least effective contributors. That drives healthy competition internally and it makes people want to do well. Maybe Susan is doing far better than Peter on closing opportunities recently; Peter could ask Susan, 'What's the method to your madness?' Competition drives funnel, it drives forecast, and it drives profit. You also need to compliment the ones that do well and celebrate wins of all shapes and sizes, giving people accolades in front of their peers. This is what makes people perform."

At ERM, Walt hosted a monthly meeting with all partners and reserved time at the end for two special awards: the "Can Kicker Heroes" and the "Sludge Slingers." The "Can Kicker" award went to the partners who kept pushing out the close dates every time an opportunity was supposed to close. The "Sludge Slinger" recognized the partner with opportunities sitting in stage one year over year. Needless to say, these weren't actually "awards" – they were a way to acknowledge bad behavior in a humorous way. Pretty quickly, people began to eliminate the sludge from the pipeline and close more opportunities (even if lost) rather than continuing to kick the can. Soon, the pipeline accuracy began to look a lot better. Walt was using data to not just track behavior, but to change it.

* * *

Jump 3 – Leading to World-class

World-class firms are data-driven machines – and they can be because their data accuracy is World-class. They measure the things that matter, and they are unafraid to course correct when they learn that something isn't working, or teams aren't performing. Culturally, every part of the organization – including those doing business development – see the value in building the firm on a basis of data accuracy and do their part to ensure this remains true. They use data to understand what resources – most importantly, people – are needed to achieve their growth goals, and they create that capacity. World-class firms take four key actions:

1. Develop an understanding of the sales capacity you need to achieve your growth goals and create that capacity in your team.

Understanding sales capacity requires firms to track two things: partners' unbilled time and sales capability. World-class firms have built the muscle to both understand and act on this information.

Step 1 is asking: "How much capacity do we have?"

Step 2 is asking: "How much capacity do we need to grow at the rate we desire?"

Let's dig into each of these:

Step 1: *Understanding your current BD capacity.*

Your current sales capacity is a combination of the following:

1. **Number of people** working on business development in some way. This is pretty straightforward and should include anyone who is responsible for renewing work, expanding clients, or winning new logo work – those bringing revenue into the firm.

2. The **capability level** of those people. We know everyone is not the same when it comes to sales capability and experience. Consider the following scale from 0–4. This is what we like to use, but you can develop one that makes the most sense for your firm.

- **0:** No sales experience.

- **1:** Experience securing renewals of existing work; limited or no experience leading a sale to new clients or sales of different services.

- **2:** Experience growing current accounts; perhaps experience selling certain services, but a lack of experience selling new or different work outside of their comfort zone to clients.

- **3:** Ample experience winning work with both current clients and new logos. Comfortable with tough negotiations and complex sales. Success in partnership with colleagues to drive sales.

- **4:** Your firm's best growth drivers. Comfortable in any sales setting, looking at the big picture, and putting together creative and complex solutions for potential clients. Excellent negotiation skills. Great at pulling in others across the firm to drive success.

3. The amount of **time** your people spend on business development. This is the percentage of their time spent on growing the firm (often a good portion of their non-billed time).

Consider the example in Figure 13.2. In this example, Natalie provides the firm with a sales capacity of 4, because she is a top business developer at the firm (capability level 4), and she has 100% of her time focused on growth – she no longer services clients directly as a billable employee. Most firms are short on the level-4 Natalies – they aren't created overnight. Hayden, on the other hand, is a growing business

ESTIMATED SALES CAPACITY AVAILABLE			
PARTNER	**CAPABILITY LEVEL**	**% TIME ON SALES**	**TOTAL CAPACITY**
Natalie	4	100%	4
Jaqueline	2.5	50%	1.25
Hayden	2	40%	0.8
Addie	1	20%	0.2
Colleen	1	20%	0.2
Avi	.05	10%	0.05
Jordan	1	20%	0.2

Total Available 6.7

Figure 13.2 Sample sales capability chart to determine available sales capacity.

developer who provides 0.8 of sales capacity for the firm. He has a capability level of 2 (has taken over leadership of a few accounts and been successful at expanding their work), and he is still billable for 60% of that time, leaving 40% available for growth activities.

If Tactical firms begin to loosely think about sales capacity and Leading firms start attempting to manage it, World-class firms optimize it to drive meaningful, predictable growth. The most mature firms map their sales capacity to their goal, toggling rainmaker time up or down based on individual capabilities and the capacity needed to grow.

In tandem with understanding your current capacity, map out the capacity you believe you *require* in order to achieve your growth goals. Getting to this number is never going to be a perfect science, but accurate, real-time, centralized data can get you really close. Figure 13.3 shows how to build out an understanding of the capacity you require, and includes the following dimensions:

- **Type of sale:** Organize your avenues to winning new work by your different types of sales; typically it will look like this:

245

Measuring What Matters

- Easy renewal

- Tough renewal

- New project (with current client)

- New project with net *new account*

- Assign a **capability level** required to close each type of sale.

- Determine the **total capability hours needed.** This is a combination of the total hours needed (often helpful to break down by hours/week over total number of weeks) times the capability level ($B \times C \times D$).

- Determine the number of projects you need to win across each type of sale to hit your growth goals (F) and divide that by your win rate to understand the **total number of opportunities you need in your pipeline** to hit your close goal.

- **Total capability hours needed** to achieve your goals with each type of sale equates to total hours times total opportunities ($E \times H$).

- Finally, we get to **total capacity needed** by dividing total capability hours by 2080 – the hours of a typical 52-week year.

	SALES CAPACITY REQUIRED								
TYPE OF SALE	CAPABILITY LEVEL REQUIRED	WEEKS	HOURS PER WEEK	CAPABILITY HOURS NEEDED PER OPPORTUNITY	NUMBER OF SALES NEEDED TO CLOSE	WIN RATE	TOTAL OPPORTUNITIES IN PIPELINE NEEDED	TOTAL CAPABILITY HOURS NEEDED	CAPACITY (FTE) NEEDED
Easy renewal	1	6	4	24	80	94%	85	2,040	1.0
Tough renewal	2	6	4	48	25	83%	30	1,440	0.7
New project	2	16	2	64	10	50%	20	1,280	0.6
New account	3	26	2	156	10	13%	80	12,480	6.0
								Total Needed	8.3

Figure 13.3 Sample sales capacity chart to determine sales resources needed to hit growth goals.

In this example, we can see that the firm *requires* a capacity of 8.3 (Figure 13.3) to meet their growth goals, but they currently have a capacity of just 6.7 (Figure 13.2). When you find that you're under-capacity, there are a few options to fill the gap:

1. Re-allocate existing resources to business development, either by adding more sellers or giving your best rainmakers more time to sell.

2. Invest in the development of your rainmaker bench to improve their capability. Increasing someone from level 2 to level 3 can make a big difference. This pays off but also takes time. New rainmakers are not made overnight.

3. Reconsider your goals for each type of sale, taking into account the capability level needed and win rate of each. If you only have a few people who have the capability to win new accounts, but far more who are good at current client expansion, perhaps you focus on winning more new projects with current clients this year while you develop those people into new logo winners, bringing down your required capacity to meet what you have.

Sales capacity modeling is a bit like predicting the weather. While rarely perfect, the most successful firms in the world harness their data to ensure they know when to bring a few extra umbrellas and who should carry them, putting the right resources against realistic goals.

2. Pilot and invest in new technologies that can enable your business development team, without over-relying on technology.

World-class firms aren't laggards when it comes to technology. They are curious and hungry to embrace enabling technologies, while judiciously evaluating the *right* investments – ones that will have an impact and that the firm will embrace. "Ignore technology at your peril" says Walt frequently. The best firms lean in – they don't lean out.

These days, Walt is as tech-forward as they come. He rode in a Waymo before many of his friends had even heard of it, he outfitted his Mercedes sprinter van with all the best technology for his cross-country road trips, and he lights up when talking about new tools PIE can use to improve visibility and performance.

Interestingly, this wasn't always the case. Early in his consulting days, he was dubious about whether technology could *really* help the sales team. "No way," he recalls thinking. "There is no way – even if you invest a boatload of money in this new CRM – that anyone is *actually* going to put their client data in there. Why would they share it?!" Walt has never been happier to be wrong. "When everyone has the same data in real-time, it's a total game-changer. You can see – for real – what is working and who is winning. The only way to do that is with technology – with a centralized CRM and dashboards that show you what is happening in the firm *right now*."

As we've outlined, the tool is only as good as its inputs. In World-class firms, management leads the charge in evangelizing its use, using it themselves, and sharing real examples of wins that come from the data. At PIE, our ability to calculate win rates across Stages 1, 2, and 3 in our CRM has opened the team's eyes to where we need to focus: pulling in additional resources to move opportunities from Stage 1 to Stage 2. The same holds true for other types of technology investments. Every firm will have key learnings – and new ones over time – when they focus on letting technology enable their business.

World-class firms also deftly avoid the "tech temptation trap" – an over-reliance on technology for things that ought not be automated can do more damage than good. We've spent much of this book talking about the importance of relationships – of human connection. Start trying to replace real conversations with technology and you've got a problem. Should you leverage available tools that can record practice sales calls and give you feedback? Yes! This is *enabling* your team and making them better at those real conversations. Should you create an AI avatar of yourself to take meetings for you and try to build relationships on your behalf? No. That's probably not who we're hiring for our most important challenges. ...

World-class firms have a team dedicated to identifying, piloting, and investing in the tools that will enable the team to meet its growth goals and stay ahead of competition. They introduce new technology when they know it can be easily adopted by the firm and provide real ROI. They constantly improve, while avoiding the easy button.

* * *

AI in Professional Services

The tech tools we use to drive business in professional services today likely look very different than the tools we used 10 years ago – and the tools we will need 10 years (or even 10 months!) in the future. Technology often moves faster than human's ability to use it and our take on what "good" looks like will be eclipsed by whatever new innovation hits the market tomorrow. However, the emergence of AI, and its impact across the world of business, is impossible to ignore.

According to Allie K. Miller, CEO of Open Machine and F500 AI advisor and angel investor with roots at AWS and IBM, the business landscape is on the verge of a major transformation. Some companies will hold tightly to traditional business models and refuse to incorporate AI into their processes. Some companies will only allow for AI and automation to touch 25–40% of their business, with a narrow focus on repetitive tasks to allow humans to thrive by enabling AI to remove the "bottom of the barrel ick." Then there will be brand-new professional services firms, or small zones of research within existing firms, where they completely

(continued)

(continued)

reinvent themselves to be AI-first firms for sales, for research, for marketing, and it's the firms in this third category that will start to eclipse those in one and two.

As a firm looking to build a growth engine, how do you capitalize on this transformation? Join group three.

- **Allocate budget for AI.** According to Allie at the time of the interview, most firms should allocate 2–5% of their annual revenue to AI efforts. This budget could be allocated to internal AI testing or AI providers that can get you faster access to tools and products.

- **Create an AI Task Force and Frontier Unit.** Having a dedicated group of leaders focused on AI ensures your firm continues to experiment with AI – this group should also nominate AI ambassadors to enable the requisite change management and launch a Frontier Unit thinking about your business 2+ years out. Says Allie, "The Frontier Unit is a powerhouse team specifically built to rapidly discover, evaluate, and unlock the highest-value opportunities in AI and emerging technologies. Executive leaders who implement a Frontier Unit can bypass traditional corporate hurdles – bureaucratic inertia, procurement delays, and restrictive data policies – that usually slow innovation down. Positioned with enough separation to move quickly and decisively, yet closely linked to core business priorities, this elite team draws the company's best and brightest. Establishing a Frontier Unit positions enterprises to remain competitive, impactful, and at the forefront of their industries."

- **Invest in change management.** According to McKinsey, for every dollar spent on AI, firms should expect to spend $5 on change management (Viswa et al., 2025). Allie agrees, "It's such an overlooked piece of it. I would recommend any consulting firm working in AI immediately spin up a change management practice integrated with AI because that is what those businesses also need. It's a constant arms race between how fast big companies can move and how much gravity the pull of past customers, past technology, past habits, and past expertise exert."

- **Dedicate time to build repeatable processes.** Too often, companies over-invest in the tools (equipping everyone in the company with access to CoPilot) and underinvest in enabling their teams to use those tools to run meetings, to review contracts, to approve invoices, or to map out 1,000 simulations of how your next supply chain plan might pan out.

- **Experiment with different pricing schemes.** Allie argues that the professional services business model is about to be flipped on its head. Historically, professional services firms have used billable hours to price work, but AI is disrupting that model both by augmenting traditional time spent on projects and billing by outcome, not time. Allie notes, "We are starting to see tools that are charged by *outcome* and charged in comparison to what a human would cost at that same scale. We will no longer be charged by seat, by consumption, or by hours." To compete, firms will need to adjust their business model accordingly and experiment with profitability models not reliant on billable time.

Where and how should World-class firms apply AI? AI typically starts with low value, high volume grunt work – things that are easily measured (example: generating preliminary lead lists from a series of pre-determined criteria or summarizing a prospective client's business performance over the last decade). Stathis Karaplios, co-founder and managing partner for EMBS, notes that with the help of AI, "You can react faster, you can get prepared to kick-off

(continued)

(continued)

meetings more easily, do more extensive research and quickly pull together information for a proposal."

Erin Michelle Connolly-Kriarakis, national marketing director at CohnReznick agrees, noting AI has helped her team build and execute their account-based marketing strategies more quickly. She says, "Our salespeople are getting meetings in hours because their messaging is targeted to exactly what they are researching and they are getting an almost immediate response back to their outreach." AI does not replace the human-to-human connection that underpins professional services sales, but it can accelerate the relationship-building process by equipping your team with better information and tools that allow you to be hyper-responsive and aligned to client needs.

Despite its many advantages, the infusion of AI presents new challenges around training and development. Notes David Fields of David A. Fields Consulting Group, "I can replace the lowest level of the consulting firm with AI but then how then do I get the next level up if I don't have anybody that's being trained in the basics? That's where I see a potential pitfall. I can now eliminate children but how do we get adults?"

According to Allie the key tipping point for the proliferation of AI in professional services firms will be whether humans legally and qualitatively put equal or more trust in AI systems than the consultants they work with, and by extension, also blame them when things go wrong.

For now, the high trust components are still human-to-human, and that is likely to remain foundational to professional services, even for AI-first World-class firms. So, use AI, learn from it, lean into it. But AI is not who a client calls at 2 o'clock in the morning on a Saturday when shit hits the fan – that's a phone call to a trusted advisor.

Part VII

Putting It All Together

Chapter 14

Managing Change

They didn't get married on the first date.

Andi met her husband, Nic, for the first time about 15 years ago. He was a colleague of both her brother, Spencer, and her friend, Michelle, so their paths crossed occasionally. Spencer and Michelle both mentioned every so often that they thought Andi and Nic would make a great match, but the timing was never right ...

... until it was. One spring, Andi ran into Nic at Blackbird, the busiest restaurant in Bozeman. During a brief chat, they realized that maybe – finally – the timing was right for them to go on a date. They had an amazing first dinner together at Saffron Table – where they talked for hours and connected over their shared love of butter chicken. As happens in a smaller community, during their dinner they ran into about three people they each knew. To make it an even smaller world, they realized on their first date that Nic was very good friends with Andi's new neighbors, Meg and Michael, so their second date turned into a double-date dinner at her neighbors' house.

By the time Andi introduced Nic to her close friends and the rest of her family, he was an easy sell – he already had fans in the form of Spencer, Michelle, Meg, and Michael. Andi flew to the Adirondacks with Nic to join his annual family reunion the first year they were together and got to meet the entire family (more than 60 people – his dad was one of seven). She worked hard to memorize their names and interests so that each year when they showed up on

Lake Minerva, they could pick up where they left off and she could keep getting to know everyone better.

By the time Andi and Nic got engaged – about two and a half years later – it was obvious for everyone. Of course that's what should happen! Family and friends were thrilled to attend their wedding and celebrate their partnership.

People need time to adjust to major changes – especially ones that impact them. We all want to feel like we have an understanding of – if not a decision in – the changes we experience. If Andi had met Nic on the street, married him the next day, and introduced him to all her friends and family as her new husband without any notice, things may not have gone as smoothly. While they would eventually come to love him, it would have been a much rockier road. Getting buy-in over time by communicating early and often with those who will experience a change will set you up for success – not just in marriage.

What Makes Change So Challenging?

"You can only change the behavior of people if those people really want to change," says Jose Bokhorst of Robert Walters Group.

Across a variety of industries and firms of all different sizes, the challenges around change management are prolific. Even when firms are aligned on where they want to go and have found agreement on how to get there, the process of actually making the change is painful. As we outlined in Chapter 1, there are five main reasons for this:

1. **Inertia:** External force is needed to act on us to drive change.

2. **Impatience:** We expect to see results far too soon and therefore give up far too soon.

3. **Sales Culture:** Getting a bunch of independent leaders to shift from running their own shows to putting on a show together is hard.

4. **Poor Communication:** Too often we start with the "what" and not the "why."

5. **Inconsistency:** We're not actually clear about what we're changing, or when or how we're changing it.

Principles of Good Change Management

As firms look to move up the maturity curve toward World-class, building a strong muscle around change management is essential (Figure 14.1). All the investments in new technology, structural reorganization to optimize business development, and fancy dashboards will fall flat if not supported with good change management principles.

1. Build it into the culture.

Successful change management begins with the people. Want to know in the hiring process whether someone is going to be comfortable with change? Try asking them about a time they had change forced upon them that they weren't excited about and how they reacted. Or consider giving them a situational example to walk through and tell you how they'd handle it. Most importantly, add this to your list of questions for your reference calls – their former colleagues or managers can tell you how well they coped with change.

Drawing on cultural norms can also be a powerful change agent. At PIE, we were eager to find a way to galvanize the team around on-time delivery of projects (realization) to improve our client experience and increase EBITDA. Too often, project deliverables bumped out by a few weeks or sometimes months, negatively

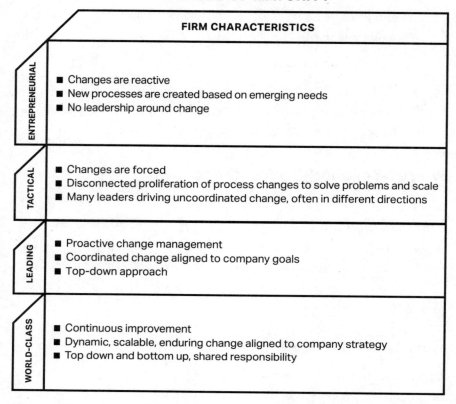

Figure 14.1 Firm characteristics at each stage of maturity – change management.

impacting realized revenue on the year. Simply saying "we need to drive EBITDA" during company meetings led to zero change. The team needed a different approach and started by printing out all of the expected and anticipated deliverables for the year, and publishing them publicly in the main conference room. If PIE delivered on each of those projects on time, they would beat their CFO's predicted forecast of only hitting 88% realization. This spurred some change. However, it wasn't until the CFO showed up to a company meeting donning a navy-blue baseball cap with white block lettering that read "EBITDAD" that company behavior really started to shift. Suddenly the message wasn't "drive EBITDA." Instead, the challenge became "PIE vs. EBITDAD" and PIE was not going to lose that competition.

2. Public recognition and peer accountability.

We spoke about the power of incentives in Chapter 10, and many of those same principles apply here. In addition to monetary and non-monetary incentives, one the most effective change management levers in professional services is the power of public recognition and peer accountability. Most business developers are competitors at heart, and drawing on that competitive nature capitalizes on both intrinsic and extrinsic motivation. When Walt was at ERM, he wanted to drive up revenue with current clients. He started calling people to congratulate them anytime they sold work to an existing client, even if it was a smaller project. He recalls, "That recognition was huge. No one had ever called any of them to say congratulations on a sale. Even when we lost a proposal to a current client, I'd recognize the efforts during our monthly key client meeting. That simple recognition led to more partners proposing work, and winning work, with current clients." Drawing on the voice of the client is another way to shift behavior, highlighting client testimonials or feedback that showcase the change you want to see.

At Edward Jones, Stuart Kaplan, general partner, Change and Transformation, explains how public recognition plays a critical role in driving their sales culture. Each year regional teams host all-hands gatherings to recognize top performers across many categories of client service. "At first when I saw this it seemed like getting a trophy on Little League Day," says Kaplan. "But as people would come up and get recognized for client service it dawned on me that these people are receiving the love and appreciation publicly of their peers. Sure, it might seem like a lot. But where else do you get that? When it is just a bonus showing up in your bank account no one ever sees that, but at these awards events it was miraculous seeing the way people react to the applause and adoration of their peers. It was remarkable!"

In addition to public recognition, sometimes a stick is required to prompt change. One firm we spoke to asks team members *not* to join their monthly BD meeting if they haven't hit their marks around actions that are in their control (e.g., updating their CRM in a timely fashion or following up on certain opportunities). Not being invited to a meeting everyone really values is a major blow.

3. Pilot, then implement, standardized processes paired with increased focus and discipline.

Process is often a dirty word in professional services because it feels like loss of freedom. And human nature being what it is, people do not like this. Resistance may come in many forms – sometimes passive aggressive and sometimes not so passive.

One way to navigate this resistance is to deploy informal leaders to help design and run pilots that can earn broader firm buy-in before widespread implementation. Employees are more likely to get onboard with something they helped design or implement. Pilots also ensure you catch road bumps early, before they become mountains. Jason Yarborough, now at Arcadia, learned this lesson while working at a company called Drift. Yarborough advises, "Don't try to train the whole team or the entire organization all at once. At Drift we wanted to drive a new process to more efficiently move leads through our pipeline. I spent the first few months working with the marketing team, and then the sales organization and finally spent a few months with the customer success organization rather than trying to scale and grow at all costs and get everything done at one time. It led to a much more comprehensive and wholesale change that actually stuck."

4. Communicate – over and over and over.

When Walt was at McKinsey, he wanted to introduce a new bonus system. He held virtual briefings for a couple of months. "I was shocked," he remembers. "Two months in, people were asking the same questions. I realized I had to say the same things many times. I kept holding the briefing sessions with an open invitation until no one showed up. In month five, when I started to give the highlights of the new system, a senior partner, and an early resister, spoke up. She said, 'Do we have to keep talking about this? Anybody who does not understand this by now is too dumb to work here.' That's when I knew I'd communicated enough. The message was clear, and the change would stick."

World-class firms have a consistent communication framework to guide change management, articulating change in a predictable, clear and consistent way. Employees know when to expect communication around change, what it will look like, and how to respond. Firms that want changes to stick also repeat the message multiple times and drive accountability through ongoing and regular check-ins to reinforce and increase the likelihood of adoption.

5. Time to absorb and process.

Andi's family took time to get to know Nic – over many meals, trips, and holiday gatherings. This is how you get comfortable with change. Expecting an entire business development function to adopt major change instantaneously is naive. Any change requires time to first process, execute, and then absorb. Don't rush things – especially the important things. While some changes are urgent, consider the cost/benefit of implementing more quickly versus having widespread buy-in.

6. Give and take.

Geese can fly independently, but it takes 50% more energy and they cannot go as far. So they fly in formation.

Even if what you need to do is seemingly obvious, getting buy-in from partners and senior leaders is often the most difficult. Mark Hawn, Managing Director, Americas at EY, advises that "Every time you take something away, you have to give something else." For instance, requiring proposals more than $1M to go through a formal approval process takes away partner independence – however, using this process gives the partner access to specialized accounting, marketing, graphics, and writing staff – a top priority for partners looking to win work.

To successfully move up the maturity curve you cannot remove all independence nor take away leadership. Consider what you can "give" if a change feels like something is being "taken." The goal is to get all the partners to "fly in formation."

7. Use the systems.

Krishnan Rajakapolan, CEO Emeritus of Heidrick & Struggles, drove a major transformation at H&S through the use of a new digital workflow platform. The new platform and processes made the work of senior recruiters significantly more efficient. Using the system required adherence to a standard approach for data gathering, documentation, and report creation. At first many partners resisted, as use was voluntary, and used manual work arounds. But over time, adoption grew to 100% as market demand and the revenue expectations could only be met one way – using the new system.

A CRM system can also be a very effective tool for driving process compliance. For example, consider requiring certain opportunity fields, like pricing, margin, or a signature from legal in the opportunity to be completed before a project can be booked. If those fields are not completed, then the project will not close, staff cannot be assigned, and sales credit will not be given. The value of the CRM is that you can build in disciplined process. When partners are frustrated with the change, they can blame the system, rather than leadership. A well-designed CRM establishes a process that must be followed – you cannot send an invoice if it is not in the system; you won't be awarded resources for proposal development if your opportunity is not in the system or does not meet the required criteria. The system demands the change in process and behavior you want to see.

There will be fallout ...

Even with highly sophisticated change management, there will always be some who resist, preferring the highly entrepreneurial firm. At some point those partners will choose a different path. But some may stay long enough to adopt the change, and when they eventually experience the benefits for themselves, may even become champions of the change.

* * *

As firms move up the maturity curve, they must navigate nearly constant change. A firm's ability to effectively steward this change is a strong predictor of its long-term success.

Andi had lived on her own for more than five years before her relationship with Nic started. Her house was set up exactly the way that suited her, and the idea of bringing all of his belongings into "her space" was a bit nerve-wracking. But she soon felt the benefits of the change: Turning the basement guest room into Nic's pottery studio meant that their kitchen would continue to be filled with beautiful, hand-thrown dishware. Reorganizing the kitchen in a way that suited him meant Nic could let his chef skills shine and cook them delicious meals. And the plants! Remember Andi's lack of green thumb? Before Nic moved in, she had one houseplant and it was already on its way out. Their home is now an oasis with thriving plants soaking up the sun near every window. Change is scary, until we feel its benefits.

263

Managing Change

Chapter 15

Going for Growth – Where to Go from Here

T en pull-ups.

Twelve weeks from her deadline, and she was barely managing two. At the start of every year, Erika joins forces with a small group of close friends to publicly declare a set of three goals for the year ahead. The goals are organized as follows:

1. Level One Goal: Must be relatively achievable, something that would take effort to complete, but with some focused time and energy, could be easily executed.

2. Level Two Goal: The stretch. This goal is a reach. It's one that's hard to achieve, that you have never done before, but it's doable. It requires a different level of planning and preparation than Level One.

3. Level Three Goal: The Big Hairy Audacious Goal – The BHAG. This is the thing you are scared to say out loud. Not only have you never achieved it, but just thinking about it prompts a mix of excitement and terror. Accomplishing this would require a huge amount of hard work (and possibly a little luck).

On January 1, Erika had declared a level two goal of completing 10 pull-ups. She'd already missed her BHAG for the year (winning a

265

running race in France), and the level one goal of reading 20 books also seemed far from her reach with just a few months left in the year (she'd been busy!). Erika had jumped on the pull-up bar a few times since January, but without any consistency. Her max number of pull-ups at any one time had capped out at four. With the end of the year imminent and an inability to conceive of a year with zero goals met, she reached out to Tschana Schiller for some tips.

Tschana, the longtime strength coach for the U.S. Ski Team, is a 5'4" powerhouse (10 pull-ups are a breeze for her). Her strength programming humbles even the Olympic gold medalists of the sport. Keen to help Erika succeed, Tschana outlined a 12-week pull-up plan that demanded five sets of pull-ups a day, five days a week, adding no more than one pull-up each day.

The first month looked like Figure 15.1.

Within eight weeks, Erika could complete five sets of eight pull-ups, but her arms kept giving out when she tried to crest the hill to 10. When Erika relayed this struggle to Tschana, she suggested a new plan. She told Erika to reduce the number of pull-ups (just five sets of six each day) and instead add a 5-pound weight between her feet. Two weeks later, on December 27, Erika completed not just one set, but *two* sets of 10 pull-ups. She happily ended the year with one goal completed (and an eagerness to dig into her pile of books in the new year).

WEEK 1	WEEK 2	WEEK 3	WEEK 4
Day 1: 2, 1, 1, 1, 1	**Day 1:** 3, 2, 1, 1, 1	**Day 1:** 4, 3, 2, 1, 1	**Day 1:** 5, 4, 3, 2, 2
Day 2: 2, 2, 1, 1, 1	**Day 2:** 3, 2, 2, 1, 1	**Day 2:** 4, 3, 2, 2, 1	**Day 2:** 5, 4, 3, 3, 2
Day 3: 2, 2, 2, 1, 1	**Day 3:** 3, 2, 2, 2, 1	**Day 3:** 4, 3, 3, 2, 1	**Day 3:** 5, 4, 4, 3, 2
Day 4: 2, 2, 2, 2, 1	**Day 4:** 3, 3, 2, 2, 1	**Day 4:** 4, 4, 3, 2, 1	**Day 4:** 5, 5, 4, 3, 2
Day 5: 2, 2, 2, 2, 2	**Day 5:** 3, 3, 3, 2, 1	**Day 5:** 5, 4, 3, 2, 1	**Day 5:** 6, 5, 4, 3, 2

Figure 15.1   Pull-up progression.

Building a growth engine doesn't happen overnight, and it doesn't happen in a perfectly linear way. Not every firm gets there at the same speed by the same means. We're all working with different inputs – maybe our baseline is 5 pull-ups, so getting to 10 isn't as hard. Maybe we've never done even 1 pull-up, so we require some other basic strength evaluation and training until we jump up on that pull-up bar. We may not all be professional athletes (like Erika!), but we can all get there – we can hit number 10. We can build a car to rival Adrian Newey's.

* * *

When Andi and Jacob had walked out of that investor meeting in Chicago, they decided their BHAG for the next fiscal year seemed nearly out of reach – hitting an EBITDA number that would give them the comfort to make real investments in new services and also make themselves attractive to outside capital. With that BHAG in mind, Erika, Jacob, and Andi set out to build a growth engine for PIE and slowly and steadily continue to move up the maturity curve.

"What do you think PIE's maturity curve looks like today?" Andi reflected as a question to Erika and Jacob. "I'm curious if we are all thinking about our next moves in the same way."

The next morning, they got together in PIE's conference room, light flooding in through the wall of windows facing the Bridger Mountains as the late winter sunrise started. "Funny," Andi said, and smiled, looking at Jacob's shabby hand-drawn lines on a yellow pad next to Erika's colorful and detailed PowerPoint slide. "We're perfectly aligned in some areas, but not in others."

Jacob's mapping of the talent discipline showed that PIE had recently moved into World-class; Erika's indicated on the talent front that PIE was not yet Leading. So they talked about it.

267

Going for Growth – Where to Go from Here

"What do you mean?! You don't think I'm World-class?" Jacob said – mostly joking – as he looked at Erika's slides.

"Don't worry, you're A+," Erika said, laughing in response. "I agree we have exceptional people here. We're full of A-players. But we know from this work that's not the whole game. Our incentive system still frustrates people, and I think we're still relying a bit too much on a smaller set of people to drive growth than we can and should be."

Jacob couldn't disagree. He'd been in charge of commission arbitration conversations in the past, and he knew firsthand that this had room for improvement. "It looks like we're in agreement that our client discipline is pretty solid," he said, "but our data and measurement still need some work. We're getting *so close* to being able to measure cost of sales – we just need to keep getting better at tracking client time. We also clearly need to be bidding on more work that's not sole source, especially with our newer services. It feels like we're leaving opportunities on the table."

And so it went. The three of them talked through all the disciplines, having healthy, caffeine-fueled debate when they disagreed, and high-fiving each other when they recounted decisions they'd made over the last decade that had helped them move toward maturity.

The three of them agreed that, right now, PIE's maturity looks something like Figure 15.2.

Then Walt entered the conversation, and it was his turn to laugh – taking them down a peg or two. "You guys have amazing client relationships, and you're excellent at client expansion, but you've never fired a client in your life, even when you should. You're definitely doing a lot of things right with clients, but you have a bit more work to do to get to World-class."

This is what matters more than the actual result: the conversation. If you took scribbled notes in the Business Development Maturity – Reader Assessment as you read, sit down with your peers around your conference table and evaluate what today looks like at your

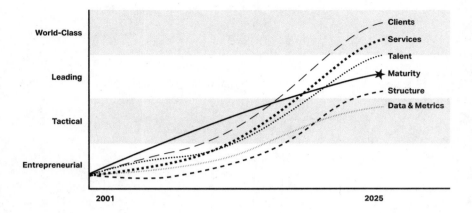

Figure 15.2 PIE's business development maturity curve.

firm. Then, more importantly, talk about where to go next. What is the lowest-hanging fruit with the highest impact?

Do you need to make an initial investment in a CRM to jump out of the Entrepreneurial phase? Is that the right investment right now, or do you need to hire a fourth employee first so you can deliver great work on the new project your budding firm just won?

Do you need to start offering more formal BD training to your team? Maybe you have a bunch of new partners who are expected to start bringing in new revenue, but they don't identify as "salespeople" and are unsure where to start.

Do you need to spend less time brainstorming 10 new service lines and focus on really building out your second? Do you need to start listening more to your clients – maybe through a formal client advisory board – to make sure this second service line is something they're excited to buy?

Your next best actions are going to be specific to you and your firm. And that's exciting. Think about the 12 months ahead: What is your 20-book goal? What is your 10-pull-up goal? What is your BHAG? Don't be bashful. Thanks to your peers who provided input for this book, you now have a map to get there.

Appendix

Business Development Maturity – Reader Assessment

Services Assessment

Step 1: Map your current maturity curve for Services (Chapters 3 & 4)

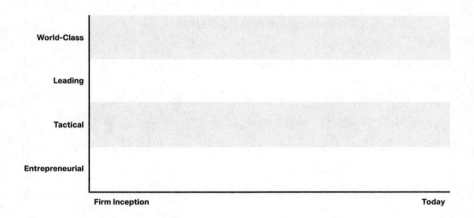

Figure A.1 Your firm's maturity curve – Services.

Step 2: Determine your next actions

Move from Entrepreneurial to Tactical:

- Define your unique value proposition. (Chapter 3)
- Identify your superpowers. (Chapter 3)
- Establish a service support team. (Chapter 4)
- Provide more than one service to a client. (Chapter 4)

Move from Tactical to Leading:

- Standardize service delivery. (Chapter 3)
- Orient your service model in the market. (Chapter 3)
- Practice saying "no" to protect the things to which you should say "yes!" (Chapter 3)
- Seek out and respond to client feedback. (Chapter 4)
  - Double up on accounts
  - Survey your clients
  - Leverage a client advisory board (CAB)
- Establish a process for deciding on new service investments and measuring their success. (Chapter 4)

Move from Leading to World-class:

- Define services by client outcomes. (Chapter 3)
- Utilize pricing to drive margin. (Chapter 3)
- Co-create highly responsive service offerings and innovate with clients. (Chapter 4)
- Position account leads as problem solvers and solution developers, not sellers of one service. (Chapter 4)
- Host an annual innovation competition. (Chapter 4)
- Engage with Alliance partners. (Chapter 4)

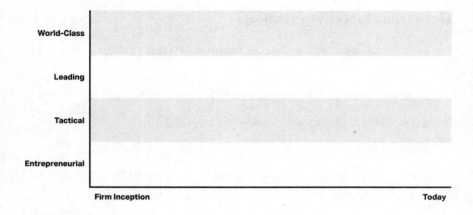

Figure A.2 Your firm's maturity curve – Clients.

Clients and Accounts Assessment

Step 1: Map your current maturity curve for Clients (Chapters 5–7)

Step 2: Determine your next actions

Move from Entrepreneurial to Tactical:

- Define your Ideal Client Profile (ICP) as specifically as possible. (Chapter 5)
- Start basic annual account planning. (Chapter 6)
- Start basic fan following. (Chapter 7)
- Leverage your existing biggest fans for referral. (Chapter 7)
- Build up your online presence both as individuals and as a firm. (Chapter 7)
- Develop your list of LEGITs. (Chapter 7)

Move from Tactical to Leading:

- Refine, review, and communicate your target client list. (Chapter 5)

- Develop an ideal portfolio profile (IPP). (Chapter 5)

- Develop a go/no-go process. (Chapter 5)

- Define an account segmentation strategy. (Chapter 5)

- Develop standardized, collaborative, comprehensive account plans. (Chapter 6)

- Build relationship action plans (RAPs) into your account plans. (Chapter 6)

- Formalize fan following. (Chapter 7)

- Establish a formal client intake process, building more relationships within a new account. (Chapter 7)

- Host value-first client and prospect executive roundtables – earning trust before the sale. (Chapter 7)

Move from Leading to World-class:

- Maintain a highly selective ICP and carefully manage your mice. (Chapter 5)

- Evaluate any potential acquisitions with ICP in mind. (Chapter 5)

- Integrate the five Ts into your account plans. (Chapter 6)

- Engage your best clients directly in your account planning. (Chapter 6)

- Develop a strong Alumni program. (Chapter 7)

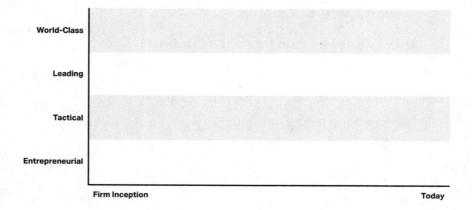

Figure A.3 Your firm's maturity curve – Talent & Performance Management.

Talent & Performance Management Assessment

Step 1: Map your current maturity curve for Talent & Performance Management (Chapters 8–10)

Step 2: Determine your next actions

Move from Entrepreneurial to Tactical:

- Expand your growth team. (Chapter 8)
- Evaluate talent against a BD competency framework. (Chapter 8)
- Begin to institutionalize your approach to business development. (Chapter 9)
- Involve junior professionals in the growth process. (Chapter 9)
- Cultivate farmers. (Chapter 9)
- Implement a simple incentive system. (Chapter 10)
- Introduce non-monetary incentives. (Chapter 10)

Move from Tactical to Leading:

- Hire for attitude, train for skills. (Chapter 8)
- Diversify your BD bench. (Chapter 8)
- Create a standard sales methodology. (Chapter 9)
- Invest in storytelling. (Chapter 9)
- Use role-play regularly. (Chapter 9)
- Evaluate talent. (Chapter 9)
- Build a wolf pack – orient your compensation around collaboration. (Chapter 10)
- Take off the "new logo" blinders and recognize cross-selling. (Chapter 10)
- Customize incentive systems. (Chapter 10)

Move from Leading to World-class:

- Establish a growth path for experts. (Chapter 8)
- Integrate lateral hires and acqui-hires while maintaining culture. (Chapter 8)
- Engage rainmakers across the employee life cycle. (Chapter 8)
- Build a training ecosystem. (Chapter 9)
- Cultivate a growth culture. (Chapter 9)
- Link incentives directly to long-term business outcomes. (Chapter 10)

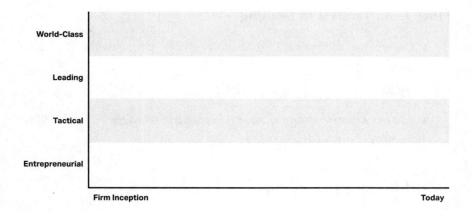

Figure A.4 Your firm's maturity curve – Operating Model.

Operating Model Assessment

Step 1: Map your current maturity curve for your Operating Model (Chapters 11 & 12)

Step 2: Determine your next actions

Move from Entrepreneurial to Tactical:

- Shift the rainmaker mentality from "*doer*-seller" to "*seller*-doer." (Chapter 11)
- Invest in basic support for business developers. (Chapter 11)
- Create a marketing role or team. (Chapter 12)
- Build a clear website that supports your brand. (Chapter 12)
- Produce basic but substantive thought leadership – don't publish just to publish. (Chapter 12)
- Establish *some* metrics and start measuring success. (Chapter 12)

Move from Tactical to Leading:

- Create an exceptional sales-to-delivery process that delights your clients. (Chapter 11)
- Align marketing with business development. (Chapter 11)
- Create clearly defined sales enablement roles – build your engine room. (Chapter 11)
- Use data to inform metrics and decision-making to drive ROI. (Chapter 12)
- Create a senior marketing role. (Chapter 12)
- Build a clear brand strategy to tell the firm story. (Chapter 12)
- Develop a clear content strategy with multi-channel distribution. (Chapter 12)
- Implement account-based marketing. (Chapter 12)
- Invest in a targeted event strategy. (Chapter 12)

Move from Leading to World-class:

- Develop a structure that supports your client needs and growth strategy. (Chapter 11)
- Engage everyone in growth. (Chapter 11)
- Build a sophisticated, data-driven revenue operations team. (Chapter 11)
- Align reporting structure with shared goals and metrics. (Chapter 12)
- Embed a client-service mindset across the team. (Chapter 12)
- Co-author thought leadership with clients. (Chapter 12)

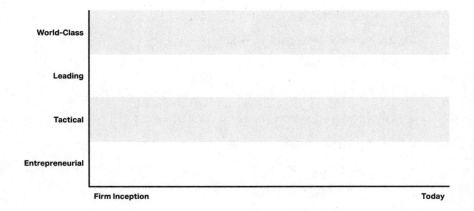

Figure A.5 Your firm's maturity curve – Data & Measurement.

Data & Measurement Assessment

Step 1: Map your current maturity curve for Data & Measurement (Chapter 13)

Step 2: Determine your next actions

Move from Entrepreneurial to Tactical:

- Invest in a CRM tool. (Chapter 13)
- Begin to develop metric visibility and accountability. (Chapter 13)
- Set pipeline goals and track your progress. (Chapter 13)

Move from Tactical to Leading:

- Set the tone at the top. (Chapter 13)
- Demonstrate CRM wins. (Chapter 13)
- Align metrics with firm goals. (Chapter 13)
- Begin tracking leading metrics. (Chapter 13)

- Cost of sales
- Competitive win rate (CWR)
- Percent of sales sole source
- Number of sales meetings
- Weighted and dated pipeline
- Percentage of business from biggest clients
- Use win-loss metrics to fine-tune business development efficiency. (Chapter 13)
- Use shared data to drive behavior. (Chapter 13)

Move from Leading to World-class:

- Develop an understanding of the sales capacity you need to achieve your growth goals and create that capacity in your team. (Chapter 13)
- Pilot and invest in new technologies that can enable your business development team, without over-relying on technology. (Chapter 13)

Bibliography

Bremmer, Ian. "Top Risk for 2011: G-Zero tops the list." *Eurasia Group*, January 4, 2011. https://www.eurasiagroup.net/media/top-risks-for-2011-g-zero-tops-the-list.

Cardenas, Felipe. "Argentina World Cup 2022 squad guide: Can Scaloni help Messi to the perfect ending?" *The New York Times*, November 18, 2022." https://www.nytimes.com/athletic/3751577/2022/11/15/argentina-squad-guide-world-cup/

Carnegie Hall. "An Interview with Jon Batiste." 2021–2022 Perspectives Artist. Last modified March 23, 2022. https://www.carnegiehall.org/Explore/Articles/2022/03/23/An-Interview-with-Jon-Batiste.

Ferrazzi, Keith. *Never Eat Alone*. Penguin Books Ltd. 2014.

Gladwell, Malcolm. *Outliers*. Little. 2008.

Grant, Adam. "Jon Batiste on the art of pushing your limits." ReThinking with Adam Grant. May 10, 2022. Podcast. https://www.ted.com/podcasts/worklife/jon-batiste-on-the-art-of-pushing-your-limits.

Maister, David. *Managing The Professional Service Firm*. Free Press. 1993.

McKeown, Les. *Predictable Success*. Greenleaf Book Group LLC, 2014.

McMakin, Tom and Fletcher, Doug. *How Clients Buy*. Wiley. 2018.

McMakin, Tom and Parks, Jacob. *Never Say Sell*. Wiley. 2020.

Merken, Sara. "Law firms' quest for market share drives New year's merger wave." *Reuters,* December 30, 2024. https://www.reuters.com/legal/legalindustry/law-firms-quest-market-share-drives-new-years-merger-wave-2024-12-30/#:~:text=In%20part%2C%20law%20firms%20are,law%20firm%20consolidation%20in%202025.

Newey, Adrian. *How to Build a Car*. HarperCollins. 2017.

Reichheld, Frederick F. "The One Number You Need to Grow." *Harvard Business Review*. 2003. https://hbr.org/2003/12/the-one-number-you-need-to-grow

Rummel, Michael. "The Complementary Fit Between Womble Bond Dickinson, Lewis Roca." *Law Week Colorado*, September 27, 2024. https://www.lawweekcolorado.com/article/the-complementary-fit-between-womble-bond-dickinson-lewis-roca/.

Viswa, Chaitanya Adabala, Zurkiya, Delphine, Zhu, Dandi, and Bleys, Joachim. "Scaling gen AI in the life sciences industry." McKinsey & Company. 10 January, 2025. https://www.mckinsey.com/industries/life-sciences/our-insights/scaling-gen-ai-in-the-life-sciences-industry.

Acknowledgments

This book would never have been written without the participation and support of an unbelievable number of people. First and foremost, we'd like to thank everyone who took an hour of their precious time to let us interview them for this book. That time wasn't billable, nor was it developing business – what were they thinking?! All of these executives – more than 100 of them – chose to be generous with their insights and stories, simply to help their fellow travelers avoid their mistakes or act on their great ideas more quickly. Many of these people were quoted throughout the book; many others provided critical insights that informed the themes you read here. Thank you.

We also want to thank Dana Roach, Yetta Stein, and Caroline Knowles – three brilliant consultants at PIE who also happen to be brilliant writers. Dana Roach is a Director at PIE and holds a master's in creative writing from Dartmouth College. She taught as an adjunct professor at Montana State University in the writing department after three years in the education nonprofit space with Teach for America. We look forward to reading her stories one day, and we are grateful for her leadership of our in-house editing team. Yetta Stein is a director and partner at PIE and our unofficial poet laureate. She is an associate editor for *Hunger Mountain Review* and has a master's in writing from Vermont College of Fine Arts. Caroline Knowles is a director at PIE and Montana native who made her way back to her hometown after living in Nairobi, Kenya, and Beijing, China. Prior to PIE, she worked in admissions and alumni relations at Stanford University and University of San Francisco School of Law. These three talented consultants came together as our in-house editing team, and they were not shy about the changes they made to our initial draft. Thank you for your wisdom, for adding what was missing, and for using your red pens liberally.

As a team of four authors, we are also grateful to Tom McMakin, the co-author of *How Clients Buy* and *Never Say Sell*, the precursors to this book. A gifted writer in his own right, Tom showed us the path from disparate idea board to structured manuscript. Thank you for lending us your compass and keeping us pointed North. We would also like to thank Carlie Auger for sharing her gift of bringing clarity to chaos. Without her, this book would be a jumble of messy quotes and disorganized content. Her eye for detail and willingness to jump in to help with anything and everything is one of her many superpowers. Thank you also to Adam Fahlquist, Emily Davis, and countless others at PIE for your help with interviews, your support, your patience, and your encouragement. We promise we are done talking about the book...at least for a bit.

Andi would like to thank the whole team at PIE for their support of this work, and would like to extend a special thanks to her husband, Nic, her mom, Susan, and her life-long friend, Avela. Nic provided the grounding, motivation, and delicious meals that Andi needed during a busy year of working and writing. As a professional editor, Susan gave Andi her love of words and writing from a young age and was generous enough to be a reader for early drafts of this book. Avela is a brilliant artist who got roped into designing the graphics you see in this book – thank you for turning our sticky-note diagrams into something our readers can understand!

Erika would like to first and foremost thank her husband, Andy. The deadline for this book coincided with the birth of their first child, Olsson Flowers Newell. Completing the manuscript on time would not have happened without numerous dedicated days of daddy day-care and seemingly endless patience. She'd also like to thank the management team at PIE for keeping the company humming right along while she took time away from the office to write and care for her new child. She can't think of a group of leaders she trusts or finds more credible than her team here at PIE.

Jacob would like to thank his wife, Amy, and his parents, Marcia and Leonard Parks. Amy is the inspiration for everything that Jacob does well and provided the encouragement and steadiness required to survive and enjoy another book-writing project. Marcia and Leonard have never seen a sacrifice they wouldn't make to give Jacob an opportunity. Thank you.

Walt would like to extend a heartfelt thank you to his family, friends, and colleagues who endured his excessive curiosity and unwarranted confidence.

About the Authors

Walt Shill is a member of PIE's Board and longtime advisor. Walt has served as a partner at McKinsey & Company, has led Accenture's strategy practice as a global managing director, and most recently, served as a managing partner and global commercial officer for ERM, a leading environmental consultancy firm. He is the author of *Friday Thoughts,* a business blog focused on professional services. He is a graduate of Virginia Tech, has an MBA from the University of Virginia's Darden School, and serves as a visiting professor of business at Emory University's Goizueta School of Business.

Andi Baldwin is the CEO of PIE. A Bozeman, Montana native, she returned to her hometown in 2014 to join PIE as a consultant, delivering work on behalf of clients like KPMG, JLL, Slalom, and IBM. She joined the management team in 2018, became chief operating officer in 2023, and was named CEO in 2025. Andi has worked in nearly every part of the business during her tenure at PIE and finds immense joy in solving the ever-present puzzle that is growing a professional services firm. Andi is proud to lead a firm that has made game-changing connections for thousands of executives around the world from its headquarters in beautiful Bozeman. She is equally proud to have built a culture that attracts exceptional talent and a partner group at PIE that is majority women. She worked on the research and editing teams for PIE's previous two books: *How Clients Buy* and *Never Say Sell*. She has Bachelor's degrees in International

Business and German from University of Rhode Island, and Master's degrees in Public Relations and International Relations from Syracuse University.

Jacob Parks is the president of Profitable Ideas Exchange (PIE), having led strategy, growth, and operations in the company over the last 20 years. Jacob headed the research team on *How Clients Buy*, interviewing more than 100 rainmakers at professional services companies, including consultants at Accenture, McKinsey, Baker Tilly, Deloitte, Goldman Sachs, and KPMG. He is also the co-author of *Never Say Sell*. Jacob has taught as an adjunct professor of business at the Jake Jabs School of Entrepreneurship at Montana State University, where he completed his undergraduate work. He also has an MBA from Gonzaga School of Business. Jacob has published research in academic journals on the topic of driving successful innovation in large corporations.

Erika Flowers serves as PIE's chief client officer, where she leads a team of consultants who deliver business development and client engagement programs for professional services firms including AWS, KPMG, Deloitte, IBM, Capgemini, BCG, and others. Erika was part of the editing and research team for *Never Say Sell* and is a former editor-at-large for Cross Country *Skier Magazine*. Erika holds a degree in geography and pre-health from Dartmouth College, where she competed in cross-country ski racing before going on to race professionally for six years. Erika returned to her hometown of Bozeman in 2018 when she joined the "PIE Pack," and simultaneously swapped the skis for trail shoes, now competing for The North Face trail running team.

Index

A

Accountability support, 189

Account-based marketing (ABM), 90, 215

Account planning, 101–104, 188

Account plans
development, 90–91
five Ts, integration, 99–100
relationship action plans (RAPs), building, 91–93

Accounts
annual account planning, 87–88
basic account planning, 87–88
doubling-up, 49–50
expansion, commission (placement), 160–161
leads, 90
positioning, 56
segmentation strategy, defining, 75–76

Acqui-hires, 53, 137–138

Acquisitions (evaluation), ICP (consideration), 79

Active coach, role, 94

Advantages (value proposition element), 33

Advocate, role, 95

Agendas, drafting, 41

Allen, Evan, 211

All-hands gathering, 259–260

Alliance accounts, 75

Alliance partners, engagement, 58–59

Alumni, program/engagement, 118–121

American Symphony (Batiste), 199

Anders, Jennifer, 86, 153

Annual account planning, initiation, 87–88

Annual innovation competition, hosting, 57–58

Annual in-person gatherings, 102–103

Annual recurring revenue (ARR), 44

Annual survey, sending, 50

Articles/white papers (resources), 35

Artificial intelligence (AI), 249–252
budget allocation, 250
task force/frontier unit, creation, 250

Attitude, hiring (relationship), 133–134

Awareness, 202, 212–213

Azagury, Jack, 97, 120

B

Batiste, Jon, 199

Batterton, Jim, 13

Behavior
change, 163
driving, shared data (usage), 241–242
rewarding, 57–58

Big Hairy Audacious Goal (BHAG), 265–267, 269

Biologics Consulting, 34

Black Box Problem, 170

Boiler-plate collateral (resource), 35

Bokhorst, Jose, 127, 133

Bonuses, 161–163

Boulanger, Paul, 41

Brainstorming, 96, 269

Brakeley, Hap, 58, 150, 188

Brand
awareness/prominence/ equity, 201
guidelines, following, 191
promise, 213
strategy, building, 210–211
support, website (building), 206–207

Brophy, Ally, 10

Buffett, Warren, 27

"Build v. buy" decisions, evaluation, 48

Burke, Ben, 134, 210

Business
developers, role/support, 126, 183–184
generation, relationships (impact), 107–108

Business development (BD)
activities, 128, 130f
approach, institutionalization, 146
bench, diversification, 134–135
bridge, marketing creation, 201
capability, building, 141
capacity, understanding, 243–244
centralized role, success, 182
competency framework, talent (evaluation), 130, 132–133
efficiency (fine-tuning), win-loss metrics (usage), 241
experience, 146
function, scaling problem, 6
Hippocratic oath, 113
identities, contribution, 149
management, 5–6
marketing, alignment, 187, 199
measurement, 38–39
meetings, occurrence/ number, 224
professional services firms, scaling failure, 3
resources, re-allocation, 247
scaling, attempt, 5
skills

assessment framework,
131f–132f

development, 143

strategy, improvement, 236–240

strength, 135

structures, development, 17

teams, training, 30

time allotment, 109

training, 142–143

Vinson & Elkins business
development types, 136f

zeitgeist, 147

Business development (BD)
maturity, 21, 268–269

curve, 16f, 269f

reader assessment, 271

stage, firm characteristics, 205f

Business Development
Representatives
(BDRs), 178–182

success, sale complexity
(inverted relationship),
179–180, 179f

Business development (BD) team
assistance, 192

enabling, 247–249

members, impact, 183

Business Development University
(BDU), 142

Business opportunity partner
(BOP), 189

Buyers
journey, marketing zone of
influence, 203f

Seven Elements, 8

C

Callahan, Greg, 64, 203

Callender, Anne, 68, 213–214

"Can Kicker" award, 242

Capability level, assigning, 246

Carnegie, Dale, 145

Case studies, usage, 35, 211

Cashflow, tightness, 30

Castino, Steven, 165

Centralized approval process, 72

Chalk talks, power, 170–171

Chambers, John, 51

Change
adjustment, 256

challenge, reasons, 256–263

creation, requirement, 13

making, pain, 13–14

Change management, 255
firm characteristics, 258f

incorporation, 257–259

investment, 250–251

principles, 257–263

Charitable priorities, interest
(display), 98

Check-the-box interview,
49–50

Chick, Caroline, 52

Clem, Kevin, 35, 209, 220

Clemons, Camille, 232

Client advisory board (CAB)
leading firm establishment, 55

leveraging, 50–52

purpose, 51

Client growth
commissions, payment, 164

Client growth (*continued*)
  engine discipline, 17
  team planning/preparation, 83
Client problems
  identification, 107–109
  solutions, sales, 126
  solving, 40–41
Clients
  access, underestimation, 92
  annual survey supply, 50
  assessment, 273–274
  base, concentration/
    diversification, 71
  buying journey, Seven
    Elements, 7–8
  case studies, 35, 211
  conversations, facilitation, 41
  creditworthiness, 74
  delight, sales-to-delivery process
    (impact), 185–187
  development, 6
  disappointment, 153
  doubling down, 81
  engagement, 9, 101–104
  expansion, 87f
  fan following, 120
  feedback, seeking/
    responding, 49–50
  focus, demand, 71
  formal client intake process,
    establishment, 115–116
  functional buyer, relationship, 68
  identification, 69
  innovation, 55–56
  inputs, 248

intake process, 116
knowledge/experience, 186
long-term value creation, 39
management, operationalization
  (approach), 4
needs, alignment, 57
needs/team core capabilities,
    intersection
    (understanding), 53
new client, winning, 105
numbers, impact, 66
organization, trust (scaling), 85
partners, success,
    134–135
percentage of work, 240
problems, translation, 183
project-based survey supply, 50
questions, asking, 51–52
relationship strength,
    spectrum, 95f
segmentation, 75–76
stakeholders, serving, 12
stories, sharing, 103
thought leadership,
    co-authoring, 220
under-listening, 49
work, winning, 244
Client-service mindset, embedding,
    219–220
Client-serving professional,
    challenge, 202
Clifford, Sarah, 111
Cold calling, failure, 208
Collaborative account plans,
    development, 90

Colleagues, meeting
(consideration), 97
Collections, increase (tracking), 235
Commissions
arbitration conversations,
control, 268
payment conditions, 164
Communication
change, process, 14
framework, consistency, 261
quality, absence, 257
repetition, 261
Company characteristics/context, 68
Compensation structure,
complement, 166
Competency, assessment, 154–155
Competitive win rate
(CWR), 238–239
Competitor advocate, role, 95
Competitors, loss/perspectives,
25, 214
Complexity, 170–171
Conforti, Christine, 202
Connolly-Kriarakis, Erin
Michelle, 252
Consulting spend, trigger events
(impact), 100f
Content strategy (development),
multi-channel distribution
(usage), 213–215
Control, loss, 228
Conversation starters, resources, 35
Cost of sales (metric), 236–238
Creativity, 36, 217–218
Credibility, 107

building, 203
requirement, 37
scaling, 85f
Cross-functional in-person gatherings,
inclusion, 137–138
Cross-selling, 168–169
Cross-team collaboration,
consideration, 57
Culture
change management,
incorporation, 257–259
firm characteristics, 129f
maintaining, 137–138
Customer knowledge,
robustness, 90
Customer relationship management
(CRM), 227–229
decision points, integration, 74
dropdown function, usage,
209–210
employee data, capture, 119
expectations, 190
follow-up notes, entry, 146
investment, 248
leverage, 114–115
marketing activity, impact, 209
opportunities, tracking, 184
system, 108, 262
tool, investment, 229, 231
wins, demonstration, 235

D

Data
assessment, 279–280
firm characteristics, 230f

Data (*continued*)

    growth engine discipline, 18

    rigor, requirement, 12

    usage, 209–210

Dated pipeline metric, 240

Davda, Arjun, 38

Day-one list, 203

Decision-making, data (usage), 209–210

Dedicated sales team, presence, 180–181

Delivery

    frameworks, resources, 35

    quality, erosion, 227

Delles, Jason, 218

Developing accounts, 75

Diamond accounts, 75

Diamond of Opportunity

    map, 90

    model, 83–87, 84f

Differentiated superpower, development, 27

Diligence practice, impact, 43–44

Disciplines, 16–18

Disrupter, role, 95

Doer-seller, change, 182–183

Dokken, Wade, 233

Domain experts

    apprenticing, 161–162

    training, 143–144

Double-poling, 25–26, 42

Downs, Jeffs, 189

E

Early-stage consultants, training (focus), 151

Early-stage firms, growth metrics management, 229

EBITDA

    increase, 257–258

    margin, driving, 226–227

    number, hitting, 267

    targets, 167

Ecosystem events, 28

Efficiency, firm reliance, 37

Elections, binary outcome, 223–224

Employees

    exit interviews, conducting, 119

    founder style, matching, 148

    lifecycle, rainmakers (engagement), 138

    retention, 164

Engagement, sealing, 9

Engine Room

    building, 187–191

    components, combination, 188–191

Engine Room, The (Brakeley), 188

Enterprise Resource Planning (ERP) system, introduction, 99

Enterprise Risk Management (ERM), 242

Entrepreneurial firms, 145–148

    experimentation, 47, 48

    hires, impact, 161–167

    impact, 110–114

    marketing, 204–208

maturation, 128–133

shift, 32

Entrepreneurial maturity stage, 18–21, 32–34, 47–48

impact, 66–68, 86–88

Entrepreneurial structure, retention, 182–184

Executive roundtables, coordination, 41

Executives, interview, 41

Exit interviews, conducting, 119

Experience, value, 36–37

Expertise, compounding, 30

Experts, growth path (establishment), 136–137

Extend work, 85

Extrinsic motivation, 259

F

F500 executives, virtual/in-person roundtables (hosting), 117–118

Fan following, 107

client fan following, 120

formalization, 114–115

initiation, 111

leverage, referral, 112

system, absence, 108

Fans

development, 116–117

winning, 117–121

Farmers, cultivation, 146–148

Features (value proposition element), 33

Feedback, 55

development, 51

getting, 49

shop floor feedback, 58

Ferrazzi, Keith, 89

Fields, David, 252

Firms

bleeding green, 109

building, value, 243

characteristics, 46f

goals, metrics (alignment), 235

growth, 177

marketing, 204–206

maturity

curve, 271, 273f, 275f, 277f, 279f

development, 47

schedule, 90

storytelling, brand strategy (building), 210–211

structure characteristics, 181f

switching, cost, 99–100

tactical approach, 208

transition, 111

triple matrixing, 44

Firmwide trust, impact, 172

First-order questions, usage, 64

Five Ts

integration, 99–100

layering, 115

Flow state, attainment, 19

Flywheel, role, 113–114

Formal client intake process, establishment, 115–116

295

Index

Fridge rights, 112
Functional buyer, client
(relationship), 68

G
Geography, client targeting, 67
Gladwell, Malcolm, 27
Goals
  organization levels, 265
Goals, reconsideration, 247
Gold star seekers, motivation, 166
Go/no-go process
  development, 72–75
  stringency, 74
Go-to-market efforts, leading, 6
"Go-To-Market" function, 220
Green, Bill, 91
Greto, Mike, 186
Groups, symbiotic relationship, 219
Growth
  absence, pain, 13–14
  consistency, 17
  culture, cultivation, 156–157
  future, 265
  goals, achievement, 243–247
  leaders, support, 177
  metrics, firms measurement, 227
  path, establishment, 136–137
  potential
    absence, 77
    unlocking, 27
  predictability, 5
  process, junior professionals
    (involvement), 146

  targets, 167
  team, expansion, 128–130
Growth engine
  changes, requirement, 13
  collaboration principles,
    impact, 199–200
  disciplines, 16–18
  importance, 5–6
  intention, 16
  world-class growth engine,
    building, 26–27
Growth engine, building, 14,
  109–114, 267
  difficulty/challenge, 6–14
  promise, 15
Growth investors

H
Hawn, Mark, 50, 187, 262
Hires, impact, 161–167
Hiring, firm characteristics, 129f
Historical performance,
  usage, 154–155
Homepage, creatin, 206
Houtman, Elisabeth, 192–193
How Clients Buy (Parks,
  et al.), 7, 202
Hunter credit, handling, 164
Hunter, Ross, 9, 147
Hutchins, Dwight, 90–91, 190

I
Ideal client profile (ICP), 78
  affordability, 69–70

clarity, 68
  absence, 72
  defining, 66–68
  determination, 64
  honing, strategies, 69–70
  selectivity, maintenance, 76–77
  strategies, 67f
  usage, considerations, 79
Ideal portfolio profile (IPP),
      development, 71–72
Immelt, Jeffrey, 15
Incentives
  characteristics, 160–173
  driving, 9
  long-term business outcomes,
      link, 172–173
  maturity stage, firm
      characteristics, 162f
  non-monetary
      incentives, 166–167
  plans, 160–161
  program, creation, 165
  seniority level, 165
Incentives system
  customization, 169–170
  implementation, 163–165
  trust, relationship, 173f
  understanding, 171–172
Industry
  mix, determination, 71
  sector, strategic fit, 73
Influencers, understanding, 68
Innovate work, 86
Innovation

annual innovation competition,
      hosting, 57–58
Innovation, requirement, 36
In-person roundtables,
      hosting, 117–118
Integration team, creation, 137–138
Intellect, requirement, 36
Intellectual capital, function, 28
Internal team, creation
      (considerations), 180
Internal training workshops, 152
Interviews
  opportunity, 106
  process, 133
Intro email drafts (resources), 35
Investments
  decision process, establishment,
      52–53
  waste, limitation, 53

J
Jiménez, Roberto, 184, 216–217
Johnston, Stephanie, 134, 215
Joslin, Murray, 167, 219

K
Kaarls, Alexander, 193
Kaplan, Stuart, 259
Karaplios, Stathis, 251–252
Keeping-in-touch efforts, 114–115
Key accounts, 75
Key decision maker, role, 94
Key performance indicators
      (KPIs), setup, 18

Khongphand-Buckman, Koree, 235
Koors, Jannice, 156

L

Langholz, Lori, 82
Lateral hires, integration, 137–138
Leadership, strategic vision,
    167–168
Leading companies, processes
    (building), 48
Leading firms
    client service, relationship,
        114–117
    formal training framework,
        adoption, 151
    integration, 218–219
    learning organisms, 135–139
    relationships, building/
        maintaining, 118–121
    talent, hiring, 133–135
    training/improvement,
        155–157
Leading maturity stage, 19–21,
    35–42, 48–53
    impact, 70–79
    usage, 55–59, 88–93
Leading metrics, tracking, 236–240
Leading move, 234–240
Leading organizations, collaboration
    (demonstration), 208–217
Leading phase, 185–191
Leading stage
    233-240
    shift, 150–155
Legg, Kevin, 96, 148

Legitimate Excuses to Get In Touch
    (L.E.G.I.T.), 96–98, 113–114
Long-term business outcomes,
    incentives (link), 172–173

M

MacEwan, Bruce, 54
Major influencer, role, 94
Margin potential, 57
Margin (driving), pricing
    (utilization), 41–42
Marketing
    alignment, firm characteristics, 205f
    business development,
        alignment, 187, 199
    efforts, tailoring, 215
    integration, 208–209, 218
    professionals, roles/
        responsibilities, 202
    role/team, creation, 204–206
    sales, separation, 219
    usage, 215
    zone of influence, 203f
Marquee clients, mix
    (determination), 71
Martin, Brandon, 130
Martin, Mike, 11
Mass-email mistake, 113, 233
Maturity curve
    appearance, 267
    mapping, 271, 273, 275, 279
    rise, 64–65, 262–263
Maturity stages, 18–21
    characteristics, 20f, 31f
    firm characteristics, 65f, 87f, 110f

Mbappe, Kylian, 197
McDaniel, Mike, 211, 242
McHugh, Caitlin, 54
McHugh, Sarah, 200
McKeown, Les, 15
McNeal, Michael, 186, 238
Measurement
  assessment, 279–280
  growth engine discipline, 18
  importance, 223
Measuring stick, usage
    (learning), 12
Meera, Shobha, 12, 134
Mentorship, 102
  programs, usage, 157
  structures, 106
Merlino, Blair, 32
Metrics
  data, usage, 209–210
  establishment, 207–208
  examples, 231
  firm characteristics, 230f
  firm goals, alignment, 235
  lagging characteristics, 232
  visibility/accountability,
    development, 231–232
Metrics, usage, 90
Meyer, Jeff, 148
Mid-market legal advice,
    providers, 27
Miller, Allie K., 249–252
Monetary rewards, inclusion, 160
Monolithic sales culture, shift, 133
Multi-channel distribution,
    usage, 213–215

N

Negative experience, risk (firm
    protection), 73
Net Promoter Score (NPS)
    methodology, 50
Never Eat Alone (Ferrazzi), 89
New business, winning, 117–121
New client, winning, 105
  maturity stage, firm
    characteristics, 110f
Newey, Adrian, 15, 21
New hires, embedding, 137–138
New logo
  blinders, removal, 168–169
  growth, 107
  winning, 120
  work, 164
Niche, 32
  awareness, 27
  dilemma, 30–31
Niching, power, 41
Niekerk, Wayde van, 185
Non-monetary incentives,
    introduction, 166–167
Non-monetary rewards,
    inclusion, 160
Non-niche work, delivery, 39
Non-relationship marketing activity,
    dependence, 233
Number of sales meetings
    (metric), 239–240

O

"One Number You Need to Grow,
    The" (Reichheld), 50

One-on-one storytelling, impact, 210–211
Online presence, building, 112
Operating leverage, obtaining, 4
Operating model assessment, 277–278
Opportunistic accounts, 75
Opportunities, creation, 119
Oracle, usage, 152–153
Organizational model (growth engine discipline), 17–18
Organization chart (org chart), visualization, 29
Organization map, 93–94
Outcome goals, process goals (contrast), 224
Outcome metrics, focus, 229
Outliers (Gladwell), 27–28
Outsourced IT function, management, 37
Outsourced sales team, addition, 186
Ownership
    overlap, 202–204
    structure, 67

P

Partnering, 59
Partners
    introduction, 78
    success, accounts (relationship), 10
    track record, 36
Partnership
    building, 116
    trust, deepening, 56

Payouts, offering, 162–163
Peers
    accountability, 259–260
    executive roundtables, 116–117
Percentage of business from biggest clients metric, 240
Percent of sales sole source, 239
Performance management
    assessment, 275–276
    growth engine discipline, 17
    maturity stage, firm characteristics, 162f
Performance visibility, absence, 226
Perry, Chris, 155
Phillips, Mike, 63
Pipeline goals, setting, 232
Pittendrigh, Michael, 11, 70, 212–213
Planning, power, 83–93
Platt, Allan, 167–168
Points-driven compensation, pivot, 167
Popler, David, 101, 139, 152
Practice leads, measurement, 241
Predictability, difficulty, 227
Predictable Success (McKeown), 15
Pre-partner stage consultants, training (focus), 151
Press, Bruce, 50
Pricing
    schemes, experimentation, 251
    selling, 44
    usage, 41–42

Priority executive, relationship action leaders (assigning), 96
Professional sales roles, need, 191
Professional services
artificial intelligence, impact, 249–252
marketing, 200–201
new logo, 82–83
winning, 120
organizations/markets, complexity (impact), 11–12
organizations, reliance, 201
scaling, attempt, 5
selling, difference, 7–9
table stakes, 206
Professional services firms
issues, 64
scaling failure, 3
types, 37f
Profit margin, consideration, 53
Progress
measurement, 90–91
tracking, 232
Proietto, Daniel, 148–149, 180
Project
implementation/handoff support, 188–189
size/scope criteria, 73
Project-based metrics, 189
Project-based survey, sending, 50
Proposal
permission, grant, 74–75
submission, permission (requirement), 73–75

Proposal development, 190–191
permission, requirement, 73
Prospect executive roundtables, hosting, 116–117
Prospective clients (nonclient incorporation), 55
Public recognition, 259–260
Publishing, reasons, 207
Pull-up progression, 266f, 269
Pure commission, pivot, 167

Q

Qualitative/quantitative goals, setting, 53

R

Rainmakers
client engagement, 36
CRM system usage, 234
development, 147
investment, 247
time allotment, 126
engagement, 138
expertise, capture, 155
identification, 147
impact, 9, 150
mentality, shift, 182–183
rewarding, 163
support, 17–18
team, egos (impact), 11
Rajakapolan, Krishnan, 262–263
Rao, Mukung, 40
Reach for Remarkable, 213

Reach work, 86

Reader assessment, 21

Real-time market feedback, generation, 33

References (resources), 35

Reichheld, Fred, 50

Relationship Action Planning (RAP), 89
- building, 91–93
- creation, 115
  - process, 93–104
- objective, 91–92
- steps, 93f
- team
  - formation, 93
  - review/update, 98

Relationships
- action leaders, assigning, 96
- building, power, 106
- business, 77
- dependence, 111
- expansion, 93
- long-term investment, 9
- statuses, assigning, 94
- strengthening, 41
- trust, 120

Reporting structure, shared goals/metrics (alignment), 219

Request for Proposals (RFPs), 188

Researching/prospecting, 190

Resnick, Deb, 155

Restivo, Michael, 169, 232, 242

Return on invested capital dynamic, discussion, 4

Return on investment (ROI)
- defining, 57
- driving, 209–210
- examples, 211
- impact, 102

Revenues
- creation, responsibility, 209–210
- forecast, 19
- growth, incent, 161

Risk
- cross-selling, relationship, 169
- exposure, increase, 72
- triggers, 74

Role-playing, regular use, 153–154

Rollman, Mary, 143, 178, 180

Roundtables, hosting, 117–121

Ruta, Frank, 217

S

Sales
- capacity
  - determination, sales capability chart (usage), 245f
  - understanding, development, 243–247
- compensation plan, reading, 167
- complexity, BDR (inverted relationship), 179–180, 179f
- cost, increase, 72
- culture, 257
  - change, reason, 13
- enablement roles, creation, 187–191
- marketing, separation, 219
- resources (determination), sales capacity chart (usage), 246f

standard sales methodology,
creation, 150–152
team evaluation chart, 154f
type, 245–246
undermanagement, 11
Salespeople
meetings, 252
storytellers, comparison, 152
Sales-to-delivery handoff,
overlap, 187f
Sales-to-delivery process, creation,
185–187
Sandman, Kira, 156, 200–201
Scale, structure, 177
Scaloni, Lionel, 177
Schie, Judith van, 183
Schiller, Tschana, 266
Self-sufficiency, importance, 78
Seller-doer
approach, 182–183
mode, 228
Seniority levels, invitation, 58
Senior marketing role, creation, 210
Senior partner, tasks, 49–50
Sensitivity modeling, 45
Service
areas, capabilities (demonstration),
47–48
definition/discipline, 25, 31f
delivery
evaluation, standardized
benchmarks (usage), 35
standardization, 35–36
development, 43
prioritization, 48

expansion, 30–31, 43, 46f
checkerboard, 45f
investments, decision process
(establishment), 52–53
lines, brainstorming, 49
mix, identification, 72
model, orientation, 36–38
offerings, 206–207
co-creation, 55–56
piloting, offering, 48
purchase, 53
scaling, resources
(investment), 35–36
selling, 44
support team, establishment, 47
Services (growth engine
discipline), 17–18
Seven Elements, 7–8, 7f, 84–85
Shared data, usage, 241–242
Shared goals/metrics, reporting
structure (alignment), 219
Short-term opportunistic
decision-making, 72
Skill sets, usage, 57
Skills, training, 133–134
"Sludge Slinger" award, 242
Smith, Aaron, 208
Soccer, 4-2-3-1 formation, 197
Social media, usage, 215
Software pricing, 45
Spam, fear, 109
Special roles, highlighting, 94–95
Speed-to-delivery, requirement, 37
Spot bonuses, 162–163
Spreadsheets, usage, 231

Staff availability, 74
Staffing mismatches, 153
Standardized account plans, development, 90
Standardized materials, building, 35
Standardized processes, piloting/ implementation, 260
Start-ups, empathy, 34
Steering committee, development, 119
Storytelling, 38, 186
   brand strategy, building, 210–211
   investment, 152–153
Stott, Jules, 216
Strategic accounts, 75
Strategic initiatives, 171–172
Strengths, strengthening, 27
Structure, maturity stage, 181f
Study halls, usage, 103
Success
   measurement, initiation, 207–208
   track record, highlighting, 4
Superpowers, 41
   identification, 34
Supplementary services, testing, 47

T

Tactical firm, 145–148
   basic account planning, growth focus, 89f
   client service, relationship, 114–117
   hires, impact, 161–167
   impact, 110–114, 204–208

internal conversations, 88
maturation, 128–133
rainmaker identification/ development, 147
service lines, brainstorming, 49
shift, 32
talent hiring, 133–135
Tactical maturity stage, 19, 21, 32–34, 47–53
   change, 35–40, 88–93
   impact, 66–68, 70–76, 85–88
Tactical phase, 185–191
Tactical stage, 182–184
   CRM system, firm investment, 229, 231
   shift, 150–155
Talent
   assessment, 275–276
   development, 141
      firm characteristics, 144f
      model, 18
   discipline, mapping, 267–268
   evaluation, 154–155
   experience, 30
   hiring/harnessing, 125
   management (growth engine discipline), 17
Target client list, refinement/review/ communication, 70–71
Targeted event strategy, investment, 216–217
Target market, conversations (facilitation), 41
Team
   capacity, creation, 243–247

304

Index

client-service mindset,
embedding, 219–220
compositions, usage, 127–128
incentives/rewards, 159
motivation, 159
Technology
piloting/investment, 247–249
temptation, trap, 233–234
world-class firm
avoidance, 248–249
Technology, firm
characteristics, 230f
Tenconi, Danielle, 219
Thornton, Grant, 212–213
Thought leadership
co-authoring, 220
production, 207
strategy, 214
Tierce, Evan, 157, 207
Top accounts, 75
Touchpoints, type
(consideration), 98
Training ecosystem,
building, 155–156
Transition, Transaction,
Transgression, Technology,
Transformation (five Ts)
integration, 99–100
layering, 115
Trigger event, 99, 100
impact, 100f
Trust
abundance, 162
building, 107, 203
earning, 116–117

incentive systems,
relationship, 173f
initiation, 120
internal building, 102–103
internal network, building, 102
maintenance, 107
requirement, 37
scaling, 85f
Trusted advisor status,
meaning, 101
Trusted Advisor, The, 145
Two-stage approval process,
consideration, 72

U
Utilization (balance), 226

V
Value
clarity, absence, 228–229
delivery, 37
long-term value creation, 39
providing, 40
quantification, 33
sharing, global conception, 173
Value-based pricing, impact, 41
Value-first client roundtable,
hosting, 116–117
Value proposition
defining, 32–34
elements, 33
Variable compensation, 161
payout, 162–163
Vinogradov, Paul, 155

Vinson & Elkins business development types, 136

Virtual roundtables, hosting, 117–118

W

Weighted pipeline metric, 240

Whitcomb, Matt, 25–26

Win-loss metrics, usage, 241

Wolves
packs, building, 168
release, impact, 63–64

Work
collection, 38
non-niche work, delivery, 39
performing, ability, 74
phase, pitching, 153
winning, likelihood, 74

World-class firms
client growth, 98–104
communication framework, consistency, 261
data-driven machine functions, 243–248
focus, ability, 103
growth, embedding, 128
impact, 218–220
incentives, relationship, 171–173
learning organisms, 135–139
relationships, building/ maintenance, 118–121
strategy, 119
training/improvement, 155–157

World-class growth engine, building, 26–27

World-class maturity stage, 19–21, 40–42, 55–59
impact, 76–79

World-class structure, 193–194

World-class symphony, role, 199–200

Y

Yarborough, Jason, 260

Z

Zero competition, 239

Zero-sum system, 168

Ziglar, Zig, 145

Zone of influence, 203f